THE POSTCOLONIAL EYE

Informed by theories of the visual, knowledge and desire, *The Postcolonial Eye* is about the 'eye' and the 'I' in contemporary Australian scenes of race. Specifically, it is about seeing, where vision is taken to be subjective and shaped by desire, and about knowing one another across the cultural divide between white and Indigenous Australia. Writing against current moves to erase this divide and to obscure difference, Alison Ravenscroft stresses that modern Indigenous cultures can be profoundly, even bewilderingly, strange and at times unknowable within the terms of 'white' cultural forms. She argues for a different ethics of looking, in particular, for aesthetic practices that allow Indigenous cultural products, especially in the literary arts, to retain their strangeness in the eyes of a white subject.

The specificity of her subject matter allows Ravenscroft to deal with the broad issues of postcolonial theory and race and ethnicity without generalising. This specificity is made visible in, for example, Ravenscroft's treatment of the figuring of white desire in Aboriginal fiction, film and life-stories, and in her treatment of contemporary Indigenous cultural practices. While it is located in Australian Studies, Ravenscroft's book, in its rigorous interrogation of the dynamics of race and whiteness and engagement with European and American literature and criticism, has far-reaching implications for understanding the important question of race and vision.

For Úna

The Postcolonial Eye
White Australian Desire and the Visual Field of Race

ALISON RAVENSCROFT
La Trobe University, Australia

LONDON AND NEW YORK

First published 2012 by Ashgate Publishing

Published 2016 by Routledge
2 Park Square, Milton Park, Abingdon, Oxon OX14 4RN
711 Third Avenue, New York, NY 10017, USA

Routledge is an imprint of the Taylor & Francis Group, an informa business

Copyright © 2012 Alison Ravenscroft

Alison Ravenscroft has asserted her right under the Copyright, Designs and Patents Act, 1988, to be identified as the author of this work.

All rights reserved. No part of this book may be reprinted or reproduced or utilised in any form or by any electronic, mechanical, or other means, now known or hereafter invented, including photocopying and recording, or in any information storage or retrieval system, without permission in writing from the publishers.

Notice:

Product or corporate names may be trademarks or registered trademarks, and are used only for identification and explanation without intent to infringe.

British Library Cataloguing in Publication Data
Ravenscroft, Alison.
The postcolonial eye: white Australian desire and the visual field of race.
    1. Social perception – Australia. 2. Ethnic attitudes – Australia. 3. Cultural awareness – Australia. 4. Whites – Race identity – Australia. 5. Ethnic relations in literature. 6. Aboriginal Australians in literature. 7. Postcolonialism and the arts – Australia. 8. Aboriginal Australian literature – Appreciation – Australia. 9. Australia – Ethnic relations.
    I. Title
    820.9'994–dc23

Library of Congress Cataloging-in-Publication Data
Ravenscroft, Alison.
  The postcolonial eye white Australian desire and the visual field of race / by Alison Ravenscroft.
    p. cm.
  Includes bibliographical references and index.
  1. Australian literature—History and criticism. 2. Postcolonialism in literature. 3. Race in literature. 4. Self in literature. 5. Other (Philosophy) in literature. I. Title.
  PR9605.2.R38 2012
  820.9'994—dc23

                                                  2011043232

ISBN 9781409430780 (hbk)

Contents

List of Figures		*vii*
Acknowledgements		*ix*
Introduction: Scenes of Race		1
Part I	**'There is and can be no brute vision'**	
1	The Eye and the 'I'	7
Part II	**When the Other Disappears From My Line of Sight**	
2	Coming to Matter: the Grounds of Our Embodied Difference	31
3	What Falls From View? On Re-reading *Plains of Promise*	45
4	Dreaming of Others: *Carpentaria* and its Critics	59
5	A Postcolonial Uncanny	81
Part III	**The Image of My Own Desire**	
6	White Men as Hidden Spectators	91
7	White Women Looking On	101
8	'Matron always carried a small whip'	115
Part IV	**Whiteness and its Veils**	
9	Darkness Casts its Light: Australian Blackface	131
10	Resisting a White Spectator's Enjoyment: *Benang*'s Aesthetics	151
Bibliography		*161*
Index		*173*

List of Figures

Pt I   Alexandra Frith 'Hand Mirror' *i*, 2009 (intaglio print),
edition 5. Reproduced with the permission of the artist.   5

1.1   Edna Walker and Doreen Barber, Cherbourg 1938, Board
for Anthropological Research Collection, AA346/4/20/1_
Cherbourg_N1476–1477. Courtesy of the South Australian
Museum Archives.   10

Pt II   Alexandra Frith 'Hand Mirror' *ii*, 2009 (intaglio print),
edition 5. Reproduced with the permission of the artist.   29

Pt III   Alexandra Frith 'Hand Mirror' *iii*, 2009 (intaglio print),
edition 5. Reproduced with the permission of the artist.   89

8.1   'Six girls in costume, late 1920s'. Courtesy of the Elizabeth
McKenzie Collection, Queensland Museum.   116

8.2   'Women posing in the costumes they wore to a fancy dress on the
settlement, mid 1920s'. Courtesy of the Elizabeth McKenzie
Collection, Queensland Museum.   117

8.3   'A ceremonial arch erected to welcome official visitors',
1920s. Courtesy of the Elizabeth McKenzie Collection,
Queensland Museum.   117

8.4   The camp at Cherbourg, 1930. Courtesy of the Elizabeth
McKenzie Collection, Queensland Museum.   121

8.5   'Both Mr Semple and his wife were keen gardeners', 1930s. Courtesy
of the Elizabeth McKenzie Collection, Queensland Museum.   121

8.6   'Jim Fisher was one of the main performers', late 1920s. Courtesy
of the Elizabeth McKenzie Collection, Queensland Museum.   122

8.7   'Jimmy Edwards in "war paint"', early 1930s. Courtesy of the
Elizabeth McKenzie Collection, Queensland Museum.   123

8.8   'Jack Semple with shield, spears and woomera', 1920s. Courtesy
of the Elizabeth McKenzie Collection, Queensland Museum.   124

viii *The Postcolonial Eye*

8.9 'Tommy Stuckey holds aloft a four-pronged fishing spear and woomera', 1920s. Courtesy of the Elizabeth McKenzie Collection, Queensland Museum.   124

8.10 'Eva Novak ... surrounded by aboriginals', 1927. Courtesy of the Elizabeth McKenzie Collection, Queensland Museum.   125

8.11 'Mr Stopford, on an official visit', 1920s. Courtesy of the Elizabeth McKenzie Collection, Queensland Museum.   126

8.12 Christmas Day, Cherbourg 1937. Courtesy of Australian Institute of Aboriginal and Torres Strait Islander Studies, Jackie Huggins Collection (Huggins. J1. BW: N5005.36).   127

Pt IV Alexandra Frith 'Hand Mirror' *iv*, 2009 (intaglio print), edition 5. Reproduced with the permission of the artist.   129

Acknowledgements

I am grateful for the generosity of this book's first readers: Claire Colebrook, Melissa Hardie, Jackie Huggins, Vicki Kirby, Philip Morrissey, Deborah Bird Rose and Alexis Wright. Without my favourite reader, Kate Foord, the book could not have been written.

I am indebted to Jackie Huggins for allowing me to quote from files produced on her mother, Rita Huggins, in the 1940s by the Queensland Government and held by the Queensland State Archives.

For their assistance in enabling archival research, my thanks to Kathy Frankland and Antje Noll, Community and Personal Histories, Department of Aboriginal and Torres Strait Islander Policy, Queensland Government; Thom Blake, Rosalind Kidd and Mandy Paul. At the Queensland Museum, Natalie Sandow, Carolyn Martin and Scott Carlile were very helpful in enabling access to and reproductions of photographs held in the Elizabeth McKenzie Collection. Cr Ken Done, as Mayor of Cherbourg Aboriginal Shire Council, kindly gave me permission to reproduce images of Aboriginal and Torres Strait Islander people held in the Elizabeth McKenzie Collection. Cr Sam Murray, as current Mayor of Cherbourg, kindly gave me permission to reproduce an image of former residents of Cherbourg, held in the Jackie Huggins Collection, Australian Institute of Aboriginal and Torres Strait Islander Studies (AIATSIS). Shannan Dodson, Access Officer, Audiovisual Archive Program, AIATSIS, assisted access to that collection. My thanks to Lea Gardam, Archives Collection Manager, South Australia Museum, for assistance in accessing and reproducing a photograph from the Board for Anthropological Research Collection held by the Museum.

For technical assistance with the photographic images used in this book, I thank Tess Flynn, Photography and Digital Imaging, La Trobe University; I thank Neal Haslem for assistance with the cover image. Thanks to Bruce Sims for editorial assistance.

Portions of Part II of this book were previously published in *Australian Literary Studies*, vol. 25, no. 4, 2010; *Cultural Studies Review*, vol. 16, no. 2, 2010; and *Postcolonial Studies*, vol. 10, no. 3, 2007.

Introduction:
Scenes of Race

This book is about the 'eye' and the 'I' in Australian scenes of race. It is about the possibilities of seeing, imagining and knowing an other across the cultural divides between settlers and Indigenous peoples but just as importantly it is also about the radical limits to vision and knowledge. It is about what falls from view. Against some current moves to erase the divides between settler and Indigenous peoples and to cover over our differences, this book insists that modern Indigenous cultures remain in significant ways profoundly, even bewilderingly, strange and unknowable within the terms of settlers' epistemologies, and it argues for aesthetic practices that allow such strangeness to be. What new ways of seeing might be possible if a white subject were to approach Indigenous cultural practices as a stranger or foreigner might, not now to trespass or colonise but instead acknowledging radical difference – sovereignty? Is that possible, or is a white subject destined always to approach Indigenous subjects and their textualities as versions of herself?

It is not only historical examples that I am speaking of here, but very contemporary, very modern Indigenous cultures and in particular the literary and visual arts that they produce. Non-Indigenous Australian and international audiences often assume to understand these when, at best, we see only traces, fragments from which we cannot assemble a whole. There are gaps in all vision; there are things we cannot see or signify. What I have been especially curious about, in writing this book, is what whites do before this gap in vision, this place where an other's strangeness cannot be tamed and assimilated.

This book is oriented by theories of visuality, knowledge and desire that assume that there is no visual field composed only through the pre-given, natural capabilities of this organ the eye. 'There is and can be no brute vision', Joan Copjec says. 'Semiotics, and not optics, is the science that enlightens us for the structure of the visual domain' (Copjec *Read My Desire* 34). This is not to free vision from the body, however. Vision, she claims, is always embodied, delimited by desire. This book aims to bring into view white subjects' enjoyment of their others, including the enjoyment of an other as spectacle, while also aiming to put under erasure what is meant by this troubling and persistent thing we call whiteness.

The Postcolonial Eye also aims to put under pressure what is meant by postcolonialism, especially those notions of postcolonialism in which colonising and settling impulses are figured as if belonging only to the past.

One of this book's emphases is on reading itself. How to read a modern Australian scene of race and its white desiring subjects? By reading I mean a visual and performative practice where the text is sometimes written on paper, sometimes on skin or canvas; it is sometimes a photograph or a film; it can be written on bodies, strokes made with paint or ochre, it is bodies in movement, in dance or ceremony. It can be the country itself.

This is reading as an act that marks and makes. When we read, we produce a scene of our own imagining. We *produce* a scene; there is no scene waiting to be seen. There is no scene before us, as it were. This subjective and subject-making practice has its limits: all readings have their aporias. This book is very much concerned with these places of illegibility for a settler-reader faced with an Indigenous-signed text. It is interested not only in how to read differently, but in the places where reading cannot go on.

Another way of putting this is: how might a settler *not* read? What are the critical and aesthetic implications of allowing the aporias to remain? How *not* to fill in the gaps or slide over them in our haste at interpretation? So, for instance, what to do before Indigenous claims that the country itself is sentient; that without women's ceremonies of dancing-up country – painting breasts, and stamping and shuffling feet – the country cannot live? What to do before 'true story' of the donkey-devil whose strange physical form and its hee-haw I can neither see nor hear, even as they are pointed out to me? What to do before the claim that a young girl has the power to bring waters flooding back to the dry lakes? In writing this book, I have been interested in questions about what remains unassimilable to a white settler subject's forms of knowing and seeing. What possibilities might be opened in the face of unintelligibility?

The idea of radical differences between white and Indigenous cultural forms and subjectivities is antithetical to much academic writing in the field. I am often told that the idea of radical differences is a very dangerous one. Of course, critics of difference are right to point to the ways that whiteness's others have been exoticised and romanticised, demonised and inferiorised in the name of difference but it is a mistake to think that exoticisation and demonisation are propelled by a logic of radical difference: it is the logic of the self-same that drives them. I do not know where one would find evidence that Aboriginal people feel anxious about claims of difference between themselves and whites except when, in the name of difference, they are represented once again as a (lesser) version of the white settler: when they are seen as 'natural' and 'native' to the settler's 'cultural'; 'lazy' to the settler's 'industrious'; 'nomadic and promiscuous' to the settler's 'rooted'; 'savage and primitive' to the settlers' 'civilised and sophisticated'. This is a kind of difference that is delimited by the settlers' own terms. On the other hand, the idea of radical difference – that is to say of sovereignty or incommensurability – is found in many Indigenous discourses. It is settlers, historically and right up into the present and in popular discourses as well as academic ones, who have insisted on the danger of difference.

This book begins with a photograph of two young girls. It is the kind of image that can be found in almost any colonial archive in Australia as elsewhere. In the course of writing this book I have often returned to this image to find that it has morphed, and morphed again, as my initial way of seeing these girls with their little faces and shaven heads has been revised. The work of writing this book

Introduction

has brought into proximity images and ideas that I have generally kept apart and this new proximity has effected a shift in my perception – it is an anamorphotic shift. These ideas and images range widely, historically and spatially, from post-war German literature and back to contemporary Australian Indigenous-signed fiction, from American blackface and back to the chromatosation of Australian race, from psychoanalytic theories of enjoyment and the visual field and back to the formation of a white, postcolonial seeing 'I', and so on. What has emerged is a book that is not so much about these girls and their countrymen and women as about the white subjects who look at them, and I am necessarily implicated as one of those white seeing subjects. This postcolonial eye is my own after all; its vision and its blindness are my own.

PART I
'There is and can be no brute vision'

Chapter 1

The Eye and the 'I'

> Things are not what they seem and should be visualised from all directions in
> order to enhance clarity. But even then there's doubt because of what's hidden.
> —Gordon Hookey in Ryan *Colour Power* (151)

There is a photograph of two young girls, barefoot and in shabby dresses; one
girl's head is shaven. In front of the other girl is placed, enigmatically, a small
card which has a number inscribed on it – N1474. Who were these girls and what
happened to them after the camera closed its eye and the photographer turned
away? What was the fate of these children and also of the photographer who looked
upon an image from which he excluded himself but in which he was implicated
nevertheless? How to bring such a scene into writing?

In attempts to bring scenes of deprivation or suffering into legibility, material
conditions often stand as condensed carriers of meaning: here, hand-me-down
clothes and shaven heads, elsewhere there might be a dirty kitchen in a broken-
down house. We all know narratives of deprivation and material ruin, of rubble
searched for two odd shoes to make a pair before the winter comes, or for a cup not
too broken to pass dirty water between dry lips. W.G. Sebald has looked to post-
war German literature and its descriptions of material poverty in Germany during
and after the Second World War in order to make a point about such narratives of
the ruins. He refers us to a passage in Hermann Kasack's novel *Die Stadt hinter
dem Strom* and the description of an assortment of junk among which dispirited
Germans rifle in search of the necessities of life: 'Here a few jackets and trousers,
belts with silver buckles, ties and brightly colored scarves were laid out, there a
collection of shoes and boots of all kinds, often in very poor condition. Elsewhere
hangers bore crumpled suits in various sizes, old-fashioned rustic smocks and
jackets, along with darned stockings, socks and shirts, hats and hairnets … all
jumbled together.'[1] But as Sebald goes on to point out, 'the lowered standard
of living and the reduced economic conditions that are evident as the empirical
foundations of the narrative in such passages do not make up a comprehensive
image of the world of ruins'. Instead, he insists: 'They are merely the setting for
the paramount plan, which is to mythologize a reality that in its raw form defies
description' (Sebald 48). This is why, for Sebald, German post-war literature, this
literature of the ruins, fails at its avowed task. In the end it is a literature that turns
away from rather than looks at the ruins.

---

[1]   From Hermann Kasack's *Die Stadt hinter dem Strom*. Frankfurt am Main, 1978,
154. Quoted in Sebald, *On the Natural History of Destruction* 48.

The Postcolonial Eye

Sebald was preoccupied with the Holocaust and the failure of post-war German literature to represent it. This may seem a long way from the subject of *this* book and yet the Holocaust's terms are touchstones in some important Australian debates on colonisation. The term 'holocaust' has been used by some historians, political scientists and anthropologists to describe the Australian scene: 'the great Australian holocaust known as colonisation' as Deborah Bird Rose has said.[2] Indigenous-signed fictional and nonfictional writings, too, do not shy from mobilising the European Holocaust's scenes and its lexicons. In figuring the horror of Indigenous experience, Indigenous authors have sometimes alluded to genocide and to concentration camps and their associated tortures, deprivations and other perversions. In Kim Scott's *Benang: From the Heart* the descriptions of reserves to which Aboriginal peoples were forcibly removed recall the camps with men and women and children in uniforms with heads shaved, lining up for 'food': 'Cold. A thick yellow skin formed across the bowl. You tapped something solid at the bowl's centre. It bobbed, and the yellow skin broke apart ... Eyeballs floated across puddles of greasy soup' (93). Men and women pressed into the cattle trucks of waiting trains, the forced work of the reserves, and then the fires to burn bodies: 'See the limbs crooked and dangling in the firelight, the limbs akin to our own but lifeless?' (172).

Leaving aside for the moment the questions that have been raised about the sense of making comparisons between disparate historical events, and indeed of the term holocaust itself, Sebald remains of interest because of his arguments against a literature of deprivation, loss and ruin that attempts to fill in the silences and gaps in historical knowledge but which all the same newly inscribes them.[3] In this book I am interested in gaps in representation, too, in the places where representation might be said to fail, and crucially, I am interested in the stitches that non-Indigenous Australian readers of Indigenous textuality tend to make

---

[2]   Deborah Bird Rose, *Dingo Makes Us Human* 2. Both the terms 'holocaust' and 'genocide' have been mobilised, albeit controversially, in accounts of Australian colonial and postcolonial history. Aboriginal historians have insisted on the fact of genocide of Australian Indigenous peoples. Kim Scott and Hazel Brown, for instance, are explicit on this in their *Kayang and Me*. Against this, Robert Manne and others have challenged the applicability of the terms to the Australian context. See Manne, 'Sorry business'. In turn, Manne has been critiqued by Patrick Wolfe, 'Robert Manne', 31–3. For arguments on the relevance of the term genocide to the Australian case, see Reynolds *An Indelible Stain?*; Moses (editor) *Genocide and Settler Society*; and Moses (editor) *Colonialism and Genocide*. Tony Barta has written extensively on this question, most recently: 'With intent to deny', 111–19; 'Sorry and not sorry', 201–14; and 'Discourses of genocide in Germany and Australia', 37–56.

[3]   Georgio Agamben refuses to use the term 'Holocaust': 'Not only does the term imply an unacceptable equation between crematoria and altars; it also continues a semantic heredity that is from its inception anti-Semitic' (31). Primo Levi did not like the term: 'Please excuse me, I use this term "Holocaust" reluctantly because I do not like it. But I use it to be understood. Philologically, it is a mistake.' Levi, quoted by Agamben 28.

The Eye and the 'I'

to cover over these gaps. In writing this book, I have been interested in what falls along and beyond the borders of seeing and knowing when non-Indigenous Australians approach Indigenous textuality. I am interested in Sebald, too, because of his own (we might say inevitable) failures to write the scene of suffering that is his object of study; the places where his methods reproduce the problems he points to, and the warning this holds for any critical practice.

To return to the image with which we began. This image[4] of two girls in rough dresses and shaved head appears in the memoir of Ruth Hegarty, a Murrie woman who writes of the conditions at Cherbourg Aboriginal Reserve in Queensland, where she grew up in the 1930s after being removed from her family. Ruth Hegarty and all the other little girls 'were treated identically', she writes, 'dressed identically, our hair cut identically. Our clothes and bald heads were a giveaway' (Hegarty 4). Such an image might have come from countless memoirs, family photograph albums, and government archives in Australia, as in other settler societies. Stories of young children's deprivations on reserves circulate now in many Indigenous life stories and fiction, accounts of being taken away from parents, of being forced by the missionaries to work in lowly paid or unpaid work far from home, of searching through rubbish dumps in efforts to scrape together the bare necessities that might make life possible. There are accounts of being 'huddled on wagons ... [with] bundles of clothes, a bowl, a cup ... a broken clock tucked under someone's arm' and of children being accorded numbers, sometimes instead of names.[5]

Of such representations of deprivation, a settler reader can often say, 'Yes, I have known such poverty'. The migrant, for instance, might say, 'I too know what it is to be separated from family, to be without a home, to be without shoes'. A British child migrant might say, 'I was also taken from my home and told that my parents were dead'. Many more readers know these stories not from immediate personal experience but from the experiences of people close to them. These are the stories of a settler society. To such readers, then, writing which can show the material signs of poverty bridges a gap between Indigenous and settler by showing places of correspondence, the places where one person can identify with another through shared deprivation. There is a danger, though, in this

---

[4] The photograph is part of the Board for Anthropological Research Collection, reproduced with permission of the South Australian Museum, series AA346. This photograph is one of thousands taken in the course of the Board for Anthropological Research's Harvard and Adelaide Universities' expedition in 1938. The number written on the card held in front of these girls provides a link between the photograph and anthropological data-cards that Norman Tindale and Joseph Birdsell produced. Most of the data-cards for the expedition to Cherbourg note Birdsell as the observer and recorder, so it may have been he who took this photograph. Birdsell was especially interested in anthropometrics: he recorded his subjects' weight and hair colour, for instance.

[5] The quotation is from Scott *Benang* 329. For a fictionalised account of Aboriginal people being assigned numbers instead of names see Wright *Plains*; for an autobiographical account, see Ginibi.

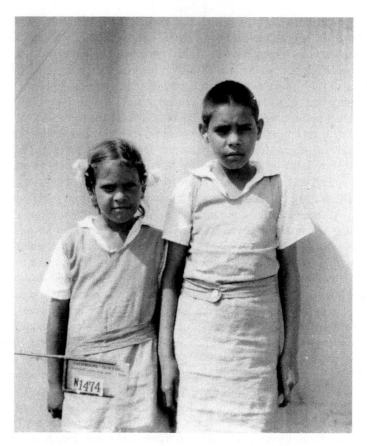

Fig. 1.1   Edna Walker and Doreen Barber, Cherbourg 1938.

kind of reading practice because the settler reader can then ask of the Indigenous author: 'What gives you reason to imagine that you are a special case?' Reading practices based on identification risk collapsing differences. They risk reading these signs of poverty – a pudding-basin haircut, or bare feet, say – as signifying the same for these Indigenous girls as they might have done for this reader. Such a reading practice cannot answer the question: how do these things come to take their meaning *here*, in the specificities of this reality? What meanings can they hold for these girls, Edna Walker and Doreen Barber, Aboriginal girls on a reserve in the late 1930s, rather than, say, for English migrant girls in the backstreets and laneways of the industrial inner cities in Australia in the same years?[6] How do objects come to carry different meanings, and what would it mean for reading and writing practices to insist on this difference?

---

[6]   See Tony Birch *Shadowboxing* for a fictional account of the lives of Indigenous men and women in Fitzroy, Melbourne.

The Eye and the 'I'

Material objects take their power and meanings in relation to the embodied subjects who bear them, who in turn press the objects into the work of carrying social values. Objects are social forms; they carry meanings between people. Sometimes they are the very thing through which a social bond is mediated – and their meanings arise relationally – their values or meanings are not absolute or immanent. The objects – here, a sack dress and shaved head – have their historical particularity, as do the subjects who bear them, and as do we as viewers.

This is in part why literatures like those Sebald points to from the post-war German scene fail: they attempt to materialise deprivation and suffering through a catalogue of sad and peculiar objects, failing to bring these objects into proximity with the men and women who once touched them. In such stories of deprivation, too, there tends to be an emphasis on those objects that are extant rather than what has been lost – a kind of positivism that necessarily fails to speak of loss, of what is missing. Thinking back to descriptions of the Holocaust for instance, the emphasis tends to be, say, on the shaven heads, or the hair itself, detached and arranged in obscene piles. There are either images of hair, or teeth, gathered in their anonymity, or images of the people to whom these kinds of things should still belong but who can never reclaim them. As Agamben asks: *where is the rest of this hair's body?* Hair and shorn head cannot be brought together again. Between what there is to be seen and what is absent is a horrifying distance, horrifying, we might say, precisely because it is unrepresentable. It is not a distance that can be given a measure in metres, or days; it is a space beyond the normal coordinates of space and time. It seems, then, that the truth of images might lie in what fails to appear as much as what is in view.

In the image of two young Murrie girls with which we began, its truth does not inhere in the material objects that are visible to my eyes. There is no *thing* that can stand as the minimal point of my considerations. This is partly because of the difference in what these things might have meant to these girls and what meanings I can give them, but it is also because of what falls from my view. I cannot see the pleasures these girls' lives hold – it is the memoirs of these years that will show me some of these – and I cannot see the power and force that, again if I turn to Indigenous writing, I am told might be there running like an electric current – the Dreaming that, we are told, is like an engine, it *pushes* (Stanner). Nor, looking at this image, do I see the girls as carriers of Indigenous Law, although Indigenous-signed fiction will bring me back to this image and make me wonder.

To turn again to Sebald and to his descriptions of the literature of that other time and place of destruction, Germany in the 1940s. This literature maintains its silence, he suggests, by recourse to either abstraction on one hand or imagination on the other – both fail to speak. He asks what it means, for instance, to represent the bombings in terms of numbers, attempting to abstract the sum of countless individual experiences. What can we discover in the fact that by the end of the war 7.5 million people were homeless, and that there were 31.1 cubic metres of rubble for every person in Cologne, and 42.8 cubic metres for every inhabitant of Dresden? 'The destruction, on a scale without historical precedent, entered the

12   *The Postcolonial Eye*

annals of the nation, as it set about rebuilding itself, only in the form of vague generalizations' (Sebald 4). The numbering of the homeless does not bring into our sights the intimacy and interiority of even a single home; quantifying rubble does not disclose any bodies which the rubble covers. We could say that the quantification itself stitches over what has been suffered or lost.

Sebald instead turns to rather different sources for information about the effects on bodies of the firebombs. He starts with the diary of Friedrich Reck, who died in Dachau. Reck's entry for August 20, 1943, describes refugees at a railway station in Upper Bavaria. Among these refugees is a young mother who, in her rush to board a train, drops her cardboard suitcase, which spills open on the platform, revealing among its contents the incinerated body of her child, miniaturised by the intense heat of the firebombs. The case falls onto the platform, 'bursts open and spills its contents. Toys, a manicure case, singed underwear. And last of all, a roasted corpse of a child, shrunk like a mummy, which its half-deranged mother has been carrying about with her, the relic of a past that was still intact a few days ago' (29). Against this, the numbering of dead or the reckoning of rubble show themselves as strange and concerted evasions of the human subject, methods that miss flesh and bone. Perhaps we can say more: that they make flesh and bone merely objects, separated once again from the subjects to whom they belonged.

But Sebald finds literature that relies on the imagination fails, too. Neither a reckoning nor an imaginative act, he argues, could bring the reader close to the subjective effects of these years. How then to write? Sebald argues that German literature had to wait for the publication of a different kind of writing, some of which carries Jewish signatures. It is a trilogy of novels by Hubert Fichte, who lost his Jewish father in the war, and the autobiographical essay style of Jean Améry, who was tortured and interred in Auschwitz, that first hold Sebald's attention.

In *Detlev's Imitations*, the second novel in Fichte's trilogy, one of the protagonists undertakes research into the Hamburg air raid. The narrative has him looking at documents held in the library of the Eppendorf Medical School. Extracts of genuine historical documents are then incorporated into the novel, appearing as discontinuous notes in a fragmentary, dense and psychically chaotic narrative. These documents include reports by a coroner on autopsies he performed on bodies burned in the fires in German cities, cold summaries of bodily effects that erupt into the otherwise interior, almost autobiographical style of writing.

Can we say that the horror of a reader's encounter with this material in *Detlev's Imitations* lies in the separation of subjectivity from body? For in these autopsies, bodies are again acted upon as if they were merely things – in this sense the whole body is made as thing-like as its extracted parts, as hair or teeth. The coroner, Siegfried Graff, endeavours to keep bodies separate from that which animated them – he misses the human subject and appears engrossed in his calculations: the size and weight of the body mass, the effects of heat on tissue and bone. He seems to hope that if only he could weigh, measure and catalogue these remains, he will have made something whole; from his accumulation of facts he will come into new knowledge. His is a kind of doctoring that will stitch up the bodies again when parts have been removed for examination.

But against this, Fichte's writing installs the human subject as incalculable, and insists that accounts of any subjective experience are necessarily fragmentary. Fichte's writing puts the fragments into proximity with each other rather than attempting to contrive wholeness, in his writing the fragments remain rather than being stitched together. Fichte's aesthetic suggests that neither the wholly imaginative writing expected in a conventional novel nor the documentary form of an autopsy report could tell the truth of the 'raw form that defies description', but once such disparate forms are brought into proximity, they together produce a most disturbing effect. Unlike the coroner, this novelist seems not to be afraid of the fragments that make up the story he has to tell; he brings together fragments gathered from disparate sources – memory, fiction, the archive – but lets the gaps between the fragments remain rather than stitching them in order to make an apparent whole. The fragmentation, gaps and silences *are* the story.

But how to write of trauma? As Jean Améry asked: how could he show readers the experience of torture without bringing them to the torture chamber to be subjected to its crimes? Améry waited 20 years to write about his body being twisted, and he reminds us of the origins of the word 'torture'. 'Torture', Améry jokes: 'from the Latin torque, to twist. What visual instruction in etymology!' Améry's response to these dilemmas of representation was to write of torture obliquely, installing a formal distance between the subject of the writing and the scene of reading. He employs a form of understatement that makes his writing (just) bearable to a reader and perhaps to himself, too. His joke about etymology suggests that in the end he could not sustain the critical distance at which he so carefully aims. Sebald puts it so well when he says that Améry's joke sounds as if his voice itself is about to crack under the pressure of maintaining this distance between reality and its representation and between this reality and his reader: 'The phrase with which this curiously objective passage concludes, provocatively deviating almost into the ridiculous, shows that the composure, the *impassibilité* allowing Améry to recapitulate such extreme experiences has here reached breaking point. Améry resorts to irony where otherwise his voice would be bound to falter' (151–2).

Sebald is interested in Améry's writing for the ways its autobiographical style enables the appearance of an embodied subjectivity. This is writing that is neither imaginative nor a kind of empiricism that refuses the body. For me, as a reader of Améry, I am also interested in the way his writing suggests that the body under torture is another body, a body that is strange to oneself. The subject loses his bearings as it were. As Sebald reminds us, the body is dislocated. This is what some Indigenous writing will show us: the torture of dislocation. There is another important aspect of Améry's writing, too: Améry points out that the Holocaust was driven by the Nazis' desire to *make* themselves: it was an act of self-formation – and no less obscene for that. When Améry looked into the face of his torturer, it wasn't hatred he saw but the face of a man in a desperate and serious act

14   *The Postcolonial Eye*

of self-formation. When Améry jokes: 'What visual instruction in etymology!' he is referring to the instruction of the torturer. It is the torturer who *looks*.

Améry's question – 'how to write of torture?' – suggests at least two meanings. One is that torture is unrepresentable in words; the body has its own language. The other meaning poses a different ethical question: why represent torture if to do so is to torture again? We might add to this: how to write, and how to read, without repeating the enjoyment of another's suffering? This dilemma goes to the heart of any writing practice which seeks to speak about violence, and it is therefore implicated in my own efforts to write, here, in this book. So, to have referred to Friedrich Reck's account of the scene on a railway station in 1943 was surely to have courted my reader's horror. Were you scared by this image, as I was when I first read of it – a scene that you might not have imagined before, a scene that was in some sense impossible for you? To repeat this story here raises the question of my own complicity in your anxiety. What writing practice are we engaged in when we tell such traumatic stories to each other, and can it be done differently?

Sebald himself mobilises this and other stories with the avowed intention of showing us what was missing in so much post-war German literature – the human, bodily effects of the torture and the firebombs – but in this move he risks making body into object – a dead child turned into a thing among the other objects that spill from a woman's suitcase. And are we too perhaps fascinated by this scene, as we might be fascinated, too, when Sebald lifts from Fichte's novel details of Graff's autopsies? These I will not repeat. Crucially, Fichte himself presents these reports in the form of fragments – discontinuous notes – and his interest appears to be on the effects the documents have on the state of mind of his protagonist, this researcher. Sebald, however, surrenders these considerations in favour, ultimately, of his own attempt to form a coherent version of the human effects of the firebombs. Despite everything he knows about the purpose and effect of Fiche's formal choices, Sebald desires to extract as full knowledge as possible from the fragments given to him by Fichte, and to do this he tries to redeem their status as archival documents.

Sebald seems in the thrall of the grotesque descriptions and calculations performed in that cold room 60 years ago by a coroner who may have been as deranged by what was before him as the young mother was deranged standing with her suitcase on a railway station. In their respective traumas, coroner and mother try to hold together what can no longer cohere. In his own way, and against his own intuition, Sebald too stitches over the gaps, wishing to be able to trust the medical archive to make sense of that which escapes his own understanding. He repeats what he critiques: the cubic metrage of the ruins, the weight of a burnt body, the number of dead or homeless.

And so what about the stories with which we are concerned here, the stories of a settler society? The continuing traumatic effects of colonisation in a settler society are so large they cannot be measured on any scale. Their reach into the minds-bodies of both settler and Indigenous subjects defies the capacity of language to give it expression. Perhaps this is why prevailing histories of colonisation, like

Sebald's examples from post-war literature, so often disappear into abstractions and generalisations or are reduced to facts and figures. Both negate the individual subjects on whom colonisation has its effects and they risk repeating, in the very act of telling the story of colonisation, the violences they purportedly merely represent.

In Australia, the so-called 'history wars' with their contestations over the numbers of Aboriginal men, women and children killed in the course of colonisation is such a case.[7] In this account-keeping approach to the story of colonisation, human subjects are once again missed even as their deaths are counted and dated. What is obscene in the history wars lies not only in the emphasis on the dead, but in their numbering, in the cold act of the body count. Numbering the dead will not tell us who these men and women and children were. It will not tell us of their relation to each other and to those who came before and those who came after. It will not give insight into the minds of those who took up arms against them. As Stuart Macintyre has said of the history wars, 'Such a grisly dispute could hardly assist a reckoning of the past' (4). Macintyre rightly refuses the terms of the history wars. I think he unwittingly re-enlivens something of their logic, though, by speaking of a *reckoning* of the past, if we take to reckon as to: 'ascertain number or amount of, by counting or usu[ally] by calculation, compute … conclude after calculation'. It is to 'make calculations, cast up account or sum, settle accounts with person'.[8] It is precisely the idea of a reckoning, of a calculability, with which this book takes argument. Rather than the number of dead, the size of suffering and other weighty calculations, in the writing that follows I take a lead from Indigenous-signed texts where enigma and doubt are put into effect, in narrative content and form. My reading and writing 'the other' will therefore favour the fragment over the whole, unsettlement over certainty. It will give a formal place to nonknowledge and invisibility. In short, I am interested in a literary practice where our gaping mouths (agape at times in horror, at others in wonder) are not stopped up with numbers and facts.

* * *

I have begun with one small black-and-white photograph. We know the time and place the photograph was taken, we know the girls' names, or at least the names by which they were known in white society, and the written record might give the time and place of their births. Yet, these girls' lives, like all lives, elude such a list of facts. There will always be places that are unreachable to us, standing here now looking on. Among the many reasons for this is this one: that the stories Aboriginal

---

[7]   Key texts in this controversy are Windschuttle's in which he disputes the extent of the damage perpetrated during colonisation as alleged by those Australian historians who have been pejoratively named 'the black armband' historians, most notably Henry Reynolds; and *Whitewash*, a collection of essays edited by Robert Manne, which made a powerful refutation of Windschuttle's arguments and methods.

[8]   *The Concise Oxford Dictionary of Current Usage* 1934, 974.

16   *The Postcolonial Eye*

men and women tell of their own lives have gaps inscribed into them because of trauma, the places where minds close like fists around memories and will not let them go. Narratives of trauma are usually arranged around the nodes of silence and speech and how each of these work to make meaning and, inextricably bound with this, where meaning fails to be made.

Indigenous authors sometimes refuse to write about events in their lives that might cast their Indigenous readers back into places of suffering and loss. This would be to speak of things that are already known by these readers and it would therefore risk repeating the hurt. In the process of producing life story for publication, for instance, a particular kind of telling and re-telling of stories sometimes goes on. There is one such telling I know very well, and this is the way that Rita Huggins used to tell stories about her life.[9] Each story had its double. There was the well-practised, well-rounded story, the one that would be made into printed form, and then there was its underbelly, a story almost identical to the first except for a single event which would be introduced into the telling. This added element was profoundly important; it had the power to utterly transform the previous account. A story previously framed as a young girl's misadventures, say, or of hardship brought about by poverty, would become a story of criminal negligence or of ritualised violence on the part of white guardians, missionaries, mistresses. However, at the next telling, this would have been replaced again by the more benign vision, the eruption of memory and feeling slipped under the surface again. Rita Huggins was usually quite insistent that the more gentle, even humorous, version be brought forward for the written account. Her Aboriginal readership already knew the painful and unexpurgated life. It was their own.

The form of address in her writing is intimate, quiet, as one speaks to someone standing close by. She addresses the reader as someone whom she knows and loves. Sometimes, humour is used as much a release for her Aboriginal readers as it is for herself, laughter's 'divine gift', to use W.E.B. DuBois's phrase. Her humour stays on the side of reason, while nevertheless also pointing to the place where reason fails.[10] This is an idea of authorship which refuses a sadistic relationship between

---

[9]   In the early 1990s I worked with Auntie Rita Huggins and her daughter Jackie Huggins on their auto/biography *Auntie Rita*, and participated in the recording and transcribing of some of Rita Huggins's stories. The text's final form and the author-editor-reader relations that are inscribed in it have been the subject of scholarly attention since its publication, most recently Michele Grossman, 'Xen(ography)' 277–301.

[10]   Rita and Jackie Huggins retell jokes told by Aboriginal country-and-western singer Kevin Carmody:

   Q: What's the difference between a computer and a Blackfella?
   A: You only have to punch the computer once.
   Q: What's the definition of an Aboriginal nuclear family?
   A: Mum, Dad, the two kids and the anthropologist.
   Another true story: A young Aboriginal mother turned to her whinging five-year-old perched in a supermarket trolley and shouted: 'Ahh, wadda ya want?'
      'Land rights!' came the loud reply. (Huggins and Huggins 145)

author and reader. Like Jean Améry, Rita Huggins understood that to figure stories of suffering is to risk inflicting it again.

Then there is the silence practised in order to protect Indigenous knowledges from the white gaze which has yet to prove itself trustworthy. Kim Scott in *Kayang and Me* repeats a story of cultural authority and traditional ownership told to him by his Nyoongar elder, Hazel Brown, in a mix of trust and warning. Hazel Brown tells Scott of having taken visitors to a special site on her traditional country, a site indelibly marked by the footprints of the *woodatji*, 'a little tiny bloke … who used to live in the hills … some people say they're still there, those little men. You can feel their eyes watching you' (255). Hazel Brown shows her visitors the marks these men left in stone, and then covers over the marks again with sand, demanding that they never show anyone what they have seen. She reminds her visitors that they are on *her* country; she is welcoming and warning them at the same time: warning against trespass, against the misuse of knowledge. Kim Scott, himself a Nyoongar, knows that in being told this story Hazel Brown is welcoming and warning him, too. In turn he asks whether we, as readers now of this story, can be trusted: 'And you, our reader?' (256).

There are also those things that cannot be written about because they are irretrievably lost. The memories that are recorded in autobiographies, for instance, are only a part of a much larger picture, of course. There are those things that cannot be remembered, or were never known. These omissions sometimes fail to be recognised, however, by settler readers, perhaps out of a hope that no such omissions exist, or, if they do, what is missing can be recovered. There is in the Australian context a hope, for instance, that an imaginative reading of the archive will recover the past.[11] In its own way this fantasy is as dangerous as the other fantasy: that *all* has been lost. This raises for us the question: how to hold together irretrievable, irredeemable loss among Indigenous nations without collapsing into a narrative of death and total destruction? How to hold the fact of irretrievable

---

[11] The Australian historian's Inga Clendinnen's efforts to describe the moments of first encounter between British and Indigenous peoples in *Dancing with Strangers* practises such an imaginative historicism. See Joan Copjec's critique of new historicism in *Supposing the Subject* (vii–viii), where she points to the wish for there to be no loss, for everything to be retrievable:

> The calculus of gain to which we are obliged ever more vigilantly to submit is grounded in notions of unfailing reciprocity and recognition. These notions dictate that every expenditure can and must be duly recorded in some symbolic register from which no entry is ever erased. The eventual profit expected from every notable expenditure is guaranteed by the complete survival – the record – of all past expenditures, to which the current one can simply be added, counted as 'everything plus one' – that is, as pure gain. The strong belief driving our information age – that everything can be/is recorded, that nothing exists outside this historical register – serves this capitalist logic of gain. Conversely, what this logic cannot abide is the notion that something might be permanently lost, utterly irretrievable for all time …

loss against the stand taken by some non-Indigenous Australians that little or nothing remains?

There are also things that cannot be spoken by Indigenous men and women because they are unknowable, or unsayable – something that is at times almost unbearable to a non-Indigenous subject, it seems. The anthropologist W.E.H. Stanner reported white men and women like himself confronted by their own curiosity about the Indigenous 'Dreamtime' in the face of their Indigenous informants' inability, not just refusal, to put the 'Dreamtime' into words. Within the Indigenous epistemologies to which Stanner referred, there is the idea that representation is always only partial and incomplete: some things escape representation. Stanner's Indigenous interlocutor reports a silence or gap which must be allowed to remain, the silence into which things must fall, the places of unknowability.

In writing this book, I aim to re-read this image of two girls by bringing it into proximity with a range of images taken from Indigenous-signed fiction and memoir, from government archives, and from photographic collections. These other images offer directions from which to gaze at the still photograph, and so 'enhance clarity', as the Waanyi artist Gordon Hookey suggests of his own methods of aesthetic production. But, as he insists, 'even then there's doubt because of what's hidden'. I aim to offer some new views on an old scene, but also to show the critical possibilities of a reading practice that works generatively with doubt.

How to Write? How to Read?

All writing must fail at perfect re-presentation, all writing has its omissions. Some writing, however, aims at showing the impossibility of bringing all into representation, into language. This is a kind of writing that endeavours to make a space for the enigmatic, not to reveal its content or size, not to give it measure, but to give it space where it can remain what it is – unknowable, unspeakable, invisible. This is a writing that points to the relation between the known and the unknown, and which asks: how is the unarticulated and inarticulable productive, how does it bring some things into hearing and into view? And, can we read for what is not articulated or shown?

I began with the literature of the Second World War and its failure, in Sebald's estimation, to figure an embodiment of trauma. The trauma of the Second World War placed new demands on European aesthetics. To rehearse Theodor Adorno's position on this question is unavoidable: what aesthetics, he asked, after Auschwitz? For Adorno, it was aesthetics such as Samuel Beckett's, where meaning itself is 'put on trial' and where the unspoken and the unspeakable are dramatised in formal absences, in emptiness: 'The violence of the unspeakable is mirrored in the fear of mentioning it. Beckett keeps it nebulous. About what is incommensurable with experience as such one can only speak in euphemisms.' In Adorno's view, writing that renders its own crises of meaning, in form as well as

The Eye and the 'I'   19

semantics, allows the unspeakable to be referred to without attempting to represent it. While Adorno has attracted many critics, including those who argue that trauma is not necessarily best figured in Beckett-like forms, his problematisation of the limits of representation remains a vital one.[12]

There exist forms of Indigenous-signed textuality which bring readers' attention to the unspeakable in a way that Adorno might have considered to be Beckett-like, or what since has come to be called modernist. That is, texts that refer to rather than seek to represent the unspeakable and unknowable. One way of describing this is through the metaphor of a circle drawn around the unrepresentable. This is a circle made of objects – that is, it is comprised of the speakable, the visible, the knowable, the representable. These objects are drawn into a circle so as to refer to the space of the unrepresentable. Not to give it specific content, size or shape, but to suggest its existence. In turn, this space, or gap, renders new meanings to that which *can* be materialised. It may turn out then, that the objects brought into a circle in efforts to point to the gap in meaning, this otherness, are not arbitrary after all, but are suggested by the nature of the gap – what Francis Bacon called the 'darkness of otherness' that enables the appearance of the objects in the circle. Francis Bacon says this of his art practice: an object is made to appear by being 'remade out of other shapes'. He goes on: 'Because if the thing seems to come off at all, it comes off because of a kind of darkness which the otherness of the shape which isn't known, as it were, conveys to it.'[13]

But does a reader – a reader such as myself, a white Australian – faced with the otherness of a text refuse its otherness, its uncertainty, in order to protect herself from its effects? There is an anxiety I have known when picking up an Indigenous-signed text: it is an anxiety about what will be discovered, a fear that what will be found will be unbearable. Is it possible that what might be most unbearable, most feared, is uncertainty itself: the opacity of a stranger's world, the places where I cannot install meaning? And what are the effects of this opacity on me as a reader? How can I make myself appear if the other disappears from view? This is my anxiety: that faced with a strange and incomprehensible text, *I* will be undone. If by reading we mean an act of making sense, of giving meaning to a text, of finding semantic consistency, then what does the non-Indigenous subject do if an Indigenous-signed text resists this meaning-making? Can we go further and ask whether prevailing reading practices are a modern repetition of the relations of colonialism where a coloniser-settler encounters an Indigenous subject as if the self-same?

---

[12]   See, for instance, Luke Thurston, who suggests realism can figure trauma and the Holocaust, 29–48.

[13]   Francis Bacon, quoted by Parveen Adams in *The Emptiness of the Image* 113. As Adams puts it: '[T]he otherness is that which has remained outside the signifying chain and only dimly seen by the artist and acceded to only with the help of "accidents" and "chance" interventions' (113–14). According to this approach, the artist does not know or see otherness; it falls from his view, too, and luminosity, when it is achieved, is achieved through accidents, interventions and inventions.

If silence and omissions are inscribed in all writing, one question that suggests itself is: how to read for what is not articulated? This is to refer to a reading practice that cannot be taken any longer to be only 'making sense'; a reading practice that finds where we can no longer read, where the text is silent – for whites at least – and where we in turn must observe our own silence. This is to speak of a reading practice that does not stitch up the gap in meaning, but lets the enigmatic and aporiatic remain. How might that silence or the places of non-sense be allowed to work on the reader? This is a reading practice, if it can still be called that, which is interested in the places where interpretation and the imaginative act fail. In the Indigenous-signed texts that I look at in this book, we have a kind of writing that works with, indeed aims at, this kind of failure. It draws it out, and shows its ethical necessity.

This is reading as a process through which we bring *ourselves* into uncertainty, through which we cause doubt to fall on our perceptions. This is an idea of reading not (or not only) as that act which brings us into knowledge, but one that puts our knowledge under pressure until we can say: 'I do not – cannot – know the other.' And then to hold with this willingness to be an unknowing reader a willingness to read anyway. That is, against a notion of knowledge as accumulative, reading instead is a shift in relations between objects in a field, and between the field and what lies outside it, a shift that implicates the viewer, or reader.

Limits to Knowledge, Limits to Vision

In writing this book, I have been interested to reapproach the question of radical differences between white European cultural forms and Indigenous ones. To speak of difference in this way is antithetical to most academic writing on Australian postcolonialism where, as I've already suggested, there is, quite rightly, a deep wariness of mobilisations of difference that exoticise and romanticise, demonise and inferiorise whiteness's others in the name of possession. There is a paradox, though: the refusal of radical difference shares the same logic upon which exoticisation/demonisation is based, and this is the logic of the self-same. In exoticisation/demonisation, an other is not so other at all. This other is made in acts of exclusion that at the same time capture the other within the logic of the self. In these moves, this other is not allowed a radical, at times unrepresentable difference from the 'I', the centred white self. The other subject becomes an object within the self-same logic, an object taken to be always knowable within the self's own terms, which are assumed to be the other's too. These commentators assume a shared 'humanity', a common 'mentality', that just happens to look very much like their own. They know what 'humanity' is, and it is the same for all of us.

What are the implications of these contemporary anxieties over difference for political and aesthetic practice? In this book, I look at many examples where, to my eyes, radical differences between white and Indigenous cultures have been disavowed by my white compatriots, closed over in efforts to make the strangeness in a scene or story intelligible within our own epistemologies. By way of an example, I'd like to take a little time here to consider Robert Kenny's *The Lamb Enters the Dreaming: Nathanael Pepper and the Ruptured World*. Robert Kenny makes what is to me a surprising move for a contemporary Australian historian: he legitimates nineteenth-century evangelicals' claims of 'One Blood', insisting on a pre-discursive humanity, a humanity prior to culture, a shared humanity. The evangelicals' 'faith in our commonality ... may still be the only way for our salvation', he writes (341). What could he mean by this?

For Kenny, the 'claim of separate but equal cultures echoes the academic ground of apartheid and shares many of its intellectual roots, which are products of the nineteenth-century assertion of the integrity of race and nation' (322). He sees poststructuralist theories of language and difference – what he calls the 'cult of difference' – as having the 'acute potential to reinvest the concept of race – and thereby racism – with legitimacy' (323). Kenny bases these charges on what he sees as their inadvertent tendency to collapse culture with nature. At the heart of these theories of cultural difference, he claims, is a premise, 'hidden, like so many premises – that a people's culture is akin to their nature' where their 'nature' is 'biological', based in 'genetic transmission' (322).

To engage with Kenny's understanding of theories of difference, we have to go a long way back: to ideas about language post the 'linguistic turn' in cultural and social theory and to the developments and departures since then concerning what is meant by the human subject as a subject of language. It is to remember that 'language' is no longer taken to be only about words – a certain lexicon or idiom, a certain grammar – but that when we refer to language now we are in the register of the visible and invisible, the known and unknowable, the imaginable and unimaginable, we are in the register of desire and embodiment. I'll be approaching some of these ideas more fully in the following chapter, but for now I will take up the matter of language in a narrower sense, in the sense that Kenny uses it, and which he attributes to theorists of cultural difference.

Kenny is keenly aware of the effects on European minds of silences and gaps – in language, in narrative. We want to fill the gaps, he says: 'We want to fill them however we can, however unjustified we are in doing so. And yet there are gaps, silences we have to learn to live with' (222). But Kenny may be one of the people about whom he speaks, for he immediately moves to close over gaps between white and Indigenous subjectivities and epistemologies, what he calls mentalities. 'We may not have absolute communication within our own language, but we manage very well, all the same, by negotiating our way through our problems', Kenny says. 'Across languages we do the same; it is just more difficult. It is not tragedy' (209). For Kenny, writing against the 'prisonhouse of language', communication is always possible after all, if only we are patient negotiators. We are all 'human', according to this view, we can find our way to each other.

To support his belief in, or hope for, this commonality, Robert Kenny offers as evidence a story of the similarities between Moravian and Wotjobaluk religious 'idioms'. Kenny begins with a series of bullet points outlining the major

22 *The Postcolonial Eye*

characteristics of evangelical Christianity of the early nineteenth century, but here Kenny is playing a trick on his reader: this list turns out in fact to be based on the general characteristics of Aboriginal religion as described by the anthropologist W.E.H. Stanner. For Kenny, this is evidence of the similarities between the two religious systems. But Stanner is writing about the Wotjobaluk in the idiom of Christian belief with which he was so familiar: of course it sounds similar. The similarity that Kenny's story shows us is between Stanner and the Moravians; it casts no light on the more tantalising question of whether or not there are similarities between the Moravians and the Wotjobaluk.

In the postcolonialist discourses that I am writing to and against, in these discourses that insist that there is no radical or incommensurable difference, the idea of hybridity is often raised: it is pointed out, again quite rightly, that there are no Indigenous cultures that exist in a 'pre-contact' zone and that all Indigenous textuality (by which I mean knowledge and its narratives) bears the marks of this contact and influence. Obviously, Indigenous men, women and children often have a profound knowledge of white culture. So, sure, in reading Indigenous-signed textuality, whites do not encounter a 'pure' 'Indigenous' artefact, we encounter things in it that are familiar to us, things that white and Indigenous share. Whites do indeed find ourselves in this writing. But this does not mean that these texts are entirely available to us, either. This book takes seriously the possibility that there are things in Indigenous-signed textuality that we do not see, even when we are told they are there to be seen. It returns to the question: are there things that subjects constituted as white cannot know or imagine? Are there some things that *fall out of view*?

In what follows, I write about those moments when I find that another subject has walked out of view, stepped into a different world of meaning than the one I inhabit, a world into which I cannot follow. I write against a pervasive fantasy that complete vision is possible, and against a desire for possession of all knowledge, a place where there is no loss, only gain. This is to work with ideas of vision and knowledge not as accumulative, and not as objective, but as always fragmented, incomplete, partial and subjective. It is to attempt to show the places where my vision shifted, and where I hope the vision of my imagined white readers shifts, too. I am aiming to offer these readers glimpses of another scene than the one we might have known or imagined, but more than this, I am aiming to show that there are places we cannot see, the aporias in our visual fields.

Jacques Lacan's theory of anamorphosis is useful for the kind of work I do here. Anamorphosis, the moment when our perception of an image shifts and the image flips and becomes another one, can be used to illustrate the visual antagonism or nonreciprocity between two points of view, and the necessarily partial, incomplete and subjective quality of perception. We are all familiar with anamorphotic forms such as the black urn on a white background that is transposed into the white silhouettes of two faces in profile: what was background is now foregrounded by our own perceptual processes as the very subject of the image. We have, as it were, taken up a different position before the image, allowing our eyes' focus to shift 'behind' the shape that we see as the signifier for an urn. In that act, the urn moves back and becomes the ground out of which another image emerges, the two human profiles. In *The Ethics of Psychoanalysis*, Lacan argued that in such a form as this – in which an optical transposition is required so that 'a certain form that wasn't visible at first sight transforms itself into a readable image' – in such a form is illustrated the radical nonequivalence of two points of view (Lacan *Ethics* 135ff). One cannot hold together both images at once, they belong in two different visual fields, in two nonreciprocal narratives, for the urn has nothing to do with the two faces. The urn and the human faces are not in the same picture, they are not in the same story. While there is pleasure for a viewer in this shift – we enjoy the sense we have of being able to see what was previously hidden – at the same time, Lacan argued, the fact that we cannot hold both images together in one visual field points to the annihilation of ourselves as all-seeing subjects. Some things remain hidden in any one visual field, even as we look and look and look again. Scarily, these things *are* there, we see hints, 'stains', 'blots', but these are merely hinges onto worlds of meanings which we cannot bring forth without relinquishing another, and perhaps which are unreachable for us even then.

The example of an anamorphotic form that Lacan worked with, Holbein's famous painting *The Ambassadors* (1533) is strangely relevant for us here. Here, two men look out (appearing to look at ourselves as the viewers), surrounded by objects symbolic of the very European progress and expansion into fields of astronomy and navigation that made possible the European 'discovery' of the land mass we now call Australia. Then, in the foreground, hovering at the men's feet is a peculiar object which only becomes discernible as one positions oneself differently before the image, as one moves farther away. This is the skull that can only be seen or read – made sense of – once the viewer moves into a different position in relation to the image. As Luke Thurston puts it, the skull, the anamorphotic object in Lacan's example of *The Ambassadors*, is not part of the picture, it is a blot or a stain through which we peer. 'It remains undecipherable as long as we remain in a position to "read" the overall image; it only emerges as an allegorical *memento mori* when we switch to a viewpoint so oblique to the main picture as to render it, in turn, opaque' (Thurston 42). Again, we cannot hold the two images together: one comes into focus as the other grows out of it.

'The secret of this picture', Lacan said, 'is given at the moment when, moving slightly away, little by little, to the left, then turning around, we see what the magical floating object signifies. It reflects our own nothingness, in the figure of the death's head' (Lacan *Concepts* 92). This is why this particular image was so hermeneutically useful for Lacan because the anamorphotic object is a skull, a signifier of death. It could have been anything else of course: it is useful for Lacan because he can make it stand in for the death, or 'castration', of the subject as all-knowing, all-seeing.

There are a number of points from this that I work with in the course of this book. The first point is that, according to this theory of vision, *there is no visual field before the subject*. We can think of this as meaning two things at once.

First, that there is no visual field in front of the subject, the subject is always implicated in the field of vision, the subject is always in the scene. And, that what is visible is always subjective; the subject produces his or her own visual field. The subject gives the scene meaning, or rather makes a scene, arranges the scene into foreground and background, object and subject, bringing some things into view, and obscuring others. We might say that the subject produces it in order to make his or her own appearance in the scene of her own making. And it is only language, or the signifier, that, in Copjec's words again: 'is capable of lending things sense, [it] alone makes vision possible. There is and can be no brute vision, no vision totally independent of language ... The field of vision is neither clear nor easily traversable. It is instead ambiguous and treacherous, full of traps' (*Read my Desire* 34).

Just as significantly, though, some things fall from view. It is only when the subject shifts position, what can be thought of as a re-subjectification, that other things enter the subject's visual field. And, a new position which the subject might take up is still *hers*. Lacan here is not speaking of a taking up of another's position: one does not step into another's position because positions are not simply there, to be occupied by this or another body. *The subject is the position*: there are no positions outside subjectivities. This movement away from one position to another is not to move into another's viewing position. The observer is within the world and within his or her body. Perhaps it is obscene then to think we can 'look through another's eyes'. This is another moment in occupation, an obscene trespass. The best we can hope for, and the only ethical goal, is our own re-subjectification: those processes through which we can stand in another position that is still our own.

Finally one more point about vision. How to understand what Indigenous writers tell us is there to be seen (or heard or felt) – the Great Serpent, say, or the Dreaming – but which fails to appear for white western eyes (ears, and other organs and tissue)? Here I want to recall the arguments made by critics of scientific positivism, going back to its founding critic, Gaston Bachelard, writing in the 1930s for whom the objects of science are materialisable concepts, not natural phenomena.[14] Bachelard's argument is that phenomena are not given to us directly by an independent reality but are rather constructed by a range of practices and techniques that define the field of truth, practices that make the object of science appear, practices that are productive of the objects that appear in the visual field, and not simply seeing and measuring what is there.

These kinds of approaches to the visual field are suggestive of the ways that the visible is produced: through desire, and through signification. But what of the invisible, what of nonknowledge? If what appears in our visual world is epistemologically produced and therefore delimited, if the visual field is shaped by the desire to know and the desire to remain unknowing, by extension we can argue that the products of any epistemology or social order, include the stuff of

---

[14] For a discussion of Bachelard's work on the subject of science, and its critique and development by Louis Althusser, see Copjec *Read My Desire* 20–21.

nonknowledge or invisibility. As Copjec argues, invisibility and nonknowledge are *produced*; some things which are invisible or nonknowable within one frame are visible and knowable within another.

If we work from these ideas about the visual field – as subjective and therefore necessarily corporealised and as only possible because of processes of signification through which things come to matter – what might we say about the visual field that a white reader produces when it is the scene of the Indigenous text upon which she gazes?

Reading and Race as Visual Practices

Reading is a visual practice, it always involves a scene, and like other visual practices it is performative in the sense that in reading we produce the scene we say is already there, waiting for us to discover. We produce a scene of our own making in both senses of that phrase: we produce the scene that appears as it were 'before' us, *and* we are made in this act of looking, as 'white', say, or as 'woman'. But such a subjective and subject-making practice has its radical limits: there are some things that my eye/I cannot, will not, see. There are some things that I do not desire to see. If there are subjective limits to what can be seen, how then to bring an other into our own scene of reading and writing? How to read, how to write, an other?

Here, I take the text as sometimes words on paper, sometimes a photographic image, sometimes art on canvas, sometimes art made on bodies, strokes made with paint or ochre; the text might also be bodies in movement, in dance or ceremony. This is reading as writing, as an act that marks and, through the mark, it makes. It is the act that brings into the visual field not only an other, though, but also the reader, this reader *cum* viewer. It is in these acts that a reader is made. The reader is made in the act of reading – marking, making – an other. So, this book asks: what of the white reader? Is this reader made white in reading her others? Might it be that in some important sense there is no white reader before the text?

To suggest that there is no white reader before the textual processes of his or her formation recalls the claim James Baldwin once made that there are no white people, only people who think they are white (Baldwin 177–80). In this sense, to imagine oneself *to be white* or as *possessing* whiteness might be fantasmatic; whiteness might be 'merely' an ideal of prevailing discourses, and as such never secured. Like all ideals it might only be approached, never arrived at (Hage, Butler *Bodies*). We might say then that there is no one who can stand in the place of whiteness, there are only subjects who fantasise themselves as being there. Instead of 'the white subject' or 'the white reader', conceived as calculable, known in advance, we might instead think of a subject-who-desires-whiteness, with all the violent material effects of that desire. A white subject then is a subject who can make him or herself intelligible as white, who is able to make an appearance, as it were. It is a subject who neither *is* nor *has* whiteness, but who succeeds in approximating it. The white subject is a subject who can pass as white – at least in this moment, in this place.

To claim that there are no white readers but only readers who fantasise themselves as white is reminiscent of some earlier feminist literary criticism where it has been argued that 'there is no woman' before the text, no fixed, stable, certain woman. According to these arguments, a feminine reading subject is instead made in the act of reading. Gender is understood in these approaches as being textually produced in the sense of being produced in differentials of meaning. It is therefore always in flux. In reading, a subject seeks to stabilise the text's meanings, including around 'the stabilising specular image of woman in the text' (Jacobus 5). To search for and find woman is, Mary Jacobus has argued, 'a form of autobiography or self-constitution' (5). Psychoanalytic and deconstructionist feminist interventions of these kinds resist those earlier Anglo-American feminist claims that a woman reads *as a woman* and instead posit reading as a moment in an unending sequence which splits the single term 'woman' before and after reading and writing: a woman reading as a woman reading woman ... and so on. In this splitting, space is made, as Peggy Kamuf has argued, for a shift, however slight, in the single term 'woman'. 'Woman' after reading is not necessarily identical to 'woman' before reading, or identical to the image of woman looked for in the text. This is an argument against taking 'woman' to be a totalising nomenclature that disavows the split in the term: the feminine subject, while experiencing the constraints, and presumably pleasures, of her name 'woman', is never wholly captured by it. The feminine subject then, according to this approach, is always reading, and always (re)making herself in textual practices.

If reading can be thought to be such a gendering practice, if the feminine subject, for instance, can be said to be made in reading (however provisionally), then can we say the same about a white reading subject: that whiteness might be effected in a process similar to the way that Kamuf suggests femininity is effected? The sequence would go something like this: a subject-who-desires-whiteness looks for those figures in a text that are recognisable to her as white in order to stabilise the meanings she can give not only to the text but to herself. She attempts, that is, to stabilise an 'I' for herself around the nodes of race, searching in the text for an image that inspires her to say 'I am this' – the image that in her eyes bears a white face – and just as significantly another image against whom this subject who aspires to whiteness can say: 'I am *not* that'. Such a reader, searching for that which she can signify as white and its others in the text is in the act of constituting herself as white. To read, then, is to write oneself; it is an autobiographical act. The reader is an autobiographer, making a life as she reads, making a white 'I' that, however temporarily, however shifting in its contours, can for that moment be imagined – felt – to be hers.

Critically, this act is a *visual* one. Reading practices, like racial ones, are ways of looking, their objects are always in the visual field. Reading concerns the production of images, it always involves a scene. It is a process of selection and arrangement in which some parts of a text are brought into view while others are allowed to fall, of finding an arrangement of the visual field in which the reader can make herself appear, stabilised around an image of herself – as white, say, as a woman. The reader makes herself white (again) in reading through a process whereby she visualises a scene of her own making, finding the places where she can install herself in the scene, seeking to stabilise an 'I' through searching out the other white faces or conversely insisting on their absence and with this refashioned 'I' she turns again to the next act of reading, the next visualisation of the scene of race, and so on.

But, such an act cannot simply repeat or re-present what was there beforehand. As a performative act, reading is a riskier, more ambiguous practice than that. It not only holds the promise of stabilising an 'I' but threatens/promises its destabilisation, too. The white reader might find herself repositioned as a result of her reading. This way of thinking of a white reader as a reading effect also recalls Judith Butler's notion of interpellation where, against its earlier appearance as a singular and even catastrophic moment, interpellation comes to be seen as a never-ending process of being called, and, usually, of answering the call. There is not a single interpellating call, and therefore not necessarily a single answer, 'yes' (Butler *Bodies*). The formation of the subject as white through interpellation is always provisional; it is not a founding act but a series of repetitions that 'both conceals itself and enforces its rules' (Butler *Bodies*). There is no certain and stable white subject, instead there is a subject in an endless process of repetition, in a continual process of coming into, and at times jostling for, a position of intelligibility in discourses of whiteness.

But, such a reader might sometimes give an equivocal reply to this call into whiteness: she might say that perhaps she is not that white image after all, and that perhaps she does not find her opposite in another, in that image she loves to hate. So, one might be read and written as white but one is not pinned down by this naming, this calling, one is never wholly captured. Crucially, then, reading is a process that opens up the possibility of change, of the old re-formed through imperfect repetition. In reading, as in any process of meaning-making, there can be a *shift* in whiteness, however infinitesimal. If the subject moves positions *vis-à-vis* whiteness, if she evinces her own split or division, then there lies in this the possibility of imperfectly reiterating whiteness, to borrow Butler's terms. Reading opens up the possibilities of something 'new': of a white subject – that tricky, slippery thing – coming to read and write itself and its racialised others differently, imperfectly.

The character of these imperfections is what is at stake. How can a white subject read and write her other so as to refuse the call to perfect whiteness, so as not to repeat again whiteness in its old forms: whiteness as trespass and possession, as refusing others' sovereignty, their difference? This is to make a different point than the commonsense view of reading as changing the subject through the accumulation of knowledge. This is instead to describe a process whereby a reader sees differently rather than sees more. This reader, rather than simply acquiring more knowledge, relinquishes some of the objects of knowledge she had previously held onto so dearly.

PART II
When the Other Disappears From My Line of Sight

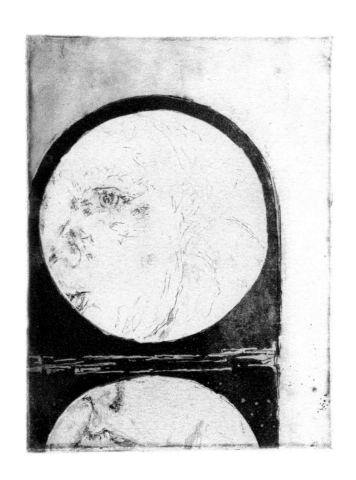

Chapter 2
Coming to Matter:
the Grounds of Our Embodied Difference

> The question of perception must take up the problem of what I want to see, and the way in which it structures the gaze which captures me. Instead of thinking of perception as just a visual field, it must be thought of as the field that is structured by the relations and forces of objects and desires.
>
> —Parveen Adams *Emptiness* (111)

The boy's elders have asked him to walk alone from one camp to another. He is an Arrente, and very young, three or four years old. The distance between the camps is several kilometres over hot country under a sky made moody by the Wet coming in. Although in one sense his is a solitary journey, he is nevertheless always accompanied, and not only by the old women and men watching him from their hidden places. He is accompanied by stories of country, stories that have already been told to him many times. He is accompanied by these stories, or one might say that he is in these stories and they are in him, and it is in this double relation that he comes to know earth and heat, and the forces that pull at him, bringing his body down, others pushing his body up. Through these stories, meanings are made. This is the way that things come to matter. These meanings are registered in the young boy's body, entered there. More than this, can we say that they make his body *in its very matter*, in ways that might never be given words as such but which make the nonetheless articulate body; and, more enigmatically again, might his body in turn make the country in its matter? Can it be said that country is made in its substance and capacities by the presence of those living forms, such as this boy, in whose bodies are carried stories of country? That is, against the Western view of country as fixed, immutable and non-sensate, as dumb and mute, the country might instead be substantiating of human embodiment, and perhaps also substantialised by it.

Within Australian Indigenous conceptions of country, country is bound with story itself: 'Stories are told to and by this ancestral land.'[1] It seems, then, that according to such a view, country writes, and might we say that bodies read?[2] If this is so, why is it then that some bodies can read this country when for others it remains illegible? For the country is filled with Indigenous men's and women's accounts of things that are clearly manifest to them but which fail to appear in the eyes of settlers, falling it seems beyond all of a settler's senses. These are 'true story' for

---

[1]   These are the words of Alexis Wright, Indigenous novelist and essayist, personal communication.

[2]   This chapter's perspectives are indebted to Vicki Kirby's writings on structuralist and poststructuralist semiotics, in particular *Telling Flesh*.

32   *The Postcolonial Eye*

contemporary Indigenous men and women, but for many if not all settlers they are mythical, fictional, fantastic. The objects to which these stories refer lack materiality, lack matter, in the settler's eye. For instance, in the following story, can you see the donkey devil that lives up in the Kimberley? Can you hear its terrifying growl?

The Donkey Devil

This story was told by Paddy Roe, a Nyigina man, and it circulates now in written form, recorded and transcribed by the white Australian anthropologist Stephen Muecke, who was there at one of its tellings (Roe 46–55). The story goes like this: two men have been drinking and are coming home in the dark when they see a strange creature, with donkey ears and the nose of a dog, and a dog's woolly tail. The look of this thing and its terrible noise frighten them, but when later they return to the site with Paddy Roe to show him what they have seen, they find the thing is no longer there and that it has left no tracks in the soft ground. There is no evidence of its ever having been there, save for the men's own witnessing. In the second part of Paddy Roe's story, the same creaturely thing is seen again a few weeks later, this time by a party of old women, all sober. Again, Paddy Roe goes back to where the creature was sighted this second time, his spear at the ready, 'tommyhawk' in his belt, but again there are no tracks except those made by the women as they fell about in fright and ran away. The women have returned to the site with Paddy Roe but hold back from approaching too closely, and are willing only to point to where the creature had lain:

> 'He's layin' down right there' [the women] say 'In dis way' –
> 'Yeah? but I can see all the road –
> two road see one turn this way nother one there and what in the middle nothing' I tell-em –
> (Whisper) 'Oh must be gone' –
> 'Oh well we go an' have a look might be dog might be donkey' –
> so we went right up there an' have a look oh all wet ground –
> can't miss seeing the track –
> 'Where youfella seen im?' –
> 'Here he's layin' down' –
> 'Where's the track' I tell-im –
> nothing no track nothing –
> ah that made me think back now that other thing this other two bloke seen –
> 'Ahh this is only, mus' be devil' I tell-im –
> 'Something live in this country you know' I tell-im –
> 'Ahh all right' they say this never worry them no more – (Roe 54–5)

'Something live in this country you know', Paddy Roe says, but can a settler see or believe it? Has any settler ever seen what these men and women say is there, what in English they call a donkey devil? Could a settler read this country in ways that make the donkey devil appear?

Coming to Matter   33

For one white Australian reader, Russell West-Pavlov, Paddy Roe's story about the donkey devil is about what is not visible or legible, it is about an absence of readable signs out of which knowledge might nevertheless come. This, he points out, is performed in the story itself. As Paddy Roe does not know what the men and women have seen when they first tell him of their experiences, neither does the reader; since Roe does not see this creature or any readable marks of its passage, the story becomes about unreadability. This is reinforced by the interjections of a young girl, Paddy Roe's great-granddaughter, who was present at the time that Stephen Muecke recorded the story, and whose interjections have been included in his transcript: 'Nothing there', the young girl says, 'Nothing there'. These interjections, West-Pavlov suggests, anticipate the story's end and point to its crucial aspect:

> What the young girl's interruptions foreground is the fact that this story is about *not* being able to read. The cornerstone of the narration is a double absence: first, that of the narrator himself as an eye-witness at the sighting of the donkey devil, and then subsequently, the absence of readable traces of the donkey's passage. (West-Pavlov 163–4, original emphasis)

'Absence', he goes on to say, 'is the crucial semiotic element in this story diptych ... Reading, in this configuration of the semiotic process, is something that happens out of a context of lack'. West-Pavlov proposes an ethics of cross-cultural reading that turns on such a gap in knowledge, where the story, indeed country itself, is unreadable 'in the first instance' for Indigenous subjects and for a white subject willing to position himself as an unknowing subject. After positioning oneself as an unknowing subject before this story, West-Pavlov suggests, one can come into knowledge. It is only when the white settler reader positions himself in the same place as Paddy Roe or his great-granddaughter that some kind of knowledge can finally be secured: 'Once we too have been *initiated* via the act of listening, and have become familiar with the absences of the text, we will be in a position, with Paddy Roe's great-granddaughter, to elucidate and activate the lacunae of this text: "Nothing there"' (West-Pavlov 164, emphasis added).

But is nothingness really the end of Paddy Roe's story? For the lack of tracks is operating not as an absence, not as 'no thing', for this traditional Nyigina man but as a sign, and a sign of a powerful presence: 'Something live in this country you know' (Roe 55). Paddy Roe reads the lack of tracks together with the men and women's accounts as a sign of the presence of the living thing in the country, this devil. For Roe, his story seems to be quite precisely about legibility rather than its absence. Roe is showing that he *can* read the country; and he knows there is something there to be seen, a donkey devil. West-Pavlov suggests that Paddy Roe comes to his knowledge about what is present by way of a reading process that puts what can be seen next to what cannot, but West-Pavlov nevertheless keeps returning only to what is not there, the donkey devil's tracks. West-Pavlov's discourse always pulls short of acknowledging what it is that Paddy Roe and his compatriots insist *is* there – this donkey devil. He never arrives at the knowledge that his own reading practice promises. There is instead a seemingly anxious repetition of the young girl's: 'Nothing there.' It seems that at this moment it is the white reader who has made some thing into no thing, who has produced an absence, a gap which he then closes over while calling semiotics to his aid.

It would seem then that Paddy Roe's story might be about illegibility only for the white settler in whose eyes surely some part of the story does indeed remain unreadable, invisible. It is in the eyes of the white settler reader that both the donkey devil's tracks and the donkey devil itself fail to appear. West-Pavlov cannot read the donkey devil nor write it into legibility; it fails to appear in his eyes. It is quite simply invisible, inaudible, and, I suspect, unbelievable, too. The white settler can neither sense it, nor make sense of it.

I can – *just* – imagine the donkey devil once its form has been described to me. I can recall images of a donkey's solid, recalcitrant body and a dog's hairy tail and, reassembling these images, make a new one. In making this new image, though, I do not make a new belief. I do not believe in the donkey devil; I certainly do not believe that it would appear to me if I stood on the same ground as the men and women who told Paddy Roe what they had seen. (Is it even right, I wonder, to think that I could stand on the same *ground*, the same 'country'?) Why can't we, West-Pavlov and I – white settlers – read the country as Paddy Roe and others do? Why can't we see what we are told is there to see?

'There is and can be no brute vision', insists Joan Copjec (*Read My Desire* 34). There is no visual field composed only through pre-given, 'natural' capabilities of this organ, the eye. 'Semiotics, and not optics, is the science that enlightens for us the structure of the visual domain' (*Read My Desire* 34). However, this is not to say that vision is freed of the body. Vision, she claims, is neither outside the body, nor is the viewer outside the world, looking on. The observer is within the world and within his or her body. If vision is corporealised, by implication there is no viewing position that one can take up outside one's own body. To move subject positions is not to stand in another's position and look out through his or her eyes, but to shift one's position in relation to other objects in a scene.[3] Any subject only looks at the world through his or her own embodied vision.

What then of the touchstone of appeals to empathic relations to others: the truism that one should stand in another's position, see through another's eyes? Might this then be a fantasy of occupation, a repetition of the colonising impulse to possess? West-Pavlov assumes to rest his vision in the eyes of the young girl. If we follow his reading practice, he claims, we will be in a position with Paddy Roe's great-granddaughter to come to the knowledge comported by the story. West-Pavlov hopes to occupy the same position as this young Indigenous girl, and thereby come to her knowledge. But, according to the argument that vision is corporealised, he cannot do this, he must remain in his own position/s, which is to say in his own embodiment, with its attendant blind spots. In this case, it is

---

[3]   See Parveen Adams on anamorphosis in *Emptiness* 109–21.

the donkey devil that falls into West-Pavlov's blind spots, this is where *his* vision fails, not the girl's.

And of course it is where my vision falls short, too. Like West-Pavlov, I can neither see nor believe in the donkey devil. Neither Paddy Roe's nor his story's protagonists' vision is mine. There is no *initiation* or other *rites de passage*, to use West-Pavlov's words, that can bring a settler into an Indigenous viewing position. What appears in our visual fields will be limited by our embodied subjectivities. There are not subject positions that are distinct from the subjects who occupy them, or, rather, there are no subject positions that are distinct from the subjects who *are* them. And if we follow Copjec and take vision as subjective and thereby corporealised, then a white subject's embodiment is surely implicated in what he can and cannot see.

A Body of Feeling

But what is 'the body'? In ethnographic discourses, 'the body' tends to be universalised so that embodiment can be understood as the same *thing* across cultures. Vicki Kirby puts this so well when she says: 'this same body reappears, its naked truth culturally clothed' (Kirby *Telling Flesh* 156). In the place of a universal body – *the* body – Vicki Kirby installs a body differentiated in time and space. Consider her vivid example: the powers of a devotee of the Hindu festival of thaipusam. Metal spokes are driven into a devotee's skin and organs, and hands and tongue, face, lips and neck may also be pierced. And yet, Kirby says, 'for the serious thaipusam devotee, none of these effects is realised. This man does not bleed, nor does he scar' (Kirby *Telling Flesh* 3). Does this mean, she asks, that the very biology of the devotee performs itself differently? Are these rituals productive in the most visceral sense: entering and constituting the delicate blood vessels and nerves perhaps, the bones and heart and other organs as well as the skin, the ears, and the other senses? Is this what Kirby suggests in that telling phrase 'culture in-corporated' whereby the cultural practices of the devotee are taken into his body, re-making it in the process, making therefore a different body than the body of an onlooker for instance?

> However it might be conveyed through the conventions of ethnographic reportage, the descriptive minutiae of this ritual's context do little to explain what makes its performance so compelling. Even if we presume to elaborate the cultural significance of this festival within Hinduism, as it is expressed in a specific geographical location, and as it might be understood and even experienced by a particular participant, such explanations cannot answer our prurient curiosity. It is not the explanations that this man or his society might make of his ritual action that fascinate us, but rather the simple fact of what this ritual action has apparently made of him. (Kirby *Telling Flesh* 3)

Kirby also looks to the example of the profoundly deaf percussionist Evelyn Glennie to suggest that bodies are differently sensate, in this case differently

36 *The Postcolonial Eye*

'attuned' to sound: 'Glennie explains that she hears certain notes through her jaws, while others sound through parts of her face or certain parts of her feet and so on.' As Kirby continues, 'Sound is thus intricately scored and played through the staff of her body, recorded and performed in the very tissue of skin, blood, and bone' (Kirby *Telling Flesh* 63). This music is not only made from the sounds that issue from Glennie's kettledrum but it is made in the bones and other tissue of her own body. This then is rhythm, or vibration, a kind of force that is read and rewritten by her body, differently than mine, for instance. If there is then no universal body, there is no universal body of feeling.

Then there are those of us who call ourselves 'hearing' and whose bones and skin are also presumably set to rhythm or vibration by the sounding of a drum yet we do not 'hear' *this* as sound in our own tissue, we do not *feel* this force in bone and skin because our bodies, unlike Glennie's, do not know how to read and write its music. In this 'sense', it is we who are deaf.

So what of the accounts Indigenous men and women give of the 'Dreaming' as a rhythm, a push, a force – as material as Glennie's sounding drum and bone?[4] W.E.H. Stanner reported an impressive experience common among white anthropologists such as himself when speaking with Indigenous men and women about their Dreaming places which they speak of in terms of such a force, a push, something they feel in their viscera. Speaking from his experiences with the Murrinh-patha and the Warumungu, he reports that the white man will often be:

> taken by Aboriginal friends to places in the wilds and there shown something – tree, rocky out-crop, cranny, pool – with formality, pride and love. Conversations follow something like this: 'There is my Dreaming ... My father showed me this place when I was a little boy. His father showed him.' Perhaps a child stands near by, all eyes and ears. What had his father said? 'He said: "Your Dreaming is there; you want to look after this place; you don't want to let it go [forget, be careless about it]; it is from the first [totemical] man."' ... What did the father do there? 'He used to come here every year with the old men, the wise men; they used to do something here [hit, rub, break off pieces, brush with green leaves, sing]; that way they made the [totem] come on, come back, jump us, spread out.' *How* did that happen? *What* is it that is in the place? 'We do not know. *Something* is there. Like my spirit [soul, shadow, invisible counterpart]; like my Dreaming [naming the totem entity].' (Stanner 165, parentheses and emphasis in original)

Stanner's anthropologist pushes the man further: 'Will he think more? What else did his father say? That there was something in the Dreaming-place?'

> The dark eyes turn and look intent, puzzled, searching. 'My father did not say. He said this: "My boy, look! Your Dreaming is there; it is a big thing; you never let it go [pass it by]; all Dreamings [totem entities] come from there; your spirit is there."' Does the white man now understand? The blackfellow, earnest,

---

[4] For a critical perspective on anthropology's coinage of this term, see Wolfe 'On being woken up' 197–224.

friendly, makes a last effort, 'Old man, you listen! Something is there; we do not know what; *something.*' There is a struggle to find words, and perhaps a lapse into English. 'Like engine, like power, plenty of power, it does hard work; it *pushes.*' (Stanner 166, original parentheses and emphases)

Stanner's anthropologist is not satisfied with the account he is given, and he demands more words as if in the hope that were the right words found they would evoke for him the feelings that the other man claims to experience. There is a force bearing upon the other man's body, there is 'plenty of power' here, something '*pushes*' and yet the white man is unable to feel it. Is there not something in the nature of his embodiment that makes him unable to sense what for the other man is simply there? Might it be that there is some material force here, one that can only be felt by certain subjects, and that this white man is not one of these? How would it come to pass that one body-subject could feel what for another is insensible?

Perhaps the white man disbelieves the materiality of the other man's experiences, too. Nevertheless Stanner does raise the question of what these things might be that are referred to in ritual and story: are they 'ultimate or metaphysical' he asks? For Stanner this isn't a question for anthropology, though. It is for philosophy to decide: 'The true anthropological approach to such symbolism is to recognize it as a category of ontological fact' (Stanner 168). For him, anthropology's proper object of study, then, is the being of the other, read through a system of signs.

A Country Moved by the Dance

The Indigenous man in Stanner's anecdote claims that the force he can feel – the Dreaming – is made to 'come on, come back, jump up, spread out' by the rituals the old men have always practised. This recalls Jennifer L. Biddle's descriptions of the women-only *Yawulyu* Dreaming ceremonies among the Warlpiri of the Central Desert, ceremonies through which the women aim at the 'livening-up of country – rejuvenating, re-vitalising, "feeding" certain places, species and persons' (24). Biddle, like Stanner, takes the objects to which the ceremony and art refer as significant ontologically. For Biddle, however, the question of whether the objects are 'ultimate or metaphysical' is rather differently posed – the rituals produce the objects which they name. In this case, the rituals *make* instead of only mark a way of being. The rituals are in this sense performative. The women's rituals – which include applying paint to the breast and, in the contemporary context, painting the same patterns on canvas – produce the objects to which they refer. That is, they *make* through *marking*, with paint on skin or canvas. Sometimes the ritual of painting on canvas is all that is available to these women who, through the ongoing effects of colonisation, are distanced from their traditional country. Again, Biddle insists on the art as being read not as representations of some thing but as bringing this into being, as performative. And, significantly, Biddle sees the viewer – including the white viewer – as part of the performance. The viewer becomes part of the processes through which country is potentially 'livened-up'.

The rituals of *Yawulyu* bespeak what Biddle describes as a breasted ontology. Paint is used to mark skin in ways that emphasise the size of the breast and its fall – concentric circles and half moons. The ideal breast is the one that points downward as if to the mouth of an infant, where that hungry mouth belongs to the ground, to country. Country will be nourished by this ritual in which woman and, it seems, country itself participate in the intimacy of pull, pause, pull of feeding:

> A certain slow-speed jump forward is made where the feet don't actually leave the ground and yet manage to slowly, measurably, compel the dancer forward, undulating the breast vertically each time – far more the point it seems than any actual distance covered. The breast rises, falls, slaps, rhythmically against the body, an action which seems designed to produce the effect of 'sagging' and 'falling' the breast ... Like arrows pointing downward, the nipples seems to aim at the ground, almost poking it, were they closer, with a thwarted start and stop so that the breast moves, vibrates and stills again, a tremulousness produced of both flesh and design. (Biddle 18–19)

In the movement of the dance:

> The breast is compelled downward towards a no-longer static or inert ground – country – that simply provides a platform for the dancing. But this is ground – country – which is enlivened by the pounding of the dancers' feet, the slapping of the breasts in rhythm with the singers' voices and the swirling of the dust engendered, which appears as almost an active partner to the dancers, almost as if it too moves, rising up to meet the breast in 'fall', like the infant, pulling for a feed. (19)

Country, Biddle says here, is 'almost an active partner to the dancers, almost as if it too moves'; country is 'enlivened by the pounding of the dancers' feet'. It is this way of apprehending country and embodiment that I want to tease out here. What is 'country', what is 'body', that they can be in such proximity to each other, in this 'almost' living and fleshly intimacy?

If we take seriously Biddle's claim that these women's rituals are performative, that they make what they name – that they make in the process of marking – then we can turn to bodies and country and ask how these are made by marking. In particular, how is body made in relation to country, in these and other cultural practices? Following structuralist and poststructuralist theories of signification, we might say that there is no body or country before the making of the marks whereby a universe of undifferentiated sound and image is cut and ordered into a chain of signification through which 'noise' or substance is differentiated and made intelligible. We would then say that in any cultural form some of this substance emerges as discernible objects through certain cultural practices – including ritual, storytelling and painting – and that different objects are thereby produced within different cultural forms. There are no things before these practices – there are no pre-given or 'natural' phenomena as such. There are no objects given to us by an independent reality, rather they are made by a range of practices and techniques.

Therefore some things that appear in one cultural form fail to appear – fail to be made – in another.

But what then of the tissue of the body, the substance of stone? Aren't these, too, made by the mark? Here I am indebted again to Vicki Kirby and her insistence on the materiality of the sign – her insistence that we follow through the logic of Saussurian semiotics to its surprising ends (Kirby *Telling Flesh* passim). For each of these white observers – West-Pavlov, Stanner and now Biddle – mobilise semiotics, albeit in their different ways, when they consider 'being' in a (post) colonial setting but stop short, I suggest, in the face of the materiality of 'body' and 'ground'.

Might it not be that body and country are different things in the Warlpiri context, for instance, than they are in the settler one? This is to say something other than that this thing called the body for instance takes different meanings unto itself depending on its habits and habitus. It is to say something other than that there is a 'cultural corporeal schema', in Maurice Merleau-Ponty's terms, defined by Rosalyn Diprose as 'a set of habits, gestures and conducts formed over time in relation to other bodies'.[5] It is instead to say that the very substance of bodies is not universal but is made differently in different places, and that country, too, is made differently in relation to different bodies. Country and body might be consubstantialising such that one does not 'have' the same body if one lives in one country rather than another. And, I want to suggest, Warlpiri live in another country to the one in which I live, even if they and I abide in the same coordinates of longitude and latitude, because 'country' is constituted differently in these two bodily contexts. (This is what I meant earlier when I asked whether I could stand on the *same ground* as Paddy Roe or his great-granddaughter.)

Thus, when in rituals of scarification Warlpiri bury earth under their skin, are they as Biddle says housing country in flesh or might this intimacy be reconceived as taking the body into itself? (Biddle 21). For if their country and flesh are not the same as mine, how can I say what is their country, what is their flesh? To put this another way, what or who is buried in what or whom? We might say at this point that country is not *like* skin, it *is* skin, but it is their 'skin' and 'country' we are speaking of, and not mine. Or, to give another example, when the country appears to move in response to the dance, again we could ask: where does 'country' begin and 'body' end? For a Warlpiri woman dancing *Yawulyu* it seems not only that her body is in intimate relation with her country, but that her body might already be comprised of and by the thing I call country but which will be body to her: her bodiliness is already countriness – but in my language not hers. Her body in-corporates what I would call country, ground say, and makes things that I see as body into country. So when the settler observes an intimacy between Warlpiri women's bodies and ground such that their boundaries seem to dissipate, we would have to ask: what does this settler see as 'body' and 'country'?

---

[5] Diprose, referring to Maurice Merleau-Ponty's idea of a cultural corporeal schema, quoted by Biddle 24.

40   *The Postcolonial Eye*

This is the scope of cultural differences between white settler and Warlpiri: they are radical, they are in the register of embodiment, they concern the very making of matter. If body and country are not allowed this radical difference in their conception, if the very substance of 'body' and 'country' are not allowed to be different, then the body is once again installed as a universal body *in its matter*. It is a *thing* before the mark.

It is not enough to speak of the differences as being in the register of belief or epistemology if by that we mean that belief or knowledge are separable from the embodied subject. One does not 'have' beliefs or knowledges, one is had by them; one is possessed by knowledge as much as one ever possesses it. To live in a cultural context, a place, is to be a particular body/subject. It is to enter/be entered into a particular arrangement of matter.

If the *Yawulyu* ceremony is performative then, Biddle argues, so too are the marks made on canvas. Speaking specifically about the art of Emily Kame Kngwarreye, Kathleen Petyarre and Dorothy Napangardi, this art is also 'increase' ceremony now and it is 'experienced as sensation – in the body of the viewer herself' (Biddle 16). This includes the body of the white viewer of this art. Moved by unaccustomed affect, this viewer is now open to the sensation of this breasted ontology out of which the art has been made and which it makes. These works operate 'to dissipate bodily boundaries between viewer and image ... between Whitefellas and Blackfellas'. More than this, the viewer of this art, including a 'Whitefella', might in an act of 'intersubjective mutuality' 'bring forth the potency, the latency of the image-experience' (Biddle 17).

There is the risk, though, that we might forget that there is no equivalence between the white 'body' and the Warlpiri 'body' so that their respective dissipation is not reciprocal or equivalent. We could go further to say that 'Whitefella' and Warlpiri cannot merge with each other on the ground of affect, experienced as bodily sensation, because 'ground' and 'body' are not the same 'things'. Whatever the meeting place here, whatever the point at which dissipation can be said to occur, is unknowable, unnameable. The risk, again, is for the settler to enter into a fantasy that, in relation to this art, she can take up an indigenous body of sense and sensation.

How can I feel, how can I be brought back to my body and its sensations, brought back to affect as a grounding on which to meet an other, even intermingle with her, experience my boundaries and hers as dissipating – how is this possible when the 'bodies' in question might not be of the same 'stuff' at all? We share neither the same body nor the same country. Whatever my embodied subjectivity looks upon, feels, hears, is limited by the stories it was told and tells, a body differently made in its very substance. For the Warlpiri, as for me, there is still 'body' and 'country', but their boundaries might (and perhaps must) be different than mine, a white 'settler'. Rather than being understood as giving up or dissipating bodily boundaries, these Desert women's performative gestures might mark different boundaries around body and country than mine. There might then still be 'body', 'country', oneself and others, even while these intermingle, consubstantialise.

Falling From View

In Western perspectival art, the so-called vanishing point is that tiny mark on paper or canvas that denotes the place where parallel lines, lines that do not converge, nevertheless appear to do so. It is among the paradoxes of Western representational art that what does not meet is made to do so; and what we might think of as huge beyond our knowing – infinity – is rendered no bigger than a dot. The significance of this dot nevertheless cannot be measured by its size, for it is nothing less than the mark around which the entire scene is arranged. The lines that radiate from this dot circumscribe the space, making it at once seemingly finite and all-encompassing. The illusion of Western perspectival art depends then on the making finite of infinitude; there is nothing outside the scene in view. Rather than allowing for infinity, the dot marks the scene's enclosure. In this art, too, the image extends to include the body of the viewer. The viewer is incorporated in the image. This is effected through the vanishing point as the mark from which the lines of perspective are drawn: that is, the lines move *from* infinity, not towards it. This projection in perspectival art is towards the viewing subject, who is included within its reach. This is how the illusion of three-dimensionality is achieved. The lines of projection move outwardly from the surface of the painting to include the viewer, who now enjoys the illusion of being there, in the scene. The enjoyment of this viewing experience lies in the illusion that the viewer is in the scene, seeing all that there is to be seen (Copjec *Imagine* 187–96).

How then do settler subjects see the art from the Central Desert, art that arises from within a different paradigm of perception than our own? Of my own experience as a settler subject, I can say this: when I am in the same room as a painting by Emily Kame Kngwarreye I turn away, I avert my eyes, or I keep the image at the periphery of my vision. Not because I am not drawn to it, not because it does not fascinate, but *because* it is so very beautiful. Unlike some other observers, though, I cannot make 'sense' of it. I cannot for instance accommodate this art into the symbolic order of Western modern art – of modernism or other forms of abstraction.[6] Nor can I tie it to anything I have witnessed: I have not seen another woman's skin painted up in such colours; I have no experience of ground being shaken by the dance; I have not heard women singing to and with country. I fail to bring this art into my own symbolic order, into the scene I can see, into the story I know. I cannot tie such an image to anything I have seen before and so it remains floating, unassimilable.

There are other settler subjects who can look upon this art, and who can find words to translate if not the art itself then their viewing experience, and in ways that lure me back to the art, who assist me in the act of looking.[7] Biddle's prose does this, abstracting for me some of the different principles on which this art and

---

[6] See, for instance, Muecke.

[7] See, for instance, Morphy; Dussart, 'A body painting' 186–202, and Dussart, 'Shown but not shared' 253–66.

its effects are founded. She points out that the recent art of the Central Desert might not, for instance, have perspective, or if it does it is vertical rather than horizontal. 'There is', she says, 'no focal point for these paintings, or if there is it is vortex-like in its draw, pull and force'. Unlike the projection of Western perspectival art, the illusion of three-dimensionality is evoked in these paintings as movement below the surface of the painting. This movement, or 'shimmer', suggestive of water and light, is produced in a technical sense through the application of paint in layers that are then scraped off, and it is in-between and around the remaining traces of paint that the figures appear, produced in the negative as it were, or they can be spotted, peeped, through traces of paint. There is a repetition of lines and other marks through which a 'rhythmic, mesmerising' movement is effected, and in this 'totalising experience and expression' there is 'no interference' (Biddle 28). These are paintings into which one falls, according to Biddle – 'one loses oneself in them'. 'Through viewing these works, as it were, one becomes vulnerable to their sensibilities insofar as they incite enmeshment, an enfolding', even an 'encapturing', experienced as endless, 'unhalting' (Biddle 16). This art, in the words now of Barbara Glowczeski, 'invites us to penetrate the texture of the canvas', and it is from this penetration, Biddle suggests, that an emergence of the painting's figures are effected (Biddle 23).

However, at some point here the lexicon has shifted and rather than the viewer *falling* into the images, she is invited to *penetrate* them. Moreover, this is a penetration from which the viewer returns bearing some *thing*. The trajectory is a double one, and rather than the figure of the painting being seen, elusively, enigmatically, under the surface of the canvas, it is brought out of it. We might ask, then, have the conventions of Western perspectival art perhaps been recuperated, shaping what can be seen by the settler viewer, shaping her viewing experience? Have not lines of projection in some way been reinstalled, so that there is a perception of a movement of a figure out of the canvas? Perhaps too the viewer can now enjoy the illusion that she is within the image's reach, that she too is incorporated within the image, seeing all there is to be seen.

The 'Whitefella' can take this enjoyment in the visual experience if she believes, as Biddle does, that the paintings 'invite' her, even 'insist' upon her 'inhabiting' a place where all bodily differentiation is denied: between body and canvas, between country and Ancestral body and, crucially, between 'Whitefella' and 'Black' (Biddle 28). An 'imperative', that is, to experience sameness: of body and viewpoint. One question then insists itself: who is the seeing 'I' who is invoked according to this view of Warlpiri art? Is it a Warlpiri seeing 'I', or does a settler viewing subject in the end re-make Warlpiri vision in the same terms as her own? Or is there something else in operation here? Might there be the hope that a settler subject can have the Warlpiri I/eye without relinquishing her own, and so enjoy the illusion of seeing all there is to see?

Theories of the phenomenon of anamorphosis are one way of approaching these questions, since they instate enjoyment and anxiety at the heart of vision. Anamorphosis, for Lacan, is that phenomenon of looking where an 'optical transposition' takes place where 'a certain form that wasn't visible at first sight transforms itself into a readable image' (Lacan *Ethics* 135). This form remains indecipherable while the viewer stands in one position before an image and only becomes decipherable when the viewer moves to another viewpoint. The viewing subject cannot see both aspects of the form at once. Each belongs to different scenes; they cannot be held in view at one and the same time.

Following Lacan, Parveen Adams takes the example of Holbein's famous painting *The Ambassadors* (1533) through which to explore the nature of the anamorphotic form. There is of course something in excess of the image of the ambassadors and their instruments of navigation and astronomy. 'There at the bottom of the picture', Adams reminds us, 'is something scroll-like':

> As I move away it comes into perspective as a skull. This phenomenon of anamorphosis involves a projection which is distorted from the point of view of the subject who is perceiving the rest of the picture. Only from another angle can the projection be deciphered. This distortion in fact unhinges the whole point of view. In Holbein's terms, death unhinges worldly pleasures. In Lacan's terms, castration undoes the uncertainty and given character of visual space. (Adams *Emptiness* 111)

What is crucial about anamorphosis is that the form cannot be seen in its dual aspects at the same time. For the subject who can see the ambassadors there is no other figure – there is no skull hovering in the foreground. There is only an indecipherable mark around or through which this viewer will look in order to arrange the scene of the ambassadors. This is the scene that makes sense to the viewer, this is the scene which the viewer desires to see. For, as Adams has commented, the image of the ambassadors 'is a masterpiece of theatrical, illusionistic space. It feels as though our vision and pleasure are at one. I enjoy what I see and I see what I enjoy' (Adams *Emptiness* 111).

The viewer sees what she can, and enjoys what she sees, dropping from her sights that which does not hold pleasure, which is not intelligible to her. The subject favours the view that confirms her own sense of the 'truth' of the scene. But the anamorphotic moment shows that there is something that escapes her vision; in the anamorphotic form she glimpses the possibility that there is another scene, another story, one in which this form belongs. To glimpse the anamorphotic form is not to be confused with seeing the other scene or world, for what is seen is only a fragment, unassimilable in the scene in which it seems to float. This is the moment when the subject's certainty in his or her vision fails: the glimpse of another, inaccessible world, the fact of otherness, and the failure of the viewing subject's story or scene to hold, to give account of everything. The moment when the form first becomes visible is associated with what Adams calls 'a momentary headiness, a sudden capacity to think' in which there is the brief hope that both views of the same form might be held together (Adams *Emptiness* 112). But they cannot hold, and so the form produces anxiety too as the subject loses certainty in his or her capacity for perception.

44 *The Postcolonial Eye*

For white viewers, the art of Emily Kame Kngwarreye might itself be an anamorphotic form: we glimpse another perspective, a figure that can only take its meaning from another scene or story than our own. This moment, when we glimpse the fact of otherness, is a moment of anxiety from which we step back, into the certainty of our own scene, our story. We step back into that position before the canvas where what falls from view is otherness rather than ourselves. In this sense, then, my failure to look and Biddle's looking might each turn on the same thing: the anxiety evoked in the face of unassimilable difference.

To return to the scene with which we began, of a small boy walking across Central Desert country. Now we must install, too, the body of the settler, the one who looks upon this scene, the one who writes it. For it is from my own body that this scene is seen, in my eyes the boy's body and country appear in the way I have written them. I can see neither *his* body nor *his* country. These are among the things that fall into the vanishing point of difference. There is a point where the boy disappears from my view – he disappears from the scene of my own imagining, the finite space that I imagine and through which I am imaginable, intelligible, to myself. To allow him his difference would be to allow for the fact that he is in another scene, another story, and therefore can move beyond the horizon of my own.[8] It would be to allow the 'vanishing point' to be not a dot through which the scene is rendered finite and closed, but a place through which he can and will pass.

---

[8] 'And if the openness in being is a horizon-structure and not the production of a void, then the seer and the visible need no longer be ontological opposites; the horizon includes the seer', Lingis *xliii*. Or, in Merleau-Ponty's own words: 'he before whom the horizon opens up is caught up, included within it' (148–9).

Chapter 3
What Falls From View?
On Re-reading *Plains of Promise*

> After all, the best way to turn someone or something into an object is to kill it ...
> But there are degrees of objectification. The process of mortification begins with
> how the other is seen, and supposedly known.
>
> —Teresa Brennan *Exhausting Modernity* (35)

Reading is a visual practice. It always involves a scene. What scenes do white readers of Alexis Wright's *Plains of Promise* gaze upon as they hold its pages in their hands, this text bearing the signature of a woman whose tribal affiliations are with the Waanji people of the highlands of the Gulf of Carpentaria? If the visual field is always structured by desire – in the words of Parveen Adams, 'I enjoy what I see and I see what I enjoy' – then a question insists itself: what scenes can white readers see when we read a text such as this one?[1] What scene will our desires produce, and what might fall from view?

Plains of Promise can be read for the vistas it opens up to its readers, the countries it invites us into, the new knowledges it offers, but here I am aiming to read the text rather differently (if reading is still the right word). I am aiming to show that there are some things that might remain unimaginable, invisible, unknowable in this text – unreadable. Of course, all texts and all readings must inscribe gaps, holes – places where meaning cannot be made, just as all visual fields have their blind spots. There is no position in which one can stand and see all; there is no position from which one can know all. Likewise, there is no reading practice that enables one to see all there is to see in a text. Generally, in reading we try to cover over these gaps, bridge them in some way. It is the particular places where a white reader might remain blind before this text, however – the places where such a reader might be unable to make meaning, where the gaps cannot be bridged – that I am interested in here. *Plains of Promise* seems to foreground such questions of vision and its imperfections.

---

[1] Adams *Emptiness* 111. It has been rightly pointed out that whites commonly assume their readership to be white, and that this is reflected in the grammatical forms we use. So, white writers will use 'we' and 'us' in ways that suggest there is no one else in the conversation; an assumed 'we' speaking about 'them'. At the very moment that whiteness is critiqued, it is newly centralised and naturalised. At the same, however, it is crucial that white writers like myself find ways to install ourselves in our critiques of whiteness, using the first person pronouns 'we' and 'us' now to implicate ourselves in the critique rather than always locating whiteness in others.

46 *The Postcolonial Eye*

Returning to *Plains of Promise* many years after it was first published, I see the text differently than I used to do. Now, in my eyes, it organises itself around the final few passages, the story an old traditional man, Elliot, tells about a waterbird. In my earlier readings, though, this story tended to fall from my view. Like so many other critics and reviewers, I failed to allow these final pages to do their work. I am interested in this shift, what in Lacanian terms can be thought of as an anamorphotic shift, in which a form or object that at first is not seen then becomes the very hinge on which a scene turns. The anamorphotic object is sometimes compared to a mark or stain such as might occur on the surface of a painting and through which a viewer peers, her 'eye' filling in the gaps in vision that the mark produces so that now the image is seen as if it were entire. But in anamorphosis, the mark turns out not to be incidental after all, but rather an object that, once seen, radically re-casts the image.

In my reading of *Plains of Promise*, this last story which I used to see as an incidental addition to the text – a fragment of a myth, a brief passage that seemed like a flourish at the end of the story – turns out to be an anamorphotic form, no longer a mark on the page that I can look through (or overlook) but an object that, once seen, produces a retrospective and radical revisioning of the novel. This is not to say, though, that the reading I can do now is complete; it is not to offer a corrective reading. From a Lacanian perspective, anamorphotic forms produce another effect again: they point to the uncertainty and incompleteness of every act of vision, every meaning or position.[2] One's vision is always partial, subjective, incomplete – in this sense, one is always blind – and what one can see is shaped by what one wants to see. They show that the confidence one might have in one's capacities to see what there is to see is a fantasy, that the visual field is a field of desire. So, this final passage, while it does open new vistas, new scenes to me, also points to the limits of my vision. There are countries onto which this text opens that as a white woman (with all the limitations of that position), I am unable to enter, worlds of meaning that I am unable to read.

There are some claims I am going to make at the outset, claims that might seem to be truisms too familiar to be rehearsed. This is not in order to undo them, as is the usual aim of this kind of move, but to reiterate their significance. First, there is the claim that reading is always a located practice. I read Alexis Wright's *Plains of Promise* from the position of a white reader with all the historical contingencies that this implies, where whiteness is always constituted in inextricable relation to other strands in a grid of cultural intelligibility, to borrow Judith Butler's terms (from *Bodies*), and therefore cannot be said to have a life separate from these. This leads to the second claim, that such whiteness of course cannot be said to originate in the colour of my skin or other bodily features but precedes such a reading of bodily difference. Once we can read race as lying in skin colour we are already

---

[2]   'Nonknowledge or invisibility is not registered as the wavering and negotiations between two certainties, two meanings or positions, but as the undermining of every certainty, the incompleteness of every meaning or position' (Copjec *Read My Desire* 18).

inhabiting whiteness's regime, we are one of its subjects. As one of this novel's white readers, I am a subject of and subject to the regime of whiteness that this novel shows us even as I attempt to critique such a regime. The third claim brings me back to my concern with reading: reading is a practice of meaning-*making*, reading is poiesis. It is a subjective and imaginative act: reading is writing.

While many Australian literary critics nod to such claims, still the idea persists that white subjects can know the meanings of Indigenous-signed texts and the intentions of their authors, if only we are careful and canny enough. There is a positivism in these reading practices that will insist on telling what an Indigenous-signed text is about, that looks for correspondences through which a signifier from one world of meaning can be tied to a signifier from another, making an equation, taking pleasure in decoding the Indigenous text with reference, for instance, to anthropological discourses, raising these as if they were touchstones of interpretation. We can, according to such practices, take recourse in biography, history and anthropology, not to unsettle a white's reading of the novel but to shore it up. This is a critical approach which emphasises a reader's capacity to see and know.

There is a body of literary criticism that does something very different to this, though, aiming to discover what a reader does not know, and more than this, to show that there is something in any text, in any field of signification, which cannot be known. In making that move, whole new scenes of possibility are opened up. What follows is an attempt to re-read *Plains of Promise* in the light of this other mode of literary criticism. It is a speculative exercise that takes as its subject white reading practices rather than Indigenous universes of meaning. To the extent that I venture to read Indigenous worlds of signification from *Plains of Promise*, I take only faltering steps: steps that can and will be retraced. And I will insist that *Plains of Promise* is not only a difficult book for many white readers to make meanings of, but that in places it is necessarily impossible, and that this is among its accomplishments rather than its failings. Some of the important work this writing does is to disorient its white readers.

This is not to claim that *Plains of Promise* can be read 'properly' only by Indigenous readers, or that they and not white readers can read it in its entirety. For one thing, this would be to claim a singular world of meaning for Indigenous subjects, as if there were a pan-Aboriginality. There is not one Australian Indigenous people, but many: these differences are after all inscribed in this novel itself. But this essay is not about how Indigenous readers view this novel but how some white readers have seen it, and in doing this I foreground my own reading and the gaps in my vision.

In speaking of white reading practices I am of course neither speaking of something that originates from an essence carried in the body nor suggesting that these practices are inevitable and unvarying. I am, instead, trying to make visible the outlines and valences of certain critical practices that persist, even prevail. These are practices that risk collapsing differences between white cultures and Indigenous ones, despite critics very strongly stating their wishes that such differences continue to live and flourish.

In Plain View?

In *Plains of Promise*, Indigenous men and women disappear from a missionary's sights. Still, the missionary continues with the illusory pleasure that he has complete and perfect vision: he believes he can see all there is to see, and that he can trust what he sees. *Plains of Promise* resists this belief, showing where his vision fails, and crucially that failure occurs before a young Indigenous girl with whom the missionary has become obscenely fascinated. I start my reading of the novel with this example as a way of opening onto the wider questions of the differentials in perception that the novel points to and enacts, questions that I take to refer not only to the novel's white protagonists but also to its white readers.

It is the 1950s and a mother and her small child, Ivy Koopundi, are forcibly displaced to St Dominic's Mission in northern Queensland. The missionary, Errol Jipp, immediately separates mother and child, interning the girl in the so-called dormitory where she will be subjected to the dormitory system's manifold disciplines and deprivations, away from her 'bad mother', Aboriginal Number 976–805.[3] The mother is now completely despairing: she has nothing left, she is a 'lost number amongst the lost and condemned ... Her heart stopped dead when they spoke to her just before taking the child' (13). If she is already subjected to the mortification of white ways of seeing and knowing that produce her as a number on the state's tally books, this process takes a final, fatal turn. Alarmed by her grief at separation from her child, Jipp incarcerates the woman in the 'black hole' – the prison cell at the Mission, a tiny space, a mere 180 by 300 centimetres (38) – in the hope of frightening her into passivity. When Ivy Koopundi's mother is released, she soaks herself with kerosene before walking into the campfire.

What can Errol Jipp see of this traumatic scene, and what drops from his view? Jipp cannot see, for instance, that in the nights before her death the woman is tortured by 'small and faceless creatures' who come in the night 'down the ropes from the story skies, lowering their dirty wet bodies until they reached the ground outside the hut where she slept'. He cannot know that: 'There in silence they went after her, pulling at her skin, trying to rip her apart ... Again and again they came back through the nights to enjoy another attack. Again and again they made her theirs nightly' (14). Nor does Jipp see what comes next, the worst nightmare, a black bird that flies in the night: 'Now the black bird has time for torment. It attacks in the darkness in the perfect moment – the moment of loss. Its attack is unrelenting. Face, back of head, shielding arms – the pecking persists as she crawls on her stomach into the shack which offers entrapment but no escape' (14).

Are these visitations only the woman's private madness, are they delusions produced by the illness that is repeatedly referred to in the text? (Some commentators suggest this is influenza, for instance.) Perhaps, and yet others witness these visitations, too; they recognise her suffering and its very particular forms.

---

[3]   For a discussion of the dormitory system on Aboriginal reserves and settlements in Queensland, see Blake, and Sutton. Also, see Kidd.

Old Maudie knows: she hears not only the woman's screams but the flapping of the wings of the bird as it escapes the old woman's efforts to strike it. On the ground of the shack, Maudie finds 'the terrified, incoherent victim bleeding and shaking, huddled on the ground' (15). Is a reader to take these marks on the woman's body as material evidence that the bird does indeed pay its deathly visit? Maudie tells Jipp what she has seen, and that she knows that the mother will die soon, but he of course trusts neither the vision nor the knowledge of this Indigenous woman. *He* will not be deluded or duped. But, then, how would a white subject submit himself to another's vision, so different to his own? How to see and hear what Old Maudie says is there? Readers, too, are presented with a choice between believing in Jipp's vision or, in this case, Old Maudie's. It is the kind of choice that is posed to a reader many times.

After her mother's death, Ivy Koopundi is entirely alone and newly vulnerable to Jipp, who repeatedly rapes her. He drags her into darkened plantations and into the vestry, pulling her sack dress over her head so that she is blinded: 'Desperate enough to keep living, she struggled to gasp enough air. But her worthlessness she swallowed to the pit of her stomach … Meanwhile, he would, by God, push the evil out of the "she-devil" who was possessing him' (32). In the course of these few sentences, the point of view has shifted suddenly to indirect discourse, carrying Jipp's interior voice to us and bringing with it a disconcerting intimacy with his pleasure too; pulling a reader into the field of his desires, with all the disturbance that this might evoke in many readers. We begin by looking upon the girl's rape from a position outside the act but we are then positioned with Jipp, looking at the girl through his eyes. One of the great accomplishments of this writing for me is how effectively it shows the 'black' girl in Jipp's eyes, recalling the disturbing powers of a pornographic text to move and arouse even as (or because) it disgusts. The moves made in the grammar of this passage do not invite readers to *differentiate* themselves from Jipp but to see and feel *with* him, potentially a far more unsettling effect.

Jipp is certain he can see and know Ivy: she is black and filthy; raping her is 'tasting the filth' (29). Ivy is Jipp's first little girl (30), others will follow. Each of these little girls is made to wear a sack dress, a dirty shabby garment that Jipp fancies covers over the 'black filth' underneath but which is a means by which the young girls are made 'black' and 'filthy'. Jipp's dressing of these girls in their dirty sacks is a performative gesture in the sense made familiar by Judith Butler (in *Gender Trouble*) – it produces that which it claims is there, waiting to be found. If we go back to Parveen Adams's formulation of the visual field as a field of desire – 'I enjoy what I see and I see what I enjoy' – we might say here that Jipp desires to see the girls as black filth. The white man dresses the girls in a uniform vestment of his own design and then says, 'You are this'.

He then finds each girl to be identical to the others.[4] He rapes them at night, when their bodily differences *from each other* are covered over by darkness. Ordering his visual field in this way, he makes the girls indistinguishable from each other: 'one cannot tell them apart', they are interchangeable objects in an unending series. This collapsing of the girls' differences from each other enables Jipp's fantasy that he can stabilise the critical difference, the difference he desires to find between himself and the girls, the difference between white subject and black object.[5]

This is not a radical difference at all but an oppositional pairing of white and black where blackness is taken to be marked by its lack. So, in Jipp's eyes the provision of the dress is a gift, one that improves on the girls' naked, native condition. It is charity, it is better than nothing. But does the dress start to take on the qualities not only of the performative act, producing what it names, but of the fetish, an object that reduces anxiety by covering over a radical difference that has been discovered? For Jipp might have discovered that these Indigenous girls do not only lack after all; in fact, for him they might be too much, threatening his own coherence, his own appearance. In dressing the girls in this way, does he not hope to cast them as familiar, covering over their radical differences from him, the differences that exceed his categories of white and black? The uniform dress does double work, then. It is performative in that it produces what Jipp says it only represents, the 'filthy black'. But it does more than this: it distracts Jipp from what he knows is there – radical difference, sovereignty – that which he very precisely does not want to see and which therefore drops from his visual field. This is to speak of difference in quite particular terms: not as that which is opposite, because that is only to capture the 'other' in one's own terms. Instead it raises the idea of a radical difference, the difference that cannot be subsumed within familiar binaries, here, black and white.

I am reading Jipp, then, in terms of a fetishistic disavowal of the kind: 'I know very well, but still I will believe ...'[6] According to this reading, Jipp knows very well that before him stands another subject, living, sovereign, *different*, but all the same he will believe that this is not the case. He knows very well that the girls exceed his knowing but all the same he will believe that they are merely 'black' – knowable within the dualistic terms of race discourses. The uniform dress covers

---

[4] For a discussion of cleanliness in this novel and in other representations of Indigenous girls' treatment, see Bartlett. For more detailed personal recollections of this regime of cleanliness and order on Aboriginal reserves and settlements in Queensland, see also Huggins and Huggins, and Hegarty.

[5] Judith Butler evokes the scene of black and white as produced by the seer in her essay 'Passing, queering: Nella Larsen's psychoanalytic challenges', in *Bodies* (167–85). This notion of interrelation between seer and seen is explored widely in psychoanalytic, poststructuralist and phenomenological approaches to the visual field. For instance, for Maurice Merleau-Ponty there is no opposition between the object and subject, between the visible and the seer. One constitutes the other. See Merleau-Ponty.

[6] For a concise definition of this, see Zizek, 'How did Marx invent the symptom?' 18.

What Falls From View?   51

over not what is lacking in the other but what *is* there – the unrepresentable – and which if it were seen would undo the structure of belief that holds the white-black binary together.

Another Look

Will white readers smooth over the gaps in the textual scene of our own imagining? What will we do when faced with gaps in our visual fields, when things fall into the rents, fall into invisibility? For as I will show, Indigenous protagonists disappear from my view, and go where I cannot follow. The text describes a visual field that exceeds my capacities; it points to objects that I cannot see. Although I am told they are there, although their outlines and details are described to me, I cannot make them appear. And, when Indigenous men and women disappear from my view, it is, as I will show, a moment of my own vanishing, too. For without *them*, how can *I* appear in this scene of race?

For the elders at St Dominic's, Ivy and her mother possess an enigmatic power. The elders do not know what it is, they do not know its source or how to remedy its terrible effects among them: the mysterious illnesses and deaths that begin to permeate the community. For instance, there is the young mother and her newborn baby who die of a peculiar kind of heat: 'The perspiration ran from her hot body while she whispered that the spirit that looked like grey smoke was in the room, drawing the life from her and her baby. The next morning both the girl and the baby were gone' (40). This is no ordinary fever: 'The hut smelt as though it had burnt down. It was hours later before anyone could go inside because of the heat radiating from the destroyed bodies' (40–41). This is a strange fire that has destroyed these bodies but touched nothing else in the small hut; its only other traces are a terrible odour and enormous, lingering heat. Over several years, the elders conduct an inquiry into the causes of such deaths. As part of their investigations, they send Elliot on a journey to the mother's country. This is the place where the text takes a decided turn away from white Western realism, towards – what? Here is a moment when Western generic codes might fail, including the code of magic realism which so often is reached for by contemporary Australian critics of Indigenous-signed texts as if it offered a way out of this fix (as I argue in the following chapter).

Elliot travels through a landscape that is stranger than anything I have known or seen. He walks to the great dry lakes, Ivy Koopundi's country, and as he approaches the lakes he finds thousands of corpses of birds in and around these dry lakes, the gaping mouths of pelicans who had mistaken, as he had done, a mirage and perished, as it seems to him he will, too. Yet, his arrival in the country coincides with torrential rain, and so the lake's transformation into a vast waterland: 'The land turned into a brilliant carpet of bright shades of green moments after the rain finally stopped … The land rejoiced. The words of the world whistled by in an endless murmur of repeated rhythms' (80). Elliot throws himself above the rising waters and among the rapidly growing grasses which entomb him and there he

52   *The Postcolonial Eye*

lies for hours – or is it days, weeks, months? – during which time he is witness to the dead in furious combat with each other: 'Their living relatives were safe from the retaliations of this battle, where lost spirits fought each other individually. The arms and hands of fathers, mothers, brothers and sisters protected their own: Elliot' (81–2).

This traditional man's passage through the time and space of this country is represented in temporalities and spatialities that are not mine.[7] It seems to me that he has been travelling for a matter of weeks when it turns out that 18 months or more have passed (115). Past, present and future are differently co-ordinated: Elliot is accompanied (as I would never be) by the dead who are still present. The 'past' is alive, present, active, the dead are here now, in this time and place where time is more extensive than time as I know it, where the dead live and rush past into the future, and where space becomes dense with their presence.[8] How can I make sense of this figuring of a differently embodied subjectivity, when the very conceptions of what constitutes the living and the dead are so different? I cannot see or believe in Elliot's dead and I cannot imagine them seeing me either; it is not a body like mine over which their battles are being fought. I will never be in this scene. Its vanishing point is the place of a white reader's own vanishment; the place in which we, as 'settlers', cannot stand, cannot see and cannot appear.[9]

Although the purpose of Elliot's journey was to come to new knowledge about Ivy and her mother, Elliot seems, at first, to have learnt very little about the women. He has from the outset attributed evil powers to Ivy and her dead mother and his first and subsequent journeys appear to effect no change in his view.

---

[7] Nor is his passage through this country the same as it might have been for Ivy Koopundi, for instance, into whose country Elliot has entered as a stranger. For Elliot the forces in this country are potentially dangerous. Jennifer Biddle writes very beautifully on Warlpiri experiences of travelling to and from country (27).

[8] Deborah Bird Rose offers a fascinating description of some Yarralin views on the living and the dead in *Dingo Makes Us Human* (especially 58–73). I recommend Rose's work not in order to suggest an equivalence between Yarralin views and those figured in *Plains of Promise*, but to show the kinds of differences that exist between white Western approaches and some Indigenous ones.

[9] Some critics might argue that this is to misread the story altogether. Instead, they might say that we should be approaching it as dream, delusion, magic, as later critics will approach Wright's second novel, *Carpentaria*. But, if so, what is dream here and what reality? Smoke that moves in a dance of suffocation and the pelicans' great flight that turns towards the lake in response to the dance – is this dream or reality? Such ceremony, the narrator of the text claims, brings about the birds' return, but surely not in the mind of a white subject made in prevailing discourses of 'nature' and 'culture', 'mind' and 'body'. The ground moving and booming with dancing feet, the dancers in white paint and black-and-white pelican feathers, disguised from the spirits they have awoken: 'Spirit and man. Man and Spirit. All the same' (84–5). This narrative, then, positions itself in another epistemology, and calls into doubt any easy reading of it as magic realist, say, or as delusion or dream. Cf. Bliss. Against reading *Plains of Promise* as magic realist, see Renes.

What Falls From View?   53

When Elliot is forced by the elders to marry Ivy, now 14 years old and made pregnant by Jipp, he is only angry and uncomprehending. He becomes excessively violent towards her, and to others: he rapes and beats Ivy, he kills another man, breaking his neck and leaving him to suffocate in the dust. He is viewed with suspicion when the incinerated bodies of two old women are discovered, and again when the lacerated body of the old man Pilot Ah King is found strung among the low bushes of a prickly pear, his neck broken.

By the end of the novel, however, a transformation has occurred. Now, Elliot protects Ivy, chooses her over others, looks after this woman grown prematurely old and fragile, reclusive, creaturely, growling in fear. Ivy has become as tiny as a child, so bent over is she, and almost entirely covered by her long white hair. Elliot arranges for her lost daughter, Mary, to meet her, claiming Mary as *their* family. But what brought about this change the text does not show, or not in ways that I can see. At a certain point in the novel, Elliot stepped out of my line of sight. When he reappears, nearly 120 pages later, the narrative has moved on 30 years. Elliot now carries with him particular knowledges about Ivy and her mother that spin everything around, recasting the story so far. I do not know how he came to this new position, and his knowledge would most likely be unintelligible to me anyway. All I can see is a small story on the closing pages, the story Elliot offers to Ivy's daughter, a story from which I can take away only this: that the story of *Plains of Promise* that I have just read is not an other's story after all, but my own, by which I mean the one I could see from my partial and invested sights.

This is the story that Elliot tells to Mary as she prepares to depart from St Dominic's. It is a story that opens onto another way of seeing, a story that Elliot insists is true.

> If a beautiful bird was to miss the moment when the rest of its kind lifted from the Great Lake as the water was about to disappear, it would be lost. It may have been ready for days, even months, alongside the others. But when each day the birds lifted to the skies, perhaps the wind was not behind them, so they landed on the water again, waiting for the next day and the day after that, and so on ...
>
> If a young bird was left behind it might have died. That is what happens when these kind of birds don't make the great flight. They die very quickly. But if it does not die, then this is what could have happened.
>
> The tribes of crows wait in the spindly bush to take over the empty lake. Near the centre a little mud hole is all that is left of the great waters. There stands the lonely bird that was left behind. The crows fight over who shall have the bird for their own. It is such a beautiful little thing. After a battle that lasts for days and nights, no one has won, no one has lost. They will battle again to claim the powers of the waterbird: it is given the gift of life.
>
> The waterbirds returned when the great lake reappeared. The young bird left behind had been able to devise a secret way to make the water flow. The crows were unable to unlock this secret themselves, even though the knowledge was theirs. They were too lazy. In any case, they had not much use for water except for a mud hole good enough for drinking.

54   *The Postcolonial Eye*

Then the young waterbird had a child. So that the disappearing lake could be made to reveal its waters each year when the birds returned. The secret was passed on to the child. This meant that they should always live near the lake.

But the crows, greedy and evil, needed to live in new places. Their magic was so strong that they could take on whatever form they wished, and they made the little waterbird and its child, and the child's child and so forth go with them; to do as the evil ones pleased. And the secret of the lake went away with them. But the waterbird's children sent the secret back to the lake each year by unsuspecting carriers.

Over time, however, the waterbird's children's children's child went mad, because she lost her daughter in a terrible place. And the secret of the lake was lost because the crows were too interested in evil things and could not control the waterbird's madness.

So the great lake dried up and is no more. (303–4, original ellipses)

This passage appears in italics in the original. Italics is a multivalent font: it can indicate an interruption to the main text, for instance a parenthetical gesture or the introduction of another writing form or voice; it can denote that the text is in a foreign language; and it can denote the importance of the particular passage, lending emphasis. In the case of this final passage, we might consider whether each of these meanings can be held together at once. That is, that the text can be read as interrupting the narrative *and* as foreign (to some readers) *and* that it should be given emphasis.

This is another way of saying that this final passage is an anamorphotic form: it is a critical element that works to interrupt the scene on which a reader gazes, showing that there is something radically foreign, something radically other, outside the scene or story that he or she can see, or read. Lacan's example is Holbein's *The Ambassadors*. Floating in the foreground of Holbein's painting, of course, is an oblique object which one looks through, ignores, in order to arrange the scene into its two smug, plump ambassadors with their worldly goods of scientific exploration and imperial expansion: globe, telescope, set square. This object only starts to shape itself into a distinct form, that of a skull, if the viewer stands at such a distance from the painting that the predominant scene blurs, and its cheerful ambassadors fall out of focus. The absolute limits of death emerge. Of course, there is no reading practice, no viewing position, where both scenes can be held in focus at the same time, and this for Lacan is the essential point: art might point to the unrepresentable, not to represent it, 'just' to point to it, to point to the gap that exists in all scenes, all stories, these places where knowledge and vision fail (Lacan *Concepts*; see also Adams *Emptiness*; Thurston).

The writing on these last pages, the story of a waterbird left behind when the great flocks of birds finally lift from the drying waterlands, is an anamorphotic form for a reader who allows it to interrupt, to disturb, his or her visual field because it introduces something foreign into the scene: something the foreignness of which, moreover, cannot be recuperated. The final passage, Elliot's story, belongs to another story altogether than the one I can see or know, or read. It points to something illegible to me, something withdrawn from the novel as I can read it, it points to another world of meaning.

For most of the novel's white critics, this final passage either is not seen at all, or it is seen as an excess, a decorative flourish to be read around or passed over. It is a mark through which a critic can peer. I did this, and most if not all published readings have done so.[10] It is as if Elliot had not spoken these lines and instead the story ends with Mary's departure from St Dominic's. In such readings, the meanings already given to the text up to this point can remain intact. Nothing in the textual scene is put under pressure, nothing is erased or made anew. The last passage is not admitted as an interruption or disturbance of the scene that has been imagined up to this point.

But if as white readers we stand at some distance from our own prevailing narratives, if this passage is focussed on rather than passed over, if it is allowed a place in the text rather than viewed as being only in excess of it, shifts in vision take place and another story starts to appear: *Plains of Promise* is retrospectively rewritten. Previously visible elements of the text fall into a new arrangement and are thereby resignified. For surely this last story offers a different view of Ivy and her mother than anything that has been seen before? Isn't Elliot's story about generations of women forced to leave their own country, who were made mad by their displacement and other mistreatments, including having their daughters stolen from them? And, rather than these women being merely abject, filthy, 'black', doesn't Elliot's story suggest that they are carriers of Indigenous Law; that through them great and generative powers work? Colonialism has separated the women from their country, they cannot care for it any longer, but it has not stopped the power of Indigenous Law that still works through them. It is these women and their messengers who bring back the longed-for waters to the great dry lakes. A reader might now, for instance, resignify Ivy's disturbing odour: she smells of water; or re-view all the little girls whom Jipp collapses into one and wonder what powers might *these* girls carry? The story turns out to be about Mary and her daughter, too, because as their departing plane flies over the country, the lake floods for the first time in 30 years. They are the waterbirds, it seems, to which Elliot's story refers.

More than resignifying previously visible elements, though, the final story opens up new gaps in vision, places where my own reading cannot go on, where, in Joan Copjec's words, the text will not stop *not* writing itself.[11] For I do not know

---

[10]   For Carole Ferrier, for instance, Elliot 'seek[s] for, but does not find, the answer to the curse that seems to be on the mission', a conclusion that can only be made if the final pages are passed over. Ferrier, 'The best Australian novel for years', Review of *Carpentaria*. Also, see Bennett; Bliss; Jose; and Sorensen. For an exceptional reading of the novel, see Renes, who does incorporate these last pages into his reading, although differently than I do here.

[11]   Of the subjective experience of the visual field, Copjec writes: 'What is being concealed from me? What in this graphic space does not show, does not stop *not* writing itself?' (*Read My Desire* 34).

56 *The Postcolonial Eye*

how to read this image of Ivy and her ancestors except, that is, within my own Western paradigms of myth, say, or magical realism.[12] I do not *know*, I cannot *see*, a world that can be inscribed thus. This way of telling, this object, is, in the end, necessarily and radically unintelligible to me as a white woman, which is to say as a subject whose racialised position cannot be thrown over by conscious will, by 'good will' or good intentions, or by education or the accumulation of more knowledge. Elliot's story is in excess of the story I can read: it is there, it exists, it has effects, but for me as a white reader these effects might best be understood as ones that disturb my certainty in my own capacities to see. It is illegible and excessive in the sense that it exceeds the scene I can see, the story that is mine. Rather than disavowing its existence, reading around and through it, we might instead ask: what *is* this object that we look upon? It is an object that insists on another story altogether than the one I can read.

These last lines of the novel show a white readership that there are things that cannot be seen, there is a story that cannot be told, *to us*. As white readers we can no longer hope that if we are careful enough, the story will fall into view. It quite precisely moves out of view, its new arrangement revealing places of opacity, vanishing points. The text shows itself to carry within it a story that is illegible, invisible, to some of its readers.

Plains of Promise has not received a great deal of critical attention. At the time of its publication it tended to be read by its white reviewers and critics as bad art.[13] One of the reasons might lie in the failure of these readers to allow for the places in the text where their own knowledge and vision fails. The elusiveness of this text can be disconcerting, certainly, but there is the risk that we will mistake our own disconcertedness for a problem of the text. If there are aporias in all texts, if there are gaps in any reader's knowledge and vision, then in the case of a white reader before an Indigenous text, the gaps might become unbearable. Faced with holes that cannot be filled, some critics have been tempted to stitch over the holes. To do this, those elements of the text that exceed or disturb the scene that *is* possible for a white critic to see – all elements that cannot be assimilated into the scene of his or her own imagining – these are excised from the text that the critic produces. The writing then appears clumsy to these critics, it is awkward, with too many ends left untied. The novel 'doesn't work', these critics argue, its images are 'almost ludicrous', the 'whole thing is out of control' (Sorensen). In the eyes of such critics the strangeness of the writing is the text's failing rather than evidence of its accomplishment, and it certainly is not seen as evidence of the failure of certain critical practices that are preoccupied with the task of *making sense*. These are reading practices that aim at orientating readers, giving them their bearings;

---

[12]   Deborah Bird Rose (*Dingo*) argues for 'myth' as encoded knowledge. After all, isn't all knowledge encoded, to be read within its proper generic conventions?

[13]   I use this phrase to refer back to the work of earlier critics who have pointed to the ways that Indigenous arts are submitted to the constraints of white notions of genre, quality, 'art' itself. For instance, Eric Michaels, and Grossman, 'Reading Aboriginal writing' 148–60.

What Falls From View?   57

we might say then that they aim not only at making sense of the text, at any cost, but at making sense of the reader too. When the text fails to be susceptible to these processes, when readers are 'disoriented' by the text, left 'without bearings', 'at a loss', critics complain of being 'besieged', 'fighting through the tangle of signifiers, like barbed wire' (Jose; Bennett). One critic for instance complains that this text does not satisfy its 'obligations' to 'provide the reader with evidence that what is happening on the page has any reality at all' (Sorensen). Against this, we might ask how the writing does work, what are its accomplishments. For me, the answer lies precisely in this power to disorient, in its unreadability for white readers. This text works to effect our disorientation, even our disappearance from the scene it imagines.[14]

---

[14] For a discussion of anamorphosis and the annihilation of the viewing subject, see Adams *Emptiness* 111.

Chapter 4
Dreaming of Others:
Carpentaria and its Critics

A nation chants, but we know your story already.
—Alexis Wright *Carpentaria* (1)

Nonknowledge or invisibility is not registered as the wavering and negotiations
between two certainties, two meanings or positions, but as the undermining of
every certainty, the incompleteness of every meaning or position.
—Joan Copjec *Read My Desire* (18)

Whites' critical efforts to make meaning of Alexis Wright's *Carpentaria* have
sought to anchor it to the big names among white Australian novelists.[1] Such
moves presume to make Wright indebted to these literary masters, assessing the
significance of her text by its proximity to theirs. Frank Hardy's name is frequently
evoked and so is Patrick White's; Xavier Herbert's name is repeated with the
frequency of a nervous tic, one critic going so far as to suggest that *Carpentaria*'s
'subversive high-spirited vernacular voice' might have been learnt from Herbert.[2]
White creativity appears in these critics' eyes as if it were the original creativity,
the inventive one, the prototype.[3] These moves are surely another way of saying
'but we know your story already ... because it is our own'.[4] They are moves

---

[1]   Syson; Devlin-Glass, 'Alexis Wright's *Carpentaria*', 'Broken songs and ecology'
and 'A politics of the dreamtime'; England, 'Small-town dreaming'; Sullivan; Anon.,
'A great divide – New fiction from Australia'. *The Economist*, 3 March 2007, 382;
Fitzgerald. In Anon., 'Ambitious prose draws on rich tradition', *Canberra Times*, 23 July
2006, p. B4, Peter Pierce is quoted as saying:

> Wright's argument is that she's trying to do Aboriginal magical-realism and use
> oral tradition ... It's a very bold effort and it's more or less successful. What
> people don't seem to realise is that one of the things she's doing is rewriting
> Xavier Herbert's [1938 novel] *Capricornia* as *Carpentaria*. Is it breaking new
> ground in some way? In some ways *Carpentaria* follows *Capricornia*.

[2]   Devlin-Glass, 'Alexis Wright's *Carpentaria*', 84. Critics and reviewers, too, tend
to nod respectfully in the direction of the publisher, Ivor Indyk, attributing to him a creative
influence that is rarely credited to a publisher of white-signed texts. See, for instance,
Pierce; Wyndham; Anon, 'A great divide: new fiction from Australia'; Steger; Fitzgerald.

[3]   The one exception I know of is Grossman in her review 'Risk, roguery and
revelation', where she positions *Carpentaria* in relation to the important body of Indigenous
literature which forms part of the book's context.

[4]   Syson raises his own experience of growing up as a white boy in Mt Isa as a basis
for judging the text's powers.

60 *The Postcolonial Eye*

that refuse the Indigenous-signed text's unfamiliarity, its strangeness to a white reader (a subjectivity whose 'whiteness' I take to be not only contingent, but made in reading).[5]

Despite this recourse to white Australian literary traditions as marks against which to measure *Carpentaria*, however, these critics nevertheless remain at a loss; they 'just don't know' what to make of it, they are 'lost in the reading'.[6] The first familiarising move has not worked after all: neither text nor reader can be held on course, and so new moves are made. One move is to blame the author who 'cannot resolve the multifarious issues she sets running', implying, of course, that she should provide such resolution, that an unresolved and irresolvable text is a failure rather than an accomplishment.[7] I'll go on to critique such a wish to find decidability in another's text. Another popular move is to fix the text within the constraints of magic realism, a move that provides a vocabulary through which the novel can be read as 'dreamscape' 'magic', 'an indigenous magic realism'.[8] This is yet another way of saying 'but we know your story already its very form is our own', for magic realism is not a form of writing that arises in another's culture, as is so often claimed: it is very much the product of a certain white, Western critical strategy. As Stephen Slemon once warned: 'the established systems of generic classification are complicit with a centralizing impulse in imperial culture' and the concept of magic realism might be one example. It threatens, he argued, 'to become a monumentalizing category for literary practice', offering 'a single locus upon which the massive problem

---

[5]   I make the argument that, in reading practices, a racialised and gendered reader is (re)made, and potentially imperfectly so, in Chapter 6.

[6]   Ian Syson writes:

> I am left uncertain as to what to think of *Carpentaria*. Is it a rambling showing-off of Wright's undoubted literary skills? Is it a mere pastiche of good ideas? Is it a book that, despite what can be taken for flaws and impasses, ends up a pleasing and important document of our time? I just don't know. The fact that when reading I kept drawing comparisons with Patrick White's *Tree of Man* – especially in relation to the sense of satisfaction in having finished what felt like at Australian epic – leads me to believe the latter ... perhaps. (85)

Don Anderson also admits to not knowing where either the book or he were going, but does not mistake this for a failure of the book. Instead he sees it as the result of his own 'self-fashioning as a white Western reader, looking for linear narrative and realistic detail'.

[7]   Devlin-Glass, 'Broken songs and ecology'. The same criticisms were made of Alexis Wright's first novel, *Plains of Promise*.

[8]   Syson, Devlin-Glass and Davison each refer to the novel's magic realist qualities. Steger asks whether it is a form of 'indigenous magic realism'. 'Dream' is often used; for instance, see Dart's review, and Sullivan. Syson uses the term 'dreamscape', Devlin-Glass 'magic' (in 'Broken songs and ecology'); Carter refers to Indigenous 'lore'; 'Dreamtime belief' is used by England; Davison refers to 'Dreamtime legends, ancestral tales and biblical stories of epic proportions'.

Dreaming of Others

of *difference* in literary expression can be managed into recognizable meaning in one swift pass'.[9]

What are the literary practices and histories to which Australian critics refer when they produce Indigenous-signed texts as magic realist? It quickly becomes clear that magic realism has been taken up in the name of literary postcolonialism's interests in the possibilities of reading and writing difference between the coloniser and the colonised. Indeed the critical production of magic realism now reads like a synecdoche for debates in postcolonial theory, exercising that body of theory's preoccupations with questions of hybridity and liminality.[10] It is equally clear though that, in the end, the difference that is insisted upon in one moment is allowed to fall in the next. In Australia, as elsewhere, the strategy becomes one more moment in the production of another as a (lesser) version of oneself.

The term magic realism was coined by Franz Roh in Germany in 1925 to describe his vision for a new post-expressionist art, where the art would give representation to a subjective experience of reality, a reality that is amplified until its own so-called magic appears in the work of art.[11] Roh's idea arose historically in the context of psychoanalysis and its interests in visibility and invisibility, in what can and cannot be brought into language, into knowledge. Like psychoanalysis, it is concerned with division and doubleness *within* any one human subject, where what Roh has called magic is always another aspect or experience of a psychic reality. It is that part of reality that hovers around, or palpates behind, what can be discerned. What Roh hoped might be made to appear in a new art as magical or strange is not *another's* reality, then, but always *one's own* – recalling Freud's insistence on the uncanny as the constitutive strangeness that is not exterior to the subject but within.[12] Roh hoped for an artistic practice that could point to that part of subjective reality that escapes representation, this magic that falls from view and is perhaps felt rather than seen, an atmosphere one might say; a part of subjective reality that artistic practice might be able to point to by, for instance, figuring

---

[9]   As Slemon has argued, magic realism might work as:
one of the paradigmatic critical tropes for justifying an ignorance of the local histories behind specific textual practices and for securing first-world postmodernism's naturalization of ... that 'casual, unmoored international audience' which claims everything in the wide world as somehow its own. (408–9, 407–26).

[10]   For examples, see Geoff Hancock's *Introduction to Hancock* 7–15; Bowers; Chanady. Zamora and Faris speak of the production of a third liminal space: 'The propensity of magical realist texts to admit a plurality of worlds means that they often situate themselves on liminal territory between or among these worlds' 6.

[11]   Franz Roh, *Realismo Mágico, post expressionismo: problemas de la pintura europa mas reciente*, trans. (from the German) Fernando Vela, Madrid: Revista de Occidente, 1927. Roh's original work is *Nach-Expressionismus, Magicher Realismus: Probleme der neuesten Europäischen Malerei*, Leipzig: Klinkhardt and Biermann, 1925. Translated from Spanish to English by Faris 'Magical Realism: Post-Expressionism', in Zamora and Faris 16.

[12]   Sigmund Freud, 'The Uncanny'.

fragmentations of the visual field, or in certain distortions and condensations in patterns of darkness and light, in shadow and aura.

These hopes and possibilities are foreclosed, however, in most contemporary literary critics' mobilisations of magic realism. The term tends now not to be taken in Roh's sense of art that represents the magic of so-called reality, the very subjective strangeness of one's own psychic reality; instead, 'magic' and 'realism' are taken to be two distinct, even oppositional, representational codes at work in a text and referring to two distinct worlds or cultures. These worlds are now keenly associated with the world of the coloniser on one hand and the colonised on the other. Unsurprisingly, the so-called magic falls on the side of Indigenous colonised subjects and so-called reality remains on the side of the colonisers.

In postcolonial literary criticism, gestures are made, of course, towards difference and the word 'dialectic' runs through this criticism like a talisman that could ward off charges of neo-imperialism. But, as we'll see, these gestures towards difference and the dialectical turn out to be merely moments of deferral in the course of a 'self-same' argument whereby others' reality is produced as if it were a version of the colonisers' own, only a lesser one: less rational, less logical. The arguments eventually arrive at the point they are supposedly contesting: that the other's understanding of reality is a poor one, it is 'subeducated' in the words of one critic; it is naïve and fantastic, it is based in beliefs in the mythic and magical.[13] The doubleness of a psychic reality which for Roh, after Freud, always has its own 'magic' within it is now arranged across two fields, with magic and its correlates – dream, delusion, irrationality – appearing in the field of the other.

In readings that produce *Carpentaria* as a magic realist text there is just this recuperation of the binary that associates Indigeneity with magic, irrationality, delusion and dream, and whiteness with realism, reality and rationality, with consciousness, a wakeful state – despite these critics aiming at something else. Such an arrangement of dream and reality, sleep and wakefulness, across a coloniser–colonised divide recalls arguments that Patrick Wolfe has made about the meanings associated with the term Dreamtime as it was conceived – we might say invented – by anthropological discourse (Wolfe 'On being woken up'). This discourse made an affinity between 'Aborigine' and 'dreams', where dream was understood to be a condition associated with sleep, or unconsciousness rather than with what might also be called (again, in English) Indigenous Law. Wolfe shows us how this coupling of 'Aborigine' and 'dream' in the Australian colonising context made for the dispossession of Indigenous peoples by taking them out of historical time and place: they were 'either effaced from the land or assimilated to it' (Wolfe 'On being woken up' 210). So, what is at stake for contemporary literary critics who, via the trope of magic realism, once more make an association between Indigeneity and dream? And, how might whites read differently so that our doubleness and division remain, so that our own magic, dreams and delusions might make their appearance?

---

[13]   Takolander associates what she calls others' superstitious beliefs with subeducation.

Dreaming of Others   63

What follows is, first, a more detailed critique of so-called postcolonial magic realism in which I point to critics' refusal to allow markers of difference in texts to be significant, indeed, to signify at all. Instead there is a habit of skipping over these places where differences are inscribed as if they were not there at all. There are some differences that are just too much, it seems. Second, I propose reading *Carpentaria* through a different paradigm, and this is the paradigm of radical uncertainty, an impossible dialectic.[14] In this might lie the beginnings of another reading practice, one that allows *Carpentaria* its difference, its strangeness, and which points to the necessary estrangement of its white readers. This is not to refuse the beauty of the text and the pleasures it offers but to suggest a reading practice that sits still with this beauty and bears its enigma. That is, the approach is against a reading that only positivises the text. Third, I look at those readings by white critics that would have this novel as offering a white reader an opportunity to acquire new knowledge about Indigenous Law. Of these readings we might ask in what sense a white reader could be said to know Indigenous Law, and how would she ever distinguish it from this text's huge, generous, imaginative playfulness?

I do not argue that this particular text, *Carpentaria*, escapes writing's limits or that its author, because she is Indigenous, enjoys absolute or perfect vision. The argument, instead, is that for each of us there are limits to the powers of sight and knowledge, although whiteness invites its subjects to forget this and to believe instead in our own powers of perfect vision. If white subjects are canny enough, smart enough, patient enough, so the fantasy goes, we will be able to see what our others see, know what they know. From such a 'white' subject position, from the position that *Carpentaria*'s white critics take up for instance, we can be tempted to approach another's knowledge as if it were always and in all ways accessible. Here, I look at white critics of this Indigenous-signed text who have mistaken the meanings they can make of it for truth, for complete knowledge, for 'reality' itself.

Can Black People Fly?

What is magic and what is reality, and by what representational codes will we recognise these? How will readers know these different worlds and representational forms when they come across them in a text? Perhaps the questions might better be posed: whose magic, whose reality? Critics have warned against the effects of using the term magic realism too freely because of the ways in which there is the risk that audiences among the Western world will read other culture's reality as magic. Arguing against reading magic realism as magic in the Western sense, Roberto González Echevarría, for instance, has said of magical realism that it has 'as its source material beliefs or practices from the cultural context in which it is set', what Maggie Bowers has called, after Echevarría, 'ontological magical realism', where what might appear to a Western reader as magical or marvellous

---

[14] Julia Kristeva uses this term to mean 'a permanent alternation: never the one without the other' 38.

64 *The Postcolonial Eye*

are qualities that are reality to the population out of which the text was produced.[15] They are 'ontologically necessary to the region's population's "vision of everyday reality"' (Slemon 407). This kind of argument points out that what is taken by a white reader to be magic in these texts might not be so for the world of the novel or in the world of the author. This is what I take Gabriel García Márquez's refusal of the term magic realism to mean: it did not, he maintained, describe his own work at all, despite his work being cited by critics as the very cornerstone of the genre. Instead, García Márquez insisted that he was a realist writer: 'I believe that in Latin America everything is possible, everything is real.'[16] The so-called magical is for García Márquez a subjective representation of a social reality. Literary critics such as Lois Zamora and Wendy Faris, too, point out that: 'Texts labeled magical realist draw upon cultural systems that are no less "real" than those upon which traditional literary realism draws – often non-Western cultural systems that privilege mystery over empiricism, empathy over technology, tradition over innovation. Their primary narrative investment may be in myths, legends, rituals' (Zamora and Faris).

But while Zamora and Faris, like other literary critics, point out that what is magic in magic realist texts might not be so for the world of the novel or in the world of the author, at the same time their argument tends to fall away from this claim, it is unable to insist itself. As I have said, gestures towards difference tend to be only pauses in the course of a 'self-same' argument. They are merely deferrals. The arguments tend to eventually arrive at the same point they are supposedly contesting: that the other's understanding of reality is only naïve, fantastic, mythic: it is 'magic' after all. A gesture is made to the possibility that what appears as magical to the Western critic might be reality to his or her others, but the narrativity that these others pursue turns out to be, in the minds of these critics, only a tale, a myth, a legend. These very terms, these genres, are the Western critics' own, and are associated in these critics' discourse with magic, fantasy, and the supernatural.[17] Then, as Zamora and Faris have done here, the 'non-Western' cultural forms out of which the narratives are said to arise tend to be characterised as mysterious, too, empathic and traditional against an empirical, technological and innovative West, making the other culture's reality mysterious – even to itself.[18]

---

[15]   Bowers cites Roberto González Echevarría, 'Isla a su vuela fugitiva: Carpentier y el realismo mágico', *Revista Iberoamericana*, vol. 40, no. 86, 35, in Bowers 91.

[16]   Gabriel García Márquez and Vargos Llosa, *La Novella en America Latina, Dialogo*, Lima: Universidad Nacional de Ingenieria, 1967, 19, quoted in Bowers 92. It is what Alexis Wright might also be insisting upon when holding reservations about the term's applicability to her own writing: 'Some people call the book magic realism but really in a way, it's an Aboriginal realism which carries all sorts of things.' Wright quoted by Dart.

[17]   For example, Takolander's paraphrase of Carpentier causes other people's 'real' to be delusional, or 'marvellous' by which she means a kind of 'unreal'; 'marvelous [sic] phenomena that people believe to be real', 88.

[18]   See Muecke's very different approach to modernity, Indigeneity and innovation.

On this question 'whose magic, whose reality?', Toni Morrison has made some claims that are worth taking a little time to consider here, not least because of the anxiety they seem to arouse among some of her white critics. Morrison claims that among African Americans there are ways of knowing that might fall into magic or superstition in the eyes of white American readers. African Americans 'are a practical people but within that practicality we also accept what I suppose could be called superstition and magic. Which is another way of knowing things'.[19] Morrison's insistence (much like García Márquez's, or, indeed, Alexis Wright's) that she aims to represent 'reality' in its complexity rather than simply producing an inventive 'magic' and rather than superstitions, causes discomfort among many of her critics.[20] They collapse the distance that is installed by Morrison's own words – '*what I suppose could be called* superstition or magic'. Morrison's own reservations about the suitability of these words 'superstition' and 'magic' are closed over, and 'superstition' and 'magic' are reinstated as distinct from 'reality'. The white Western critics' reality has become the only one.

I'd like to tease out an example of Morrison's critics' refusal to take her at her word, even while claiming to do so. P. Gabrielle Foreman insists on interpreting as mythic Morrison's *Songs of Solomon*, where men and women have the power to fly. There is a surprising frequency with which this particular story is referred to by literary critics, as if there might be something about the story that disturbs more than might be admitted in accounts of it as 'merely' magical, or as a rhetorical move. Foreman insists that this story be read within the mythic and magical even while she offers a quotation from Morrison which suggests something quite different. Morrison herself says that if this story of men and women flying 'meant Icarus to some readers, fine; I want to take credit for that. *But my meaning is specific: it is about black people who could fly*'. White readers' own story, the myth of Icarus, is taken by these readers to be the prototype on which Morrison's story is based, whereas for Morrison, whether her story rightfully belongs in the genre of myth at all is rather more doubtful. '[F]lying', she says, 'was part of our gifts. I don't care how silly it may seem … it's in the spirituals and the gospels. Perhaps it was wishful thinking … *But suppose it wasn't?*'[21] There are possibilities that Morrison seems prepared to consider – that flying once belonged in an African American reality, although perhaps not her own.

Morrison's claim, then, that Black people could fly becomes quite enigmatic: what can she mean? And what can the magic/realist divide do with this sort of claim? Returning to Stephen Slemon on magic realism: he insists that the importance of magic realism for a postcolonial project lies in its refusal to resolve or translate

---

[19]   Toni Morrison, 'Rootedness: the ancestor as foundation', 342, quoted in P. Gabrielle Foreman, 'Past-on stories: history and the magically real, Morrison and Allende on call', in Zamora and Faris 342 (285–303).

[20]   Alexis Wright is quoted as saying that *Carpentaria* might be an example of Aboriginal realism by Dart.

[21]   Morrison, in interview with LeClair 26–7, and cited in Foreman 300, my emphasis.

one representational system into another. Realism and fantasy are 'each working toward the creation of a different kind of fictional world from the other'.[22] Slemon argues for an incompatibility between these fictional worlds that prevents either coming fully into being, 'each remains suspended, locked in a continuous dialectic with the "other", a situation which creates disjunction within each of the separate discursive systems, rending them with gaps, silences and absences' (Slemon 409).

Surely Slemon's point would lead us to ask: in what nexus of signification is the notion of men and women 'flying' given its meaning? In what other world of meaning does this possibility arise? And how would we read across the time and space between our world and this other one? Surely we can't. The claim that Black people could fly belongs to another story than the one Morrison's white critics can read, and of that story, that scene to which 'flying' belongs, all they can see is that signifier – 'flying'. We might say that the signifier itself flies; it floats like the skull in the foreground of Holbein's *The Ambassadors*.[23] To name it as magical, or as deluded, as wish-fulfilment, as fantasy, is to refuse the division in the visual field, which is to say it is to disavow the critics' own division: it is to disavow the incompatibility between worlds that Slemon insists on. It is to refuse a world of meaning, another story, which remains inaccessible to the white critic, indeed as it may remain inaccessible to Morrison herself. The difference between Morrison and her critics is that Morrison is prepared to consider that there are other worlds of meaning and she invites us to 'just suppose' with her. These words are ignored by Foreman, written over, as if the utterance had never been made. The gap in the white critic's knowledge is closed over.

Similarly, Maggie Bowers, after a discussion of 'ontological magical realism', drops realism out of her interpretation of Morrison's story of flying men and women, and the story becomes only magic or mythic again: 'Her magical realism includes characters who can fly back to Africa when they die. This was a commonly known myth amongst African American slaves' (Bowers 93). What would happen if that word 'myth' were dropped out here? Bower's statement would suddenly be made bolder, more epistemologically challenging, and closer to Morrison's own claims. It would become: 'This was commonly known amongst African American slaves.' After all, this is what Morrison says. *Her* claim is not about a myth; she claims that it was the power of flight that was known and not a myth about the power of flight. This would be to follow through the logic that these critics of magic realism have themselves established: that one's reality is not another's; that there are other ways of knowing. It would be to point out that Maggie Bowers

---

[22] Bowers distinguishes between magic realism which, as the term's inventor puts it refers to 'the mystery [that] does not descend to the represented world but rather hides and palpates behind it' and magical realism, understood by Salman Rushdie as the 'commingling of the improbable and the mundane', quoted in Bowers 3.

[23] For an illuminating discussion of the skull in *The Ambassadors* from a Lacanian perspective, see Adams *Emptiness* 109–21. For an important mobilisation for Australian literary criticism of Lacanian ideas on modern art and emptiness, see Foord.

Dreaming of Others 67

is not necessarily or exclusively occupying the same world of meaning as Toni Morrison and that she is certainly not occupying the same world as the Africans about whom Morrison writes.

Morrison, like Alejo Carpentier and Gabriel García Márquez before her, has been condemned by some critics for these kinds of propositions.[24] Morrison's insistence on a distinctly different African American reality, subjectivity, indeed corporeality, has provoked particularly powerful antagonisms. She has been accused of participating in her own cultural prostitution (Takolander 170), inventing an 'enchanted village called blackness',[25] and surely many readers will find the notion of Black men and women taking to the skies and returning in this way to Africa as entirely fanciful. What is just as clear, though, is that a writer like Morrison might be aiming to put under strain white readers' assurance that they can decide what is real and what is magical, or when it is a reality represented naturalistically and when it is figured in code.

* * *

While the magic-realist novel's subversive capacities lie for many critics in the pressures brought to bear on a hegemonic, colonial reality on one hand, and on realism as a naturalised mode of representing it on the other, this hegemonic reality is once more reiterated in the very assurance with which the real and the fantastic are determined by white critics as being across two cultural locations. What would be more productive would be to return to the idea of the 'magical' and 'reality' as subjective experiences that are available in any cultural location.[26]

---

[24] Takolander explicitly argues against reading magical realism as a representation of another culture's reality, or 'marginal realism'. She argues against 'many critics and writers of magical realism, including García Márquez, [who] have suggested that magical realist fiction is so relevant to its cultural origins as to be inherently specific and mimetically faithful to them. This is a ... prominent misconception about magical realist writing' 17. Takolander is not sympathetic to advocates of a Carpentierian theory of the magical margins who, in Camayd-Freixas' words, typically 'lean towards an ethnological version of Magical Realism', a magical realism that 'issues from an alternate world view one might call "primitive" ... which is unique to a particular "ethnic and cultural enclave"', Camayd-Freixas quoted in Takolander 159.

[25] Bayles quoted in Takolander 170. Bayles continues: '[T]his attempt by Morrison to transform black folklore into painless enchantment comes dangerously close to reviving the spirit of antebellum nostalgia, updated as a Disney cartoon full of yam-spinning "darkies" with droll names.'

[26] This is a kind of writing that might be what Alejo Carpentier referred to as *lo real maravilloso* which he distinguished from surrealism or the fantastic 'on the ground that it does not explore another or second reality, but rather amplifies the parameters of our present reality'. Quoted by Foreman 298. In this sense, Carpentier might be taken to refer back to Roh, and the idea that the so-called magic is another aspect of reality; that is, Carpentier's claims would deliver the Indigenous-signed text into a notion of reality as always having these two parts.

68   *The Postcolonial Eye*

As Freud said, there is only one reality, and this is a psychic one, where 'fantasy' and 'reality' are one and the same. But the idea of magic realism as an aesthetic form that might give expression to the division and doubleness of the subject is precisely what drops from white critical efforts to read *Carpentaria* as magic realist. Instead, reality and magic are once more divided between ourselves and our others, disavowing the white subject's own doubleness, her own 'magic', her own strangeness to herself.

Carpentaria effects its own resistances against the exclusive coupling of 'dream' and 'magic' with 'Aborigine'. To start with, it is populated with white men and women who are irrational and illogical. They are naïve believers in their own nonsense, where newfound legends and lores, folktales, lullabies and children's verse, miracles and creation stories stand in for knowledge of their own history and of the country around them. They believe for instance in 'an original God who had come along with all the white people, who created everything for them' (Wright *Carpentaria* 55–6 and following references). These are men and women who are looked upon in wonder by the Aboriginal men and women for being historyless: their white worldview is a failure of history and of origins, theirs is a timelessness, of men and women wandering without recourse either to origin or destination, without culture, song or sacred places, ghostly men and women arriving with no past they could remember (58). When a white man arrives in their midst in a most unusual way, walking in across tidal mudflats after a storm, coming with no name and no memory, these white folk recall the arrival of their own forebears. This man who will in the end be known by the name of Elias Smith recalls '[t]heir original forebear, a ghostly white man or woman, simply turned up one day, just like Elias. On the scale of things, their history was just a half-flick of the switch of truth – simply a memory no greater than two life spans' (57).

The white men and women watching Elias coming in from the sea wonder what he is. Is he, after all, a man, or something else, equally believable to their minds: 'An angel carrying the message of the one they called the Almighty? A ghost, spirit, demon or sea monster?' (62). In the eyes of the white citizens, the arrival of this man is a vision of 'a marvellously hideous *other kind*'. They believe they are 'witnessing the emergence of an aquatic aura, a God-sent water angel', and 'downright proper, respectable Uptown women could not escape the spell the mariner had cast on them' (63, original emphasis).

Here, whites desire to find magic in the other, they seek it out, they produce the supernatural in the 'other kind' so as to bring it into their everyday world. They hold hopes of their lives being enchanted by the other. Out of their own incapacity to acquire a working knowledge of the world they find themselves in – they cannot read the weather, for instance, or fish the seas – they read others' knowledge and skills in the register of magic. So, Norm Phantom's powers to navigate great bodies of water, to know stars and storms, the currents of the air and the sea, to know where great schools of fish are still to be found: these powers cannot be imagined by the white citizens of Desperance to be based in rationality, in acquired and practised intelligence. It is their own rationality that fails.

Dreaming of Others 69

The white citizens of Desperance are captured by their own dreams and delusions; they are 'netted'. They believe that the town is protected by an invisible net:

> made up of prayers and god-fearing devotion – a protective shield, saving the town from a cyclone ... every November, at the onset of the Wet, at night, when some of the Council men could be seen congregating in secret. You knew the net was being drawn, because you could see the mysterious flashing of torchlight in the long grass. In the Pricklebush, everyone stopped to listen when the bush creatures became silent. Crickets and frogs were the guardians of the night for generations of Pricklebush folk. The old people said, *Don't worry*. They explained the men were checking their magic nails in the fence posts in case anyone was stealing them. (82–3)

Among the whites there are those who 'could tell you the stories of how they had been taken away for weeks on metallic-disc spacecraft with red lights flashing across the sky, and who knows, they said when they came back, if aliens were invading the whole countryside' (73). The difference in 'dreaming' between whites and Aborigines in Desperance is noted by the Pricklebush mob, too. Where the 'Pricklebush mob saw huge, powerful, ancestral creation spirits occupying the land and sea moving through the town, even inside other folk's houses, right across any piece of the country', they see the white citizens as having 'puerile dreams of stone walls, big locked gates, barred windows, barbed wire rolled around the top to lock out the menace of the black demon' (59). The Pricklebush look on in disbelief at the Uptowners who not only believe in these strange dreams of their own making, but believe they can be 'masters of their own dreams' (58).

And, crucially, this novel not only points to its white protagonists' wish to find magic in others, and so enchant their own world, but implicates those white readers who also possess a similar desire. A white reader and not only the white residents of Uptown might find herself drawn to the others' magic, desiring to find the magical as resting in her cultural others – lured, as to a hook, by hopes of finding magic and the dream in the other, saying it was always there, that it was written for us, that it is *just there*, on the page. Many white readers have delighted in making others the repository of magic, wanting to believe. *Carpentaria*, then, is a text that inscribes a white reading practice into its narrative: it is we who are pointed at and challenged. 'Do you', the text seems to ask, 'dream of others and then say it is their fantasies rather than your own?' When a white reader determines the text's placement in her own genre of magical realism, what is this but a determination to read her own bewilderment as the other's magic?

A Poetics of Uncertainty

But *Carpentaria* does more than reverse the colonialist distribution of rationality and irrationality between white and Aboriginal. It does more than tell tales of white irrationality on one hand and Aboriginal logic and intelligence on the other.

70 *The Postcolonial Eye*

It accomplishes its political work through an aesthetics of uncertainty, a radical, irresolvable equivocality in language and form. This is not a dialectic that can be resolved: there is no unitary resolution, no dialectical synthesis. It instead raises, for me as a white reader, an aesthetics reminiscent of modernism rather than magic realism. This is an aesthetics that recalls James Joyce, whom Alexis Wright admires, rather than Xavier Herbert whose novels she 'has no time to read; she is too busy learning from other people.'[27]

Carpentaria is over 500 pages of labyrinthine narrative that opens onto one scene and then onto another, one story folded between others as if in parentheses. Past and present intermingle in the space of a page or even less: time expands into the cracks and crevices of the here-and-now, bringing with it a proliferation of images and sounds that belong now to a man's broken marriage and now to *land woman devil Gardajala* (276, original emphasis), now to a dead white man being returned to the giant old gropers in their secret place in the deep seas, now to a small boy whose mother Hope has been dropped while still alive from a helicopter at a great height over water. *Carpentaria* is a novel so full of images it will take many returns to its pages before a reader could boast of more than a slight acquaintance. So, how to keep reading and rereading this text that surely exceeds a white reader's easy knowing? How to resist the call to bring this novel into the white Australian literary canon on one hand, or into an imperialist magic realism on the other? What other ways to read Norm Phantom's journeys through stormy seas into country populated by *yinbirras*, among them toothless old women 'dressed in crumpled leaves, bush blossoms, tangled strands of grasses' (303); or his son Will's experience in the flooded Desperance hotel in a cyclone, visited by an old lady in a knitted beanie and floral dress who 'had every right to grab her turn in a countryman's dreams' (467)? I ask myself again, like an incantation: how to 'make sense' of this? How to read?

Clearly not within the monologic of conventional Western literary realism; on this point there would be few dissenters. There is, for instance, no easy narrative outline that I could provide that would be at all supportable. *Carpentaria* exceeds the narrative elements I could name and order, and it does this crucially through its form and language. To my reading, *Carpentaria* puts into effect an aesthetics of uncertainty; in its language and form there is a radical doubleness, a poetics of equivocality. It is 'unpinnable'. It inscribes different worlds and representational modes in the space of a few lines or phrases; it brings different objects, different worlds, into such close proximity that their placement in a rational or magical mode is undecidable. It makes the very division into magical and rational, living and dead, body and country undecidable – at least for this white reader. This is not an undecidability that resides (only) in the Aboriginal protagonists, as some reviewers have suggested: it is not just Normal Phantom or his son Will who can't

---

[27] Personal communication with the author. Herbert's *Capricornia* and Wright's *Carpentaria* might, Alexis Wright suggests, be read productively together for the historical differences they figure.

always tell what is living and what is dead, what is dream and what is waking, where one's own mind ends and another's begins.[28] This undecidability is produced in me, too. The conventional European arrangements of objects into reality and fantasy, interiority and exteriority, country and culture, earth and body – these can no longer hold, and the text moves and morphs, it shimmers. This movement, this doubleness, troubles my sense of knowing: it is the 'hinge' through which another scene opens, one I cannot see/hear/know, one I cannot signify. It belongs in another story than the one I can know or imagine.

To show something of this, we can look to the musicality of the text as a starting point. It is from this that we might be able to tease out what I am suggesting might be the text's uncertainty, its irreducible doubleness. For there is an impossible doubleness to its music, at least as it sounds – and fails to sound – to my senses. The text brings sounds I can hear – opera, country & western, choral music – into proximity with sounds I cannot hear even as I am told they are there to be heard. I cannot hear *Glory! Glory!* from the gills and scales of fishes. I cannot hear opera or sacred music issuing from the country itself. Although I can recognise each of the elements in a scene, I can't bring them together into the one scene. They remain unassimilable to each other. The text seems to require of me that I hold the two together rather than resolve them, holding them as distinct, in a relation of tension.

Music is an important part of *Carpentaria*'s form. The text opens with music, and music continues to its very close, ranging in tone and timbre, mood and form. The novel's epigram is: 'A nation chants, but we know your story already. The bells peal everywhere. Church bells calling the faithful to the tabernacle ...' The novel closes with another kind of song altogether: 'It was a mystery, but there was so much song wafting off the watery land, singing the country afresh ...' (519). The country sings, the crickets sing, wind and water, birds and fishes, humans too are all moved to sing, to give voice to ... what? It's hard for me to say. At times *Carpentaria* is a libretto, at others a requiem, at others it follows the lyrics and rhythms of country & western, and then again it refers to sounds that elude me: the country's own song.

Then there is the Irish priest in his old black souped-up Valiant driving in a storm across a flooding plain, who turns his car's cassette player to full volume and triumphant trumpets and the Philadelphia Tabernacle Choir flow out into the surrounding saltbush (186). Pulled over by the local mine's security guards, he addresses his antagonists in furious speech accompanied by the 'heavenly voices in a Te Deum of three massed choirs'. Another choir occupies Norm Phantom's fishroom, where he practises his taxidermy, turning dead creatures into exquisite jewels. Secretly, Norm himself believes these miracles are not his own work but

---

[28]   According to England: 'Norm Phantom, who has difficulty differentiating between dead and living visitors to his fish room, subscribes to a wonderful synthesis of scriptural Christianity and Dreamtime beliefs, and Will Phantom is calmly lectured during a town-razing cyclone by an impossible succession of beanie-clad elders.' For Sullivan, too: the 'old people in beanies are more [Will's] hallucination than reality'.

72   *The Postcolonial Eye*

the work of some God who uses 'the room as an experimental studio, a type of exposé for life in the decaying world, where the air smelt like a beach' (206). Into this room, the winter winds blow

> south-easterly in weekly rhythms after midnight. Like nobody else, Norm loved the grand old composer, the rapturous melodies which swam along the tin walls of the corridor from the house to the fishroom. The music arrived in the middle of the night and tapered off after midday ... Norm sang *Gloria*, alongside the old composer conducting his mass choir of crickets that sang *Glory! Glory!* In time with the rattling walls. The crickets, part of the fishroom's metamorphosis, lived in the dark, musky, fish-smelling environment. (209)

And Norm's resurrected fish, gleaming among the rafters where he has hung them, 'sang eerie songs in shrilled, mezzosoprano voices that floated out of their mouths from the crickets' hidden nests, from deep inside the fishes' horsehair bellies' (210). If all texts are tissues of quotation, then here we have a selection of musical forms that, for all their familiarity, are nevertheless made scarcely legible, or audible because of their arrangement.

Then there is Big Mozzie Fishman singing country & western to soothe and settle himself and his followers in his 'never-ending travelling cavalcade ... bringing a major Law ceremony over the State border' (119). 'Their convoy continued an ancient religious crusade along the spiritual travelling road of the great ancestor, whose journey continues to span the entire continent and is older than time itself.' The writing at this point takes on the feel of Fishman's tune:

> In the middle of the day, the vehicles were travelling along a narrow, hilly road, twisting like a goat track out of Mozzie's fishing nightmares. This stretch of road always caused Big Mozzie to break into nervous singing with a great deal of soul to the spirits. 'Goodbye Joe, me got to go, me oh! Myo! Me got to go for the codfish ladies down the Bayou.' Seriously, he told Will Phantom, a young man in his mid-twenties, who was travelling in the same car right next to Big Mozzie as his driver, he was a living expert on every Hank Williams song known to mankind. Older convoy members pretended this was true. It saved the peace. However, they knew, he knew, he never remembered the lyrics of any song, and simply invented new words to suit himself. But why not! 'The son of a gun, hey, Will?' And he broke into a jitterbug, singing on about some place as if he knew where it was: 'A buzzin, having fun down the Bayou.' (144)

I am puzzled not only by song but by the entire scene. To my eyes, the image of Mozzie Fishman and his men brings with it a mix of medieval Christian crusades and indigenous practices, and puts them altogether in a convoy of a hundred 1980s Falcon sedans and Holden station wagons, a 'long line of battered old cars heavily coated in the red-earth dust of the dry country ... leaving in their wake a haze of petrol fumes and dust' (119). This is strangely beautiful, an evocation of persistence in motion, at once full of earnestness and humour, of the musicality of a circus and the violence of a vocation, Christic images of the sick being healed on one hand, and Fishman's refusal to perform any miracle of the loaves and the fishes on the other; and running through it all is surely the cold-edged reality of political resistance, all moved, like the cavalcade itself, by the engine of something enigmatic – to me, at least. Perhaps it is driven by the inventiveness and determination of these religious devotees who double as mechanics with artisans' hands and genius minds, fashioning tools as well as spare parts from nature, and so 'all of these vehicles survived over thousands of kilometres of the country's hardest rock and gravel' (120). I do not know how to distribute power and pathos, humour and forcefulness among the elements of such a scene. Do I show myself as a fool to take any of it seriously; am I misreading the significance of what might in fact be a 'cult'?

To point to the musicality and indeed the triumphalism of the narrative is to risk failing to point to its tragedies and its insistent story of resistance. It would be easy to overlook, say, Norm's suppressed violence when faced with his hatred of the policeman Truthful who sexually abuses Norm's daughter. Truthful knows how to make 'Girlie scream for being mean to him. Well! She knew what she was asking for, he thought, if it was pain she wanted' (226). 'The handcuffs in his pocket pressing into his groin aroused the sensation of good times ahead' (228). There are the three little boys, petrol sniffers, who die after being left to languish forgotten in a prison cell for a crime they did not commit. Then there is the torture of Kevin Phantom, the 'coon boy', by white men under white hoods (343).

> He heard his bones break with a pain that forced him to open his shock-sealed lips, and call out through the muffling bag to his father ... He was wet and hurt, and his arms, stretched out in front of him, they were being dragged off his body. His skin was burning, he was being skinned alive, pulled behind the car, its exhaust fumes choking his breath. (344)

It is tempting to resolve these different moods and rhythms of the text into two distinct registers. If we were to follow those critics who advise us to read *Carpentaria* within the genre of magical realism, the parts of the text that appear as wondrous, or theatrical or triumphant would fall to the magical and fantastic; and tragedy, loss, and violence to realism – this despite the claims made for the genre's dialectic between so-called magic and realist forms.[29] If, as Slemon claims, the magical realist genre at its best offers a dialectic that points to the gaps and silences in each of the two representational forms, then in *Carpentaria* we might say that we have a text that inscribes an impossible dialectic: one that emphasises that these gaps and silences *cannot* be filled. This is the dialectic's

---

[29] In magic realism, the two parts, fantasy and realism, are described by Slemon as: each working toward the creation of a different kind of fictional world from the other. Since the ground rules of these two worlds are incompatible, neither one can fully come into being, and each remains suspended, locked in a continuous dialectic with the 'other', a situation which creates disjunction within each of the separate discursive systems, rending them with gaps, silences and absences. 409.

74   *The Postcolonial Eye*

impossibility: the dialogic necessarily fails to produce a whole. This might be the most threatening of possibilities for a white reader. That is, the endless movement that for Slemon is the dialectic never results in full knowledge. The dialectical is a recognition of the uncertainty of all knowledge. So, unlike the conventional trope of magical realism which ultimately resolves two worlds or forms, and beyond Slemon's important intervention in that tendency which nevertheless suggests a movement in a particular direction, that is, towards knowledge – instead we might think not of a continual movement between knowledges, not using one to fill in a gap in the other, but the gap in all knowledge. If this is true, whites cannot hope to look to another to fill in the gaps in their own knowledge, of themselves or their others. There are things an other knows (there are objects that are made) that we will never know/see/hear. The question of how to read, then, becomes this: how to bear such partial vision?

'A tree can act very strangely, if it wants'

In prevailing white Australian discourses, Indigenous Law is still read as if it were a form of fiction, an infantile, naïve fiction holding no explanatory power. By 'fiction', I mean an unreconstructed notion of fiction as an act of the imagination that bears no truth, as against 'knowledge' held to be factual. Indigenous Law is read in this unreconstructed sense of fiction. It is translated as legend, or myth, or children's story;[30] or as the Dreaming where Dreaming is taken to be the kind of dreaming one does on one's pillow, a fantasmatic distortion of everyday life without geographic or historical coordinates (Wolfe 'On being woken up'). Another's epistemologies are reduced to an irrational or primitive naïvety, belief rather than knowledge, lore rather than Law.

For an Indigenous author interested in referring to the Law in her fiction, this kind of interpretation of Law poses peculiar problems. How will her figuring of the Law be read by white Australia? Does it once more risk being dismissed as fantasmatic, or naïve? This is especially so if the author is also attempting to figure distortion, the fantastic, the fabulous and the dream in her fiction as Wright seems to be doing in *Carpentaria*, for how would a reader distinguish such playfulness from representations of Indigenous Law if she already reads the Law itself as only a dream, a fantastic story of magic powers, a naïve story of origin? So, while one critic warns us against reading Indigenous-signed fiction ethnographically because, she says, there is no 'ethnic authenticity' in its pages, we might counter with another claim: that the danger might lie elsewhere, in white reading strategies that persist in producing other knowledges as already a kind of fiction.[31]

---

[30]   For discussion of Indigenous story popularised as children's story, see Morton.

[31]   Aboriginal writers become peddlers of a 'maban' reality which, according to Takolander, sits very close to a capitulation to the pressures of publishing houses' commercial interests, including the selling power of 'magic realism', rather than a representation of subjectivity that arises in another cultural location (Takolander 171).

Against the idea that Indigenous-signed texts cannot be read ethnographically and against, too, the idea of Indigenous Law as a naïve epistemology, Frances Devlin-Glass urges us to read *Carpentaria* as 'a powerful contribution to understanding of indigenous knowledge' (Devlin-Glass 'Politics' 392). According to this critic, white readers can acquire new knowledge of Indigenous Law from the pages of *Carpentaria*. This new move – to read *Carpentaria* as a 'true representation' of Indigenous Law – presumably comes out of a desire to take seriously the claims made by Indigenous authors themselves that their texts are Aboriginal realism, say, or 'true story', or as Alexis Wright is quoted as saying of *Carpentaria*: 'It was the voice that Australians have never listened to. It's the voice of Aboriginal elders speaking about people and country, talking about what Aboriginal culture is, what it means and how it might work in the future.'[32] And, for sure, the idea that Indigenous-signed texts might in some way inscribe Indigenous Law, where Indigenous Law itself inscribes sophisticated knowledges, is often too much for literary critics. Devlin-Glass's critical move also comes out of a concern that Indigenous narratives are read not as primitive knowledge but, following anthropologists such as Deborah Bird Rose, as the complex encoding of ecology and natural history – a vital concern for any postcolonial critic (Rose *Dingo*). Devlin-Glass wants white Australia to take Indigenous narratives very seriously – as important forms of knowledge.

So, why shouldn't whites read *Carpentaria* in the way that Devlin-Glass proposes? Why not read *Carpentaria* as a 'powerful contribution to understanding of indigenous knowledge', as a text that 'mobilises and modernises indigenous narratives of the Gulf of Carpentaria, in particular the multifarious Rainbow Serpent and associated mythological beings of the region'? (1) (Devlin-Glass 'Politics' 392). After all, the great serpent is represented on the book's cover in an image reproduced from the skin of Indigenous activist and Wright's countryman Murrandoo Yanner: this is his tattoo. The serpent is there in the opening pages where the narrator makes his claims that in a tidal river in the Gulf of Carpentaria, the great serpent lives still, its body taking breaths that are the size of tides. Its moods change the river's course, with its intake of breath it draws the tide inland, towards the gorges of a limestone plateau, and its exhalation turns the tide back to the giant water basis separated from the open sea by a folding-in of the mainland.

Takolander's confidence that the 'magical' events in magical realist novels do not arise from any cultural belief system (201) – she cites the return of the dead child in *Beloved* as an example – puts another kind of pressure on reading Indigenous writing. The so-called maban or magic realist elements she finds in Indigenous women's lifestory for instance – she refers to Sally Morgan, Ruby Langford Ginibi and Roberta Sykes – are dismissed. Takolander is not sympathetic to advocates of a Carpentierian theory of the magical margins who, in Camayd-Freixas's words typically 'lean towards an ethnological version of Magical Realism', a magical realism that 'issues from an alternate world view one might call "primitive"' … which is unique to a particular 'ethnic and cultural enclave' (Camayd-Freixas quoted by Takolander, 159).

[32] Wright quoted in England and Bogle.

76   *The Postcolonial Eye*

This river snake is the ancestral serpent that still lives 'deep down under the ground in a vast network of limestone aquifers. They say its being is porous; it permeates everything. It is all around in the atmosphere and is attached to the lives of the river people like skin' (2). This serpent:

> came down those billions of years ago, to crawl on its heavy belly, all around the wet clay soils in the Gulf of Carpentaria. Picture the creative serpent, scoring deep into – scouring down through – the slippery underground of the mudflats, leaving in its wake the thunder of tunnels collapsing to form deep sunken valleys. The sea water following in the serpent's wake, swarming in a frenzy of tidal waves, soon changed colour from ocean blue to the yellow of mud. The water filled the swirling tracks to form the mighty bending rivers spread across the vast plains of the Gulf country. (1–2)

According to Devlin-Glass, this serpent is an 'expression of the Waanyi Rainbow Serpent' and the novel 'elaborates, from a Waanyi point of view, an understanding of the Indigenous sacred' (Devlin-Glass 'Politics' 394). This Waanyi point of view emerges for her, she claims, out of her familiarity with Indigenous knowledges – she can recognise the Waanyi imagination and its representational forms by bringing these into proximity with ethnographic material not with the Waanyi as it happens but with the Yanyuwa, whom she says 'share songlines in the Gulf of Carpentaria with Waanyi, especially secret and sacred women's business and Rainbow Serpent ceremonies'. It is 'a legitimate manoeuvre' she claims, 'to read this Waanyi novel in the light of Yanyuwa material ... since they share Rainbow Serpent songlines, and in particular the stories of Bujimala and Walalu, the Whirlwind Serpent, both relevant in this novel' (Devlin-Glass 'Politics' 394–5).

Well, is it? Who is it that has legitimated a move that collapses Waanyi and the Yanyuwa? Where does this legitimation lie? These questions, though, I have to put to the side. The question I can ask, the question I will insist on, is this: how would a white subject ever be able to read either Yanyuwa or Waanyi narrative, to read the country, to read skin and tattoo, to read the country as Waanyi might? How do we *see*, or *know*, or *imagine*, from a Waanyi point of view if we are not Waanyi? The answer that many white critics are offering is this: whites don't need to 'think Black', as W.E.H. Stanner once wished we might – itself an impossible and fanciful wish. Instead, whites can refigure Indigenous thinking as our own: in this formulation, our others' thinking is like ours after all, it is a shade of white. That is, we are called, by these critics, into a belief that we can push Indigenous knowledges into the shapes we can see, into the shapes of our own thinking.

To accomplish this, however, white readers must install themselves into the text, rewrite it so that it once more becomes another version of our own stories. So, for instance, Devlin-Glass is one of *Carpentaria*'s critics who insists on likening Alexis Wright and Xavier Herbert, so that Wright's alleged insistence on the congruence of science and mythological knowledge is seen to be similar to Herbert's in *Poor Fellow my Country* (Devlin-Glass 'Politics' 397).

Dreaming of Others

According to this view, Xavier Herbert, Alexis Wright and by extension Devlin-Glass can each stand in the same place in relation to Indigenous 'mythological' knowledge.

Devlin-Glass's approach is reminiscent of standpoint theory where researchers seek to position themselves in relation to their material: 'I need to position myself in relation to this material', she says (Devlin-Glass 'Politics' 394). She has worked 'for over a decade with Aboriginal elders, mainly women, from a neighbouring community in the Gulf of Carpentaria, the Yanyuwa ... I've been instructed in women's business, most recently in 2004 for the purpose of proofing a women's ceremony grounding'. However, the so-called standpoint – the coordinates by which the researcher's position is known – are always the ones that are knowable, visible to the researcher herself. This is the paradox of standpoint theory. This method does not, cannot, aim at the researcher's blindspots, which are disavowed. The coordinates that one can name are always in the field of one's own making, the field one can see, the field that one's own epistemologies describe. Such a declaration of a position cannot render visible one's position in the field of the other. And, what standpoint is it that a white critic could possibly take up in order to understand what Alexis Wright says it has taken her a lifetime to understand, the stories her grandmother told about the Gulf country, stories about places and people and things: 'A person could be something else; a tree could behave very strangely, if it wanted to' (Wright cited by Sullivan). I wonder what a white reader can make of that.

My argument here is that Indigenous Law cannot be 'seen' from a Waanyi point of view if one is not Waanyi, and that time and again the Law falls out of the scene of white Western imagining, it falls out of the scene we can see or know. Indigenous Law remains as a fragment, distorted by the light cast by the scene we *can* see; in our scene it cannot appear. It makes no sense in a white Western epistemology, and at best its traces are translated into English, into modern western discursive frames such as 'ecology' or 'natural history' or 'science'. That is, it is translated into our own grid of intelligibility – a process through which Indigenous Law as an object of knowledge is made into a different object. So, rather than 'taking Wright's representations', as Devlin-Glass says – rather than seeing for instance river and cyclone as 'an expression of the Waanyi Rainbow Serpent' – we might better look at how this text positions a white reader in relation to these and other stories of Dreaming and Indigenous Law. Rather than presuming to know 'how the Rainbow is imagined' by Yanyuwa, by Waanyi, by Alexis Wright, we might be better put to examining the limits of our own imagining.

Rather than reading *Carpentaria* as a resource from which we can know others – as ethnography purports to be, for instance – we might read it as a novel that presents a white reader with its own quite specific qualities of unknowability and undecidability. We cannot read it ethnographically, but not for the reasons that Maria Takolander suggests, not because it has no 'ethnic authenticity' in its pages. We cannot read it for its ethnic authenticity because we could not recognise this so-called authenticity if it bit us. But as white readers, we do not need to read ethnographically to allow the Law a place in the critical production of

Indigenous-signed texts. We do not need to know the answer that Devlin-Glass poses, for instance: 'Is this new rubbish-island a playful (and deeply serious) reformulation of Bralgu (or in Yanyuwa, Garrwa and Waanyi, called Jingkula), the "spirit land", located in an indeterminate place in the Gulf where the spirits of deceased people travel?' (Devlin-Glass 'Politics' 401). How could she or I know? And even if we were given an answer, what would we be able to make of it? Would we know any more than we did before?

Rather, the Law might be better admitted into white readings as an enigmatic possibility, one that cannot be anchored to the meanings a white reader can produce. That is, the Law is very precisely unreadable to a white reader, and our efforts at translation must always fail. For, how do I know what it means to say not only that Indigenous Law is law in the sense of protocols that must be followed, the laws that order the social bond, but also the law of the country itself, forces to which all living things are subject,[33] a conception of the Law as inevitable, irrepressible?[34] My world and the world from which Indigenous Law emanates cannot be melded, to use Devlin-Glass's word, because they are incommensurable. We can't assume, as Devlin-Glass seems to do, that because the narrator uses the lexicon of the Indigenous sacred at one moment (Serpent, Spirit, Dreaming) and the lexicon of modern geology, meteorology and marine biology in the next that this represents a hybridisation of these respective epistemologies – or that the language of modern science is a translation of Indigenous sacred terms such as the Serpent – because the mobilisation of either lexicon is an act of translation, into English, of Indigenous knowledges. Whether the narrator speaks of the 'serpent' or of the movement of water through 'limestone aquifers', in either case he is translating Indigenous knowledges, including Indigenous Law, into English.

This is not to argue that because a white subject cannot know, for instance, Waanji cultural texts as a Waanji might that a white subject should not approach these; it is not to argue for that kind of silence between Indigenous and settler. It is important to keep moving towards Aboriginal culture, art and law, but this is a movement towards understanding rather than an arrival. This is to argue for knowledge as always provisional, not a thing one possesses but a position – a situation.

Indigenous-signed literary figuring of Indigenous Law presents a white reader with an anamorphotic form: that is, an object which we cannot see. For the Law cannot appear to us, it belongs to another scene than the one of our abiding, the one of our formation as subjects. In art – again, in *The Ambassadors* say, or in Roh's hopes for a post-expressionistic art practice – the unseeable is made to

---

[33] Deborah Bird Rose on the conception of the Law among the Yarralin of the Gulf of Carpentaria: 'Law is a serious life and death business for individuals and the world; it tells how the world hangs together. To disregard the Law would be to disregard the source of life and this is to allow the cosmos to fall apart.' *Dingo* 56.

[34] Wright, *Carpentaria* 11. See Deborah Bird Rose's story about the law that is being in the ground in *Dingo* 56.

appear – as a fragment, an aura, an echo of another scene altogether. Art points to this other scene, it does not render it, it can only refer to it. This other scene cannot be rendered: it cannot be seen, its existence can only be pointed to. This is one way of thinking about art. It is one way of thinking about *Carpentaria*: as art, as art that makes the gap in all knowledge *appear*, but as a gap. The holes cannot be filled.

It is very tempting to put anthropological discourses into proximity with a novel such as *Carpentaria*, as Devlin-Glass has done, and look for one-to-one correspondence: to look for the objects of knowledge from one world that will fill in the gaps in another. If we resist that temptation, though, ethnography and anthropology can offer literary critics something very important, and this is a sense of our own profound bewilderment, the places where our own knowledge, our own senses, our own capacities to see and imagine as another does, must fall. Consider what Deborah Bird Rose reports for instance of Yarralin embodiment:

> … my brother is equivalent to my right calf; my sister to my left calf. My right thigh is my mother's brother; my mother is my left thigh. My mother's mother and mother's mother's brother are my forehead (brain); my mother's father is my belly (indicating liver); my breast is my child (and sister's child), and my chin (whiskers) is my father. (Rose *Dingo* 58–9)

What body is this? It is not mine. I do not live in a body arranged thus. When I say that the death of a loved one means I have lost a part of myself, I do not feel it to be located in my right calf, or my thigh. Similarly, I do not know what the *manngyin* is for the Yarralin. *Manngyin*, as Rose tells us, is connected to flesh and organs and when a person dies and is buried it *gets up again!* (Rose *Dingo* 71). What strangeness is this? How do I signify it? Perhaps within the Western notion of spirit? It would be easy to start connoting these kinds of accounts of the living and the dead with Western notions of body and spirit, but to do so would surely mean that we have once more fallen into Western mind-body dichotomies and Western religious notions. As Rose goes on to say, 'spirit' 'cannot but signal a body-soul dichotomy which is inappropriate to the Yarralin context' (Rose *Dingo* 58). Translation fails, and into the gap so easily slips our own vocabulary and generic codes: magic and superstition, myth and magic realism. We make others objects of knowledge 'magic' in a move that paradoxically tames and familiarises.

To close, I turn to a highly personal account of contact with Indigenous 'magical' objects from another world that the cultural historian Tom Griffiths gives in *Hunters and Collectors: The Antiquarian Imagination in Australia*. The story that Griffiths tells is about his experience of transporting Aboriginal artefacts to the State Library of Victoria but it might speak also of white readers of *Carpentaria* and our wishes to invest another's objects with magical powers, while divesting them of their difference:

> Even parcelled in a dusty box they were, I suspected, still full of power ... During the long drive back to Melbourne I felt increasingly conscious of the boxes in the back of the station-wagon enclosing the secret/sacred objects. Whose were they? What meanings did they hold? What processes had brought them here, a process that now implicated me? I thought of a scene at the end of *Raiders of the Lost Ark*, a film about the archaeologist-adventurer Indiana Jones, where the immensely powerful ark of the covenant is casually wheeled into the vaults of a state museum. Was I participating in the dispossession of a people and the disenchantment of the world? (Griffiths 278–9)

Ken Gelder and Jane Jacobs have argued that the enchantment, power and charisma that Griffiths feels these objects hold, and which perhaps are transmitted to Griffiths himself, occur not because of the place these objects have in their original world of meaning but because of their position now in Griffiths'.[35] According to this view, the thrill Griffiths feels, then, would arise from his possession of these rare objects: from *his* power rather than theirs. The other's power is translated into a Hollywood cinematic version, a translation in which Griffiths figures as possessor of the other's magical power rather than possessed by it.

This is an ambivalent moment, for whatever pleasure we might recognise in this scene, pleasure is not all there is. The scene has its terrifying aspects, too. These magical objects from another world are so very proximate to Griffiths – they sit just behind his back in the small enclosed space of his car where he cannot see them but he reports feeling their power. This is not entirely benign, surely – strange objects that seem to possess power? What might be truly terrifying in this scene is not the power that a white subject sees in an other's objects but what he cannot see, even if he were to crane his neck, look back over his shoulder. That is, what might be most unbearable before another's objects is one's own necessarily partial and imperfect vision.

---

[35] There is, they suggest, a 'dramatic articulation of charismatic power – charisma gained through these dusty objects, not because of their location in the "Aboriginal system" (their "authentic" location) but because of their position in the back of Griffiths' station-wagon'. Gelder and Jacobs 84.

Chapter 5
A Postcolonial Uncanny

Heimlich is a word the meaning of which develops in the direction of ambivalence, until it finally coincides with its opposite, *unheimlich*.
—Sigmund Freud *The Standard Edition* vol. XVII (226)

I want to stay a little longer with the idea of Indigenous knowledges and artefacts as seeming to possess a 'spooky' or uncanny power, as Tom Griffiths's story points out. There is a thrill in these kinds of stories but fear as well, including the fear that this enigmatic power might exceed its own domain and intrude into settler society. Such uncanniness has been of interest to Australian postcolonial critics, notably Ken Gelder and Jane Jacobs in their work *Uncanny Australia: Sacredness and Identity in a Postcolonial Nation*. Whereas other postcolonial theorists have reached for the metaphors of hybridity and creolisation, Gelder and Jacobs evoke the Freudian uncanny as a productive way of approaching the irreducible doubleness of postcolonialism.[1] Freud's famous example of the uncanny where he shows that the meanings of homely and its opposite fold into each other is a very rich one for thinking about a postcolonial nation where home and homelessness, belonging and unbelonging have become newly uncertain.

Because I take very seriously the main proposition that Gelder and Jacobs make in *Uncanny Australia* that *unheimlich* and *heimlich* are inextricably entangled in Australian discourses of nation, I feel invited to direct that proposition to a consideration of their own work and ask: where does the desire to be at home, to be in place, insinuate itself in Gelder and Jacobs's own text, what they call an 'uncanny postcolonial narrative'? Where does an argument for the generative possibilities of settlers' unsettlement and the defamiliarisation of 'home' nevertheless install a promise of (re)settlement? This is an important question because *Uncanny Australia* remains among the foremost meditations on the subject of the uncanny in the Australian postcolonial condition and many critiques of Australian postcolonialism are indebted to it. It has enjoyed an uncommonly generous reception. Indeed, very little debate has gathered around this text, which at first is puzzling considering the importance of its subject and the text's stance as provocative and political. Might the surprising acquiescence with which this text has been met lie in this: that it offers pleasures to its settler readers that we do not wish to relinquish; that *Uncanny Australia* soothes and restores settlers, furnishing us with new reasons to feel 'in place' in Australia after all?

---

[1]   Bhabha *Location*; *Nation*; 'The Third Space'; 'Cultures in-between'. Fanon *African Revolution*; *Black Skins*.

82   *The Postcolonial Eye*

To give these pleasures is not its authors' avowed aim of course: they are more critical than that. They take argument, for instance, with another Australian postcolonial writer, Ross Gibson, for what they see is his pleasure in the fantasy that a colony 'would gradually "belong", it would eventually be "in place", and it would cease to be a colony'. This is a fantasy of being at home that Gibson himself critiques but which Gelder and Jacobs maintain he nevertheless continues to enjoy (Gibson quoted in Gelder and Jacobs 2). But Gelder and Jacobs's own desires to be in place inevitably escape their sights and knowing, escape their control, in much the same way as Gelder and Jacobs see Gibson's as having done, showing again that settlers' desires to be at home will not be subordinated to our avowed political aims. The desire to be at home, to be in place, still slips into our writing and our reading, even as it slips from our view. My own is no exception.

* * *

Freud tells the story of his experience of travelling in a train at night when a particularly violent jolt swung open the door to a restroom that adjoined his sleeping compartment. An elderly man stood there, in dressing-gown and night cap, and stepped towards Freud as if to enter the compartment, mistaking it for his own. Then, to his dismay, Freud discovered his own mistake: there was no other man there, only Freud's reflection caught in the mirror on the back of the swinging door. Freud had not been disquietened by a stranger: he had seen himself. He discovered what is strange in himself: something of his own is reflected to him, returns, reappears. This image is undesirable, even hateful. At that moment, Freud saw some aspects of himself that he wished not to see: 'I can still recollect that I thoroughly disliked my appearance' (Freud fn 1 248).

Freud offers this story for heuristic reasons: the experience, he suggests, is not enough to define the uncanny but it does hold its vestigial trace. Through other and more complex examples, notably E.T.A. Hoffmann's story 'The Sand-Man', Freud will go on to theorise the uncanny experience as something other than a feeling of dislike or discomfort.[2] It is anxiety, even terror, that marks the uncanny. This is the anxiety that is felt when what is ancient and repressed in oneself comes again into view, although now as if it were in an other. As Freud says: 'the *unheimlich* is what was once *heimisch*, familiar; the prefix *'un'* is the token of repression' (245). This is an understanding of the uncanny as an encounter with *one's own*

---

[2]   In 'The Sand-Man', the terrified Nathaniel mistakes the appearance of the lawyer Coppelius for the Sand-Man, a monstrous figure in a tale from Nathaniel's childhood who has the power to render children without sight by tearing out their eyes. In Freud's telling, Nathaniel's encounter with the Sand-Man figure is terrifying, the encounter with him uncanny, not because of the Sand-Man's otherness, or strangeness, but because of his familiarity. The Sand-Man doubles as Coppelius who doubles as Nathaniel's father and the terror lies in a reawakening of a fear that he has had from childhood. This fear is that his eyes would be stolen when the Sand-Man/Coppelius/Father figure appears.

alterity, not the alterity of an other; it is an alterity that cannot be torn out. There is no operation that can be performed that will excise this. The subject is made in his own doubleness, which is to say in his own division. Both 'parts' are *his*. The experience of the uncanny, then, is radically subjective – it is not generalisable – and it is always an effect of repression.[3]

While Gelder and Jacobs attribute their notion of the uncanny to Freud, repeatedly writing his signature over it as if to lend it his authorisation, their uncanny is a surprisingly tamer, less unambiguously homely notion than his. This is because they invert his logic. Freud showed how the uncanny is experienced in a recurring encounter with one's own alterity, whereas Gelder and Jacobs see the uncanny in encounters with a stranger, in this case an Aboriginal other. At the same time, though, Freud's notion of a radical alterity is refused, so an Aboriginal other is not so *other* after all. Not only does an Aboriginal subject *appear* to settlers as a version of themselves; in Gelder and Jacobs's postcolonial narrative this subject *is* much like a settler subject. Gelder and Jacobs's Aboriginal other turns out to be very much like themselves with no more claim to be 'in place' or 'at home' in Australia than they do.

The authors of *Uncanny Australia* make very different claims and for every sentence I present here in support of my own reading they would be able to pull out a sentence that works in the opposite direction. But one sentence does not cancel the other out, as Gelder and Jacobs themselves insist. Freud's own methods, too, are very literal ones in the sense that all utterances are taken seriously. There is an equivocality in this text that the act of claim and counter-claim would miss: there is a disavowed prevarication in *Uncanny Australia* that points to a different truth about postcolonial Australia than the one Gelder and Jacobs mean to point to. This prevarication turns on settlers' irreducible fear of and desire for Indigenous peoples: a fear as well as a desire that differences between Aboriginal and settler will fall away.

To show how *Uncanny Australia* has another, disavowed, narrative inscribed within it, I turn firstly to Gelder and Jacobs's reading of a particular Indigenous-signed text, Percy Mumbulla's 'The Bunyip' (1958) – a story that is for Mumbulla not a ghost story but 'true story', a memory from his own childhood. Here is Mumbulla's text:

> Old Billy Poddam was a real bugeen, a clever-old-man. He used to have a half crown. He would go and play cards. He would go through all his other silver and then play his half a crown. He'd lose it. But the next day he'd have it back in his hand again. No one could get that half a crown from him.

---

[3] Freud 241. The uncanny for Freud does not lie in finding in the other that which one has lost and wishes to recover; it is not envy. It is not covetousness. It is not the desire to dispossess the other of that which one believes is rightfully one's own. It is not finding in the other that which is familiar in a comforting way, nor is it enough for something to be unfamiliar, or novel. Defamiliarisation is not itself uncanny. There is no enjoyment offered by the uncanny, except perhaps in its artistic representation. An encounter with the truly uncanny is frightening.

84　　　　　　　　　　　　　　*The Postcolonial Eye*

This old fellow had a bunyip. It was his power, his *moodjingarl*. This bunyip was high in the front and low at the back like a hyena, like a lion. It had a terrible big bull-head and it was milk white. This bunyip could go down into the ground and take the old man with him. They could travel under the ground. They could come out anywhere. They could come out of that old tree over there.

Old Billy Poddam never did no harm to no one all the time he was at Wallaga. He went out to Brungle, the home of his tribe, the Red Hill tribe. Out there he did something wrong that hurt his sister's feelings. His sister caught him with the *guneena* stones. She was as clever as he was. So, when he knew that his own sister had caught him, he caught her with the *guneena* stones.

'Well,' he said, 'you'll die; I'll die too.'

That bunyip, he went away, he went back to the swamp, back to the water. If he was coming out of the swamp you'd see the water bubbling and boiling. He'd make the water all milky.

My old dad was smoking his pipe by the chimney. Mum heard this bunyip coming, roaring. The ground started to shake. He was coming closer. He came out of the ground underneath the tank-stand. Went over to the chimney and started rubbing himself against it. He started to get savage. He started to roar. Mum told Dad to got out and talk to him in the language, tell him to go away, that we were all right.

Dad went out and spoke to him in the language. He talked to him: 'We are all right. No one doing any harm. You can go away.'

Dad followed him across the road, talking to him all the time in the language.

I looked out through the window. That's when I saw the bunyip. He was milk white. He had a terrible big bull-head, a queer-looking thing. He had terrible eyes, big as a bullock's eyes, and they were glaring and rolling about. Every time Dad spoke to him, he'd roar. My old-man was talking: 'Everything is all right. Don't get savage here.'

The bunyip went down into the hill and down into the salt water. I have never seen that bunyip since my poor old Dad died. It was the last people of the tribe who left him there. You don't often see him. He only shows himself to certain fellows. You can hear him panting: 'Hah-hah-hah.'

He travels around, up and down the coast as far as Kempsey, looking for anyone who has done anything wrong. When he bites you, you die. He's even been seen in Victoria, at Lake Tyers Mission.[4]

Gelder and Jacobs read 'The Bunyip' as having all the attributes of a postcolonial ghost story: 'rudimentary, gross, luxurious ... hysterical, histrionic, spectacular, overflowing, meandering, "creaky", indulgent' (30). It is an uncanny cultural text, they say, the product of a modernity that inscribes the old and the new, the Aboriginal and the settler, irreducibly. But whose uncanny does this text inscribe? According to Gelder and Jacobs, the ghost of the story is the bunyip, and it is the Aboriginal protagonists who are haunted by it. It is *their* uncanny, *their* repressed returned. But perhaps something spooks Gelder and Jacobs after all because they have made a couple of quite extraordinary slips.

4　　Mumbulla transcribed and translated by Roland Robinson (1958): 124–5.

A Postcolonial Uncanny 85

To show this, I want to look first at a moment in Mumbulla's story that according to Gelder and Jacobs carries the *unheimlich* – for Mumbulla. They read Mumbulla's story as figuring a promiscuous relation to place that is typical of ghost stories. Ghost stories, they say, do not respect 'the "localness" of their sites; they are by no means constrained in this sense' (31). Accordingly, they read 'The Bunyip' as telling of a 'wild' and 'unpredictable' relation to place: 'there is no telling where the old man and the bunyip will end up' (33). But is this insistence on a promiscuous relation to place borne out? The bunyip's travelling was wide-ranging but at the same time its coordinates are specified. In fact, if we go back to the text, we see a remarkable specificity of place for such a little story. The bunyip travelled 'up and down the coast as far as Kempsey … He's even been seen in Victoria, at Lake Tyers Mission'. The story names Wallaga and Brungle, and is specific which peoples were visited. It is Gelder and Jacobs's reading that eliminates these specificities of place or people, making the bunyip entirely free-ranging, without limits or localities. More, they take Mumbulla himself out of place. Details of his own placement, his belonging to specific country, that are given in the text's earlier publication are excised from their reading. Just at the moment when we are given a story intended to show the doubleness of the postcolonial position – of being in and out of place simultaneously – this doubleness is resolved. Aboriginals are only 'out of place' in an '*unsettled* geography'.

But we can bring this together with another moment in the story, as they retell it, a moment of *heimlich* when Gelder and Jacobs install an Aboriginal family at home, in place. This is not any old place, though; for Gelder and Jacobs this is the place of the white man. Gelder and Jacobs call the family's home a *homestead*, an extraordinary misnomer, for whoever heard of an Aboriginal family with a homestead? Is the Aboriginal family at home in the white man's *home* in *stead* of their own? Gelder and Jacobs make the family's home enviably 'homely'. I can smell the damper and the roast mutton. Here the Aboriginal couple are more akin to a white farmer and his wife with their own bit of freehold or lease. The historical reality of the deprivations of Aboriginal families in the South Eastern states at the time this story was told ('true story' for Mumbulla) makes this reading truly fantastic. They read the family 'at home' rather than displaced, as the settlers rather than the settled, in the homestead rather than on an 'Aboriginal settlement'.

Gelder and Jacobs offer Mumbulla's story as an example of an Aboriginal uncanny – an Aboriginal encounter with an uncanny modernity. But in the text Gelder and Jacobs produce it is their own uncanny that is necessarily, inevitably, figured. Their text inscribes the return of the settlers' anxiety that Aboriginals will once more be 'at home', displacing the settler, claiming as *theirs* that which as settlers we wish to believe is *ours*.

86   *The Postcolonial Eye*

* * *

'An "uncanny" experience', Gelder and Jacobs say, 'may occur when one's home is rendered, somehow and in some sense, unfamiliar; one has the experience, in other words, of being in place and 'out of place' simultaneously ... *This simultaneity is important to stress*' (23, my emphasis). This stress cannot be borne, however, by their own argument which strains and breaks, resolving itself again into distinct parts.

There is, for instance, the way Gelder and Jacobs work with Jean-François Lyotard's idea of the *differend. Uncanny Australia* starts out arguing for the differend as productive in discussions of the Australian postcolonial because of its emphasis on poly-legitimacy where two legitimate claims are made, and one does not cancel the other out. 'For Lyotard', Gelder and Jacobs claim, 'the differend speaks directly to this issue of poly-legitimacy in the law courts'. Gelder and Jacobs go on to quote from Lyotard: 'As distinguished from litigation, a differend ... would be a case of conflict, between (at least) two parties, that cannot be equitably resolved for lack of a rule of judgement applicable to both arguments. One side's legitimacy does not imply the other's lack of legitimacy' (Lyotard quoted in Gelder and Jacobs 17–18). The virtue of these concepts, *Uncanny Australia* claims, is that no judgement needs be made 'that one or the other group is wrong, as the differend observes' (18). White legitimacy is not undone; no such judgement needs to be made: in contestations over place and belonging, white and Indigenous claims can be seen to be equally legitimate.

Lyotard's notion of the differend, though, turns out to be a bit of a stumbling block, because he will insist that the differend 'retains a sense that the parties involved do not fundamentally recognise each other. That is, the differend presumes a condition of incommensurability, of mutual misunderstanding, where the one can never hope to comprehend the other's point of view' (18). For Gelder and Jacobs, this won't do: Lyotard's notion of incommensurability – that there are places where one must fail to understand an other – must be jettisoned. In its place, Gelder and Jacobs install a commonsense notion of dialogue. After all, they insist, 'there is always someone to speak to and there is always someone to answer back' (20). Gelder and Jacobs refuse the notion of incommensurability, but it is the very premise of Lyotard's differend: it can't be cut off. Having raised the notion of differend, because it offers the convenient idea of poly-legitimacy, the differend's crucial term – alterity – is excised.

The next move is to introduce a preference for a Derridean notion of 'solicit' (21). The Aboriginal sacred 'solicits' 'us', where solicit means 'to incite', 'to allure' (21). Other meanings are offered, too. Embedded in the word 'solicit', we are reminded, are the following, quite different meanings: '"to disturb", "to make anxious", "to fill with concern" ... *"to shake the whole, to make something tremble in its entirety"*' (original emphasis). They then go on to suggest the possibility that 'sacredness – a claim for an Aboriginal site, for example – can "shake" the entire nation' (21).

A Postcolonial Uncanny 87

But, can it, in Gelder and Jacobs's view? For at the very moment when such a possibility is promised/threatened, just when it has been suggested that, indeed, an entire nation might be made to tremble, which of these meanings will be borne out in their reading? Not the meanings of solicit that bring unsettlement to the fore, it turns out. They refer, for example, to the famous decision made by the Hawke Government in 1991 not to mine uranium at Coronation Hill, which for some white stakeholders in the mining industry was a 'shocking defeat', as Gelder and Jacobs report, 'along the lines of the fall of Singapore'. Gelder and Jacobs urge these disappointed white Australians away from such a 'cataclysmic reading' of the decision. They urge instead a more 'positive' reading, one that recalls 'the more obvious meaning of the word "solicit": "to conduct (a lawsuit)", "to press or represent a matter", "to transact or negotiate"' (21). That is, the Aboriginal sacred 'is always in a position of negotiation', usually through the law courts: the possibility of a 'cataclysmic' defeat of white mining interests is small. That this is more positive depends very much on where one is standing; it depends on one's point of view. At the very moment when the Aboriginal sacred might be read as powerful enough to 'shake the nation', this meaning of solicit is dropped and the more reassuring meaning is returned to. There is no threat, only negotiation, happily enough in the courts. Gelder and Jacobs rush to soothe our white anxieties that we might be displaced, unsettled. We are reassured in a belief in the old order.

Simultaneity is also thrown over for an historical approach that locates the formation of an uncanny Australia in particular moments. For instance, Gelder and Jacobs claim that settler Australians' taken-for-granted feeling that this continent was home was unsettled, was made uncanny, by the claims of native title and sacred sites. Gelder and Jacobs name claims over Coronation Hill, Uluru, Kow Swamp and Hindmarsh as causing non-Aboriginal Australians to doubt whether we had exclusive claim after all, or whether what we took to be ours was not always already theirs. Locating the uncanny in such historical moments resolves the uncanny into 'home' and 'unhome', as if there were a time when settlers were at home here, comfortably settled. There was no such time. I think we could go further and claim that white Australians' disquiet and discomfort are the bases of our formation as whites, as settlers.

The effects of Gelder and Jacobs placing the uncanny in such relatively recent historical events is that it newly narrativises the white subject as the one who was once at home in Australia but who was unsettled, intruded upon, by the Aboriginal. The Aboriginal becomes the foreigner, the stranger. Gelder and Jacobs know perfectly well this is not the case: they might counter with the claim that this is a wilful misreading of their argument. They have, though, mobilised the Kristevan formulation of the stranger, the foreigner, at this point in their argument. The non-Aboriginal is the national, the citizen, the one whose sense of home is unsettled by the arrival of the stranger, now the Aboriginal. Kristeva urges the citizen to welcome the stranger. In a bizarre slippage, either the non-Aboriginal is at home and should welcome the Aboriginal as foreigner, or the Aboriginal is at home and should follow Kristeva's injunction and *smile* at the foreigner who just happens

88 *The Postcolonial Eye*

to be an invader, too. In this 'happy' formulation (in their words), it is men and women like Gelder and Jacobs whom, if Kristeva's injunction were followed, will be smiled upon. Such an uncanny Australia is a nation that can smile again.[5]

But perhaps it is rather that Gelder and Jacobs see settler and Indigenous subjects as equally foreign in this place, another kind of poly-legitimacy, and that if settlers are not at home neither are the others. There is no place, no home, no belonging, for either of us without the other. 'They need us too.' If there are no places that are wholly ours, if this is the outcome of the legal cases in native title and sacred sites, there are no places that are wholly theirs either. We can 'share'. At this moment, the notion of the irreducible, the irresolvable, the permeable, is conveniently returned to; it is re-enlivened to new effect: all claims, all distinctions, all boundaries between 'theirs' and 'ours' are permeable. They can be crossed. As Jacobs puts it elsewhere:

> The conventional colonial distinctions between self and other, here and there, mine and yours, are no longer clearly determinable and a certain unboundedness occurs. This is why, for example, boundaries designed to distinguish the one from the other (say Aboriginal land from settler land) are so hard to draw in contemporary Australia, and if they are drawn they are immediately absorbed into a process of use (a politics). (Jacobs 405)

Uncanny Australia enacts what it describes: its form is profoundly ambiguous. This ambiguity, though, is not the ambiguity, the uncanny double, to which its title refers. *Uncanny Australia* inadvertently inscribes the ambiguity of a postcolonial Australia that fears and desires its Indigenous others, irreducibly, including desiring/dreading that which belongs to Indigenous Australians. Indigenous claims to country – the claims of sovereignty – are as unbearable to the authors of this postcolonial narrative as they are to the authors of a more conventional colonialist one, despite the promises of that word 'postcolonial'.

---

[5]   This is a reference to Kristeva: 'To recall Julia Kristeva's comment, we can wonder whether to "smile" or to "worry" in response to these unsettlements' (135).

PART III
The Image of My Own Desire

Chapter 6
White Men as Hidden Spectators

> ... this vision is *mine*.
> —Maurice Merleau-Ponty, *The Visible and the Invisible* (5)

This book has argued that a reading subject is made in reading, not once and for all but made and made again; and that the white subject in some crucial senses is fantasmatic. The white subject might be better thought of as the-subject-who-desires-whiteness. A white subject is that subject who can make him or herself intelligible as white, who is able to make an appearance as a white subject. This kind of claim recalls those cultural critics who have insisted that there is no such thing as race. Race is taken to be so inextricably bound with other strands in the cultural nexus in which subjectivity is constituted that it cannot be separated out. We know no racialised reader who is not also gendered, for instance, or who is not also a sexually desiring subject. And, as Judith Butler has insisted, strings of nouns, commas and conjunctions of the kind: 'race, gender, class, etcetera' always fail to add up. There is always the strategic retreat offered by the 'etcetera' that I have included at the end of my own list, that little word that stands in for all the things I do not know and cannot name. Neither 'gender', nor 'class', nor 'etcetera' can simply be added onto 'race', they are part of its constitution, as it is of theirs. In this way, race does not exist separate from or prior to other mutually constitutive forms – forms which themselves always require qualification, as is evoked by inverted commas for instance. On this, Walter Benn Michaels goes further to claim that there is no such thing as whiteness: 'It is instead – like phlogiston – a mistake' (Michaels 'Autobiography' 143).

What, then, of readers-who-desire-whiteness – this mistake, this fantasy – when they are engaged in practices of meaning-making before an Indigenous-signed autobiography? Such readers might claim to read the other's life in order to discover difference but instead end up looking for the reassuring image that will confirm their own faces as white. For such a reader, is the act of reading an Indigenous other's lifestory an autobiographical act, a moment in the formation of this subject as white, a moment of his or her own self-writing?

It has been said that in autobiographical writing, a self and a life are made; that autobiography is constitutive of the self and the life that it ostensibly describes (Smith 17). As Sidonie Smith argues, there is no 'I' or 'life' waiting to find expression in the text, rather this 'self' and its telling are made in the writing act. Sidonie Smith has argued that any autobiographical act is performative: the self and the life are made in these acts which purportedly describe what is already there. Autobiographical acts, she says, take place every day in those moments when in front of an audience, even if only an audience of one, speakers

92 *The Postcolonial Eye*

'assemble ... a "life" to which they assign narrative coherence and meaning and through which they position themselves in historically specific identities' (Smith 17). In these acts, Smith points out, the autobiographical speaker is a performative subject. There is no 'self' as a 'thing-in-itself' waiting to find expression in the text. Rather, the self and its telling are made in the autobiographical acts. Similarly, we might suggest that reading an autobiography is such an act of 'self'-formation.

Sidonie Smith's point that the life is formed in the telling takes a particular twist in the case of Indigenous autobiographers in a settler-coloniser context such as the Australian one. If we were to take a leading example of Indigenous-signed autobiography, Rita Huggins's acclaimed *Auntie Rita*, we would find that indeed the 'self' and the 'life' were remade in this autobiographical act, in part by the fact that, in the course of the writing, Rita Huggins discovered, as many Aboriginal men and women have discovered, that she had been under surveillance for 32 years by one or other government agency (Huggins and Huggins 5). Reading the files produced from this surveillance opened the 'I' and the life to new significations in the light of what was discovered there. In this case the autobiographical act becomes not only a matter of memory and its failure, it is more than a matter of the selection and arrangement of elements to cohere into a narrative, it is also the introduction of new elements and, significantly, ones written by others. In these files Rita Huggins read her life as it appeared in the eyes of strangers. She found a record of her being in arrears in her rent, of an unpaid account with a department store. This elderly woman in her late years discovered herself to be written into the subject position of 'black', 'native', 'inmate', 'thief'.[1]

There were many men who surveilled Rita, reporting on her lovers, her children, her financial circumstances, the tidiness of her home. Who were these men who looked upon this woman and assembled an archive of intimacies on one hand and police reports and bank accounts on the other; who were these secret readers and writers of her life, her covert biographers? We can in turn read these agents in their act of reading Rita Huggins and writing down what they saw, which is to say what they thought was there to be found but which they themselves produced through their narratives of whiteness and blackness. For in these men's acts of surveillance and record-keeping they did not simply document what was there to be found, they made the 'I' and the 'life' they purportedly re-presented. Biography is performative, too.

But biography is productive not only of its avowed biographical subject – the thing-in-itself that is imagined to be there, waiting expression – but productive too of its author. In reading and writing an Indigenous woman, these men aimed at making themselves 'white'. To write the 'life' of this Indigenous woman is an autobiographical act: it is a moment in the formation of a white 'I' that turns

---

[1]   The term 'inmates' was used in government records to describe residents of the Aboriginal reserves and missions; it is used in the personal files on Rita Huggins nee Holt compiled at Cherbourg and at the Head Office of the Department of Native Affairs, Brisbane.

out not to be a thing-in-itself either but something produced in the very reading and writing practices in which it is engaged. We might say then that the violence of colonisation that Rita Huggins found in the archive – in these records of surveillance – should not be understood only in terms of the impulse of a colonising subject to control, order and discipline an Indigenous subject. It is this, and more. At the very heart of these acts of surveillance are acts of interpretation and inscription, of reading and writing, and their imperative lies in the desire of colonising subjects to secure their own claims to whiteness. To show this, I want to describe a little of the contents of files that two particular men – the Deputy Director of Native Affairs in Queensland, and William Porteus Semple, the Superintendent at Cherbourg – kept on Rita Huggins between 1942 and 1944 when she was interred at Cherbourg Aboriginal Settlement in Queensland, files that Rita Huggins saw when, 40 years later, she came to write her own life.[2]

An Extravagant Purchase of Undergarments

Among the very first folios in the file composed by Semple, Rita Huggins née Holt will have discovered her own letters to him, intimate, handwritten letters now bearing the impersonal mark of his date-stamp. 'My Dear Boss' her letters begin: 'I write because I had not time at home to get an order for some clothes which I needed so badly. So I was wondering if I could draw about £5 out of my account. I promise not to spend it foolishly.' Rita Holt's letter prompted no reply, and so she is pressed to write again: 'My Dear Boss, just a letter to say I arrived down here safely and was glad to see Mrs Semple again. She will have a good rest now, as I am going to help her all I can.' She goes on: 'Boss, I wrote you a note the first week I was here, asking for £5 –, as I did not get any clothes, or order for either my baby or myself. I would like to get some things down here, I won't spend it foolishly –.' She writes again: 'Hello, Boss … Boss, I wrote to ask could I draw £3–3 out of my account, as I am in need of it urgently. May I please receive it as soon as possible.'

When Rita Huggins came to look at another file, compiled by the Deputy Director of Native Affairs in Brisbane, she will have seen correspondence between the Superintendent and the Deputy Director written in 1946 at the time that Rita applied for exemption from the restrictions imposed on Aboriginals under the so-called Dog Act.[3] In their deliberations over her eligibility for exemption,

---

2   File no. 123, A/55079 was compiled at Cherbourg; File no. 8R/35 was compiled at Head Office, Department of Native Affairs, Brisbane. Both files have been consulted and are quoted here with permission of the family.

3   The Queensland Government was empowered under the *Aboriginals Protection and Restriction of the Sale of Opium Act 1897* to confine Indigenous people in missions and reserves where officials had 'total control, and exercised great powers tyrannically, while residents were deprived of civil rights, economically exploited, reduced to abject dependency … The Act required Aborigines on reserves to work compulsorily at the

94   *The Postcolonial Eye*

the men discussed what Semple called the extravagance of her private purchases. Was she financially responsible enough, earnest enough, they pondered? In reading their correspondence, Rita might have registered Semple's especial interest in the precise value of her 'undergarments' and in how much she paid for a pair of shoes. While the two men reckoned Rita's eligibility within the narrow economies of their ledgers, surely some unspoken desires were also in play here, structuring her chances.

It is these men's unspoken desires that I will point to here, not in order to pin them down, not to define them, but to point to their possibility; to show that the order of the reserve system and the records it produced were driven by desire other than efficiency, say, and to propose that this included a desire to look upon the other, a desire to know her – a knowing look. As I will go on to suggest, in their desire to look, and in their assumption of their entitlement to do so, is inscribed an imbrication of 'race', 'gender' and 'sexuality'. Indeed, these intersect so inextricably that, after Butler, we would have to wonder whether they can still be thought of as distinct categories of subjectivity, or whether, instead, they would be better thought of as strands in a grid of cultural intelligibility, to use Butler's phrase. It is this nexus that is the condition of a subject's appearance – as raced, as gendered, as sexually desiring. This is to say that these men's whiteness, their masculinity, and their sexual desire do not have separate lives, none has a life without the other. These men's ideal of whiteness, the one to which they aspire, is a masculine one; their ideal of masculinity is a white one; the form that their sexual desire takes is in turn shaped by their ideals of whiteness ... and so on.

In the files these two men composed is a narrative of their own making – in two senses. First, in the sense that the narrative is one they have made, it is one they have written through processes of selection and arrangement, for the archive is after all a creative project, it inscribes a story, however unwittingly. That the archive is itself a narrative, rather than merely the bare bones out of which an historical narrative might be written, has been refused by some historians for whom the archive is valued precisely because it is not written as a story, it is not organised, it is not motivated, or so some maintain. Second, I mean to imply in the phrase 'a narrative of their own making' a return to where we began, to the idea that the men are being made in their acts of narrativising. They read and write Rita in order to make themselves appear as white masculine and heterosexual desiring subjects. Their production of an archive is an act of self-formation.

---

direction of the managers in return for accommodation, a clothing issue and food rations ... The legislation was frequently revised, but it remained essentially the same until 1984'. B. Rosser in Horton 914–15. The act was called the Dog Act by Indigenous people, and dog tags or dog licences were their terms for the certificates which, if successfully applied for, would exempt them from the Act (and similar acts in other states). These certificates carried entitlements including the right to vote, drink alcohol, use hotels and so on. However, these certificates came with new restrictions, including the prohibition against 'consorting' with Aboriginals, including one's own family. See Ian Howie-Willis, in Horton 298–9.

Their files are a story of their fascination with Rita's body which they submit to their record-keeping – the details of her physical health, the minutia of a dentist's visit for instance. This is a woman whose personal purchases are available to their knowing: they enjoy their entitlement to know the price of her underwear, the price of her shoes, they annotate their correspondence with figures in pounds and pence and that word 'undergarments' is reiterated – one might ask with what pleasure. They are entitled to know with whom she has sexual relations, and to intervene in and control these relations. (The latter of course applied to all Aboriginal men and women living under *The Aboriginal Preservation and Protection Act 1939*. I work with Rita Huggins's files not in order to suggest that they are exceptional, but exemplary.)

The narrative in these files explicitly makes Rita a woman caught, bound, captured by the regulatory system legislated through *The Aboriginal Preservation and Protection Act 1939*. This is a woman who is 'under their control', or so they wish. But Rita runs away. She is a young woman of 20 and she runs away with a lover. She 'absconds', in the language of the files with the 'half-blood [J.]'. She and J., these 'half-caste Aborigines', these 'half-blood abo. absconders' allude recapture. On 20 August, 1941, Superintendent Semple writes to the Director of Native Affairs in Brisbane: 'Rita Holt had absconded from this Settlement, presumably to join J. ... somewhere. I will be glad to know the result of your investigations. I have also advised the Police at various centres to be on the watch for this Girl.'[4] The file then maps the pursuit of Rita and her lover across Queensland's police districts as reports come in from South Brisbane, from Woollongabba and Redbank, from Ipswich and Blackall, Winton and Longreach, from Rockhampton, Woorabinda and Charleville. The Inspector of Police of the South Coast District reports his 'extensive inquiries made with the view to locating [Rita]': 'I have made inquiries', he writes, 'at all residentials, boarding houses, and other places that the coloured fraternity frequent in this division, but with negative results ... It is very difficult to obtain information about the movements of the coloured class in this division as they are very reluctant to divulge any information about each other'.[5]

Then, in February 1942, Rita is found in Clermont, without J., who has somehow escaped. The Director of Native Affairs arranges for Rita's forced return to Cherbourg. His order, addressed to 'all officers and constables of police, prison officers and others whom it may concern', cites 'Section 22 of "The Aboriginals Preservation and Protection Act of 1939" [where] it is enacted that the Director may cause Aboriginals within any District to be removed to any Reserve or District, or from any Reserve or District, to any other Reserve or District, and to be kept there for such period as the Director may direct'. Rita Holt will 'be kept within the limits of [Cherbourg], in such manner and subject to the conditions prescribed hereunder, for the periods specified'. That period is for the length of the 'Deputy

---

4   22 August 1941; 8R/35 NATIVES RITA HOLT.
5   Report dated 29 August 1941.

96 *The Postcolonial Eye*

Director's pleasure'.[6] He then orders 'native escort' for Rita;[7] the Superintendent sends a 'black tracker'.[8]

On 9 March 1942, in his last missive on this matter, Superintendent Semple advises the Director of Native Affairs 'that Rita Holt is now on the Settlement. I presume that the Military Authorities got the man J.'.[9] Semple is now reunited with Rita, who is 'settled' again at Cherbourg, and forcibly separated from J. She is returned to Cherbourg, but we might also say she is returned to Semple, and to Semple alone, her lover now gone.

These two men take Rita Holt to be the subject of their reports and in many ways, of course, she is. She is subjected to the constraints of their narrative, as it is written here in these pages, and as it is written on her body and its incarceration. But in their narrative they inscribe themselves, too. Partially, only in fragments, but can we work with the fragments and enquire into the logic that might underlie them, that structures them? When we look, now, at the language and the form of the story these men tell, we register the desire that erupts, that we might even say insists itself. So, Rita is in their eyes a young woman whom they may hold at their pleasure; she is theirs in some important way, to look upon, to hold, to gather in these pages.

Of course, one reply to my speaking here of desire, pleasure and possession is to evoke considerations of the law: these men were, after all, only acting within or under the law, specifically the *Aboriginal Preservation and Protection Act 1939*. These men were subject to this law, too: as public servants, they were driven to act. Perhaps, too, it seems excessive to be working with that word 'pleasure' since it is a commonplace in legal discourse: 'to be held at the Deputy Director's pleasure'. Some might want to insist that, in this context, the word 'pleasure' has nothing to do with pleasure.

But let me open this up a little more. I am struck for instance, looking at the files now, by a particular distinction between the way the men represent themselves and the way they represent Rita Holt: where she is always named, the men rarely are. Their letters are written under the sign of the Superintendent, or Director of Native Affairs, the impersonal nomenclatures of office bearers. As they exchange details that are of Rita's body and its vestments, at the same time, do they try to hide their own distinct embodiment, the ways that as living flesh they must exceed the titles of office? Do they act as if they have no desires, or at least that their desires are not legible?

---

[6]   Order number 15, 19 February 1942.

[7]   Memorandum from Deputy Director of Native Affairs to Secretary, Commissioner of Police, Brisbane, dated 19 February 1942.

[8]   Memorandum from Superintendent at Woorabinda Aboriginal Settlement to Director of Native Affairs, Brisbane, dated 2 March 1942.

[9]   Memorandum from Superintendent Semple to Director of Native Affairs, Brisbane, dated 5 March 1942, 'Reference 42/48 Arrivals'.

White Men as Hidden Spectators 97

Perhaps, but another reading is possible, too, and this would be that the desires these men feel for this Aboriginal girl are shared between them, that they may assume to know what the other man desires and, more than this, that this desire is not peculiar to one or other of these men but belongs to a wider discourse, itself inscribed in law. That is, is their desire and its narrativisation made possible because of a narrative of race in which Aboriginal men, women and children are made into objects that are then, in turn, available for a particular kind of scrutiny, and that this is sometimes (but perhaps always) sexually perverse? Senior men commenting on, and documenting, a young woman's purchases of underclothes, say, or her sexual relations with men, would be regarded as perverse, surely, under other circumstances. The perversion of white masculinity in the postcolonial scene of race takes its particular enjoyment in an Aboriginal woman who is not protected by law from these men's gaze but very precisely made its object. It is the law, then, and what pleasures it allows, that is perverse.

These men's hold on the coveted position of white is secured in the act of looking at another, when they enjoy the pleasures of spectatorship that their role affords. Indeed, they not only watch but are unseen by those whom they observe – sometimes really so, sometimes only in their imaginations. They look upon this scene of race which is the scene of their own imagining, producing the Indigenous subject as the object of their looks in a tableau framed in such a way that they are always outside it, looking in.

Crucial to the subject's appearance as white, though, is another look altogether. For these subjects who write themselves into narratives of whiteness by imagining themselves as spectators of an unseeing other do, nevertheless, imagine themselves looked at, not by the racialised other but by the gaze of the Other. This is the 'big Other' fantasised as *white*; indeed, as *whiteness itself*.

Jean-Paul Sartre evoked the seer's double position in this way (here recalled by Joan Copjec):

> A voyeur peering through a keyhole is absorbed in his own act of looking, until suddenly he is surprised by the rustling of branches behind him, or the sound of footsteps followed by silence. At this point, the *look* of the voyeur is interrupted by the *gaze* that precipitates him as an object, a *body* capable of being hurt. (*Imagine* 209; original emphasis)

For Sartre, this Other as gaze is quite precisely *not* 'an omnipresent, infinite subject *for whom*' the subject exists. The gaze of the other is not a 'transcendent eye'. For Sartre, as Copjec explains, 'the gaze is not an object in the ordinary sense':

> While it is always met with among objects, is always 'manifested in connection with the appearance of a sensible form', which can be seen (in the slight parting of curtains on a window in a horror film, for example), or heard (the creaking of a door), or smelled (an exotic perfume), the gaze itself would quickly evaporate were any of these sensible disturbances to become the index of a determinate observer, that is, were the Other of the gaze to become a determinate person, a

small other. The reference to a specific seer remains in suspense in the encounter with the Other's gaze ... There is no reciprocity between the observing subject and the Other of the gaze whereby each could come to recognize the other. (*Imagine* 210–11)

Taking this back into our considerations of the government men looking upon an Indigenous woman and writing down what they see, we can say that these subjects are poised between two visual fields: the scene upon which they look, imagining themselves unseen by their racialised other, making themselves appear white in their own eyes by taking up the position of spectator of another who is made, in the men's eyes, into the 'black' to their 'white'. Then there is the other visual field, the one in which these men figure now as objects of the gaze of the Other, this imagined white spectator for whom the men imagine themselves to be the spectacle, the one in whose eyes they hope to appear white.

But, there is no one there. The Other of the gaze is inapprehensible. As Sartre puts it: 'he flees me when I seek him and possesses me when I flee him' (Sartre 529). Copjec shows how Lacan took up Sartre's notion of the gaze, insisting on the fact of the gaze as illusion. The Lacanian gaze, Copjec says, 'looks at me, but I can never catch sight of it there where it looks, for there is no "there", no determinate location, no place whence it looks' (Copjec *Imagine* 209–10). There is, then, '*no bearer of the gaze, there is only the gaze*' (216, original emphasis) – and the gaze is blind.

> Lacan does not ask you to think of the gaze as belonging to an Other who cares about what or where you are, who pries, keeps tabs on your whereabouts, and takes note of all your steps and missteps, as the panoptic gaze is said to do. When you encounter the gaze of the Other, you meet not a seeing eye but a blind one. The gaze is not clear or penetrating, not filled with knowledge or recognition; it is clouded over and turned back on itself, absorbed in its own enjoyment. The horrible truth ... is the *gaze does not see you*. So, if you are looking for confirmation of the truth of your being or the clarity of your vision, you are on your own; the gaze of the Other is not confirming; it will not validate you (Copjec *Desire* 35–6).

As readers of race in a colonial and postcolonial setting, subjects-who-desire-whiteness imagine a scene in which they are the viewing subjects, seers of an unseeing other. Yet, at our backs, do we imagine an Other, looking upon us, this Other in whose eyes we imagine ourselves as appearing white, perhaps quite precisely because we are caught in the act of looking at another? But if there is no Other who bears the gaze, as Sartre and Lacan insist, there is no whiteness either, except as a fantasy of perception.

Black Looking

bell hooks describes how 'black looking' in the American scene was strictly controlled under the slavocracy and then the antebellum era: 'Black slaves, and later manumitted servants, could be brutally punished for looking, for appearing to observe the whites they were serving, as only a subject can observe, or see' (hooks 317). hooks and other commentators of the US scene of race have argued that this remains the case. Looking, it seems, is what subjects do, which is to say it is a defining right of whites. These subjects might be said to be white not only because they take upon themselves an exclusive right to look, but because they assume that the 'black' other is unseeing. The 'black' is not another subject, according to this view, and is therefore unable to return the look.

In his introduction to *Black on White: Black Writers on What it Means to be White*, the white American critic David Roediger invites his reader to:

> Consider a slave on the auction block, awaiting sale. Imagine the slave being seen, indeed examined, by the potential bidders. Imagine what she felt. Imagine her trembling and crying, breaking down, even fighting back. Such attempts to imagine looking in on the auction block and to empathize with those for sale have found a hard-won place in the mainstream of American culture. But little prepares us to see her as looking out, as studying the bidders. And yet … slaves on the block often searched out every clue in sizing up the whites who would own them. Did that scar represent a history of violence? What did that leer suggest? Was that accent familiar, or did it point to the possibility of being transported great distances, away from family and to the master's home? What could be learned of the buyers from other slaves? What strategies of self-presentation would discourage the attention of the bidder most feared, or encourage the potential buyer judged to be the best of terrible options? (3)

Neither Roediger nor his assumed reader is prepared for the woman looking back: 'little prepares us', Roediger writes, 'to see her as looking out, as studying the bidders'. Roediger's assumed reader is therefore white and, surely, another white *man*, caught, as Frankenberg has pointed out, in the nineteenth-century European narratives of the suffering female victim?[10] Roediger's hopes are that his reader will be shifted from a position where the 'black' female other is unseeing. At the moment that Roediger can see (read) this woman on the auction block returning the bidders' gaze, and at the moment when his narrative achieves the same shift in his readers, then whiteness has been imperfectly repeated. The reader before the text is not the same as the reader after; and the reader will perhaps differently read the image of another in the next act of reading. The white subject is not the same subject as before reading; in particular, the white subject has been installed in the scene as appearing in another's looking.

---

[10] Frankenberg (78) critiques Roediger for mobilising nineteenth-century European genres of the 'suffering female victim'.

Or has he? For neither Roediger nor his assumed readers appear in front of the woman: his assumed readers are – again – lookers, according to Roediger. If we stand in the position Roediger has given to his readers, we can only see the woman and the bidders, looking at each other but not at us. The shock and the shame of being looked at by the woman on the block is reserved for the anonymous bidders. Roediger's assumed white readers – *still* – escape the moment of the woman's gaze falling upon us. As his readers, we are invited to stand at a critical distance from the scene, looking upon both the woman and the bidders, tracking an exchange of looks, a gaze that, in Roediger's imagining, cannot fall on us, even as he claims that it does. In the scene that Roediger has written and in which he invites his readers to install themselves, a 'white' is once again located in the position of observing the 'black' unseeing other.

And in the Australian scene, do 'whites', too, imagine ourselves as spectators of a 'black' other, one who drops her gaze? Are we aspiring to make ourselves white – again – in a reading process whereby we fantasise that we look upon another who does not see us looking, who does not look back? How then to read – in the broadest sense of that term? How to read such that an other, an Indigenous other, becomes the seer, our interlocutor, seeing and writing us?

In Roediger's account, we might find, though, a moment of imperfect reiteration of whiteness, nevertheless. For at the moment that Roediger can see the woman on the auction block looking back at a white man (but not at himself, it seems) Roediger is already in a different position in relation to the whiteness of the bidders whom, Roediger's scene implies, cannot see the woman's look. At the moment that Roediger's writing has accomplished its aim of making his reader 'see', perhaps for the first time, that this racialised other sees, if not himself then another white man, that she is an observing subject – at that moment Roediger's writing has opened up a split, a shift in whiteness, an imperfect repetition of whiteness. If the woman can be seen as looking, her 'blackness' in the reader's eyes and the reader's own 'whiteness' have been shifted. This white subject is not the same subject as the one for whom the woman for sale is not a seeing or speaking subject, but is blind and mute.

Chapter 7
White Women Looking On

'The subject of the dream is the dreamer'
—Toni Morrison *Playing in the Dark* (17)

Among the stories that Rita Huggins liked to tell is the story of her courtship by Jack Huggins, an Aboriginal man from northern Queensland.[1] Thursday evenings, she said, they spent at the Boathouse, the old haunt where a couple of hundred people, more on a good night, would dance to the old music, waltzes, pride of Erin, the foxtrot. The Boathouse wore huge verandahs on three sides where lovers 'spooned', and others flirted, or spoke softly to each other and watched smoke from their cigarettes drift on the moist darkness of a Brisbane night. But in the daylight hours, without any better place for their intimacy, they would hold hands and kiss in the park in George Street, behind the statue of Queen Victoria and her stone skirts. Jack Huggins was 'tall and handsome … and free'. He 'had a string of white lady friends chasing him' but it was Rita Holt, 'this little black duck', whom he loved. They were married the next year, in 1951, at the All Saints Church at Wickham Terrace, and spent their wedding night at the railway hotel before boarding the train to Jack's hometown of Ayr, sugar cane country. And so a new life began for Rita, away from the working life she had known since she was a girl of fourteen, as a domestic servant taking care of Boss and Mistress. The Boathouse has gone now (the Expressway passes over the site) but the trees remain, the giant Moreton Bays under which, until not so long ago, old Aboriginal ladies and men still gathered (Huggins and Huggins 51–2).

How to understand this story, as an everyday love story, small and benign, or is there something hidden in its seemingly innocent folds? And whose story is it – Rita and Jack's, mine, yours? What is missing from the story as I've told it here; missing, that is, from my own eyes? What is said, and what is found?

There are many things that are not spoken here but which give Rita's story some of its meanings: it is a love story set in a time when Indigenous men and women in Queensland lived under the so-called Dog Act; there were profound restrictions on their movements and with whom they could associate, and whom they could marry; it was a time of police raids, curfews, secret and overt surveillance.[2] These are condensed by Rita Huggins here into one brief phrase: Jack was free. He hadn't lived as she had done on one of the reserves or 'under the Act', although the circumference of his life would have been delimited by it nevertheless.

---

[1]   Rita Huggins told me this story personally; a later version appears in Huggins and Huggins 51–2.

[2]   For details of the Dog Act, see fn 3, Chapter 6.

102 *The Postcolonial Eye*

It is within the wider context of the Act and the radical impoverishment it enacted – the denial of Indigenous sovereignty – that the little love story takes place.

In profound ways, though, this part of Rita and Jack's story will always escape my knowing: I do not know the effects of the Act on the possibilities of this couple's intimacy. What I can add to their story is an interrogation of what settlers can and cannot see in this story and its *mise-en-scène*. Here, in my considerations of white settlers' powers of vision, I implicate myself: indeed, I make myself one of my subjects of critique. For, as the collaborating editor of Rita Huggins's autobiography, reading early drafts, pausing over the photographs that Rita passed to me, I was among the text's earliest readers, and I produced, like any other reader, a scene limited as well as enabled by my own desire, however unconsciously. In my case, this desire (that I scarcely recognised at the time so naturalised was it) was a desire – immediate, pressing – to position myself as a white woman.

In what follows, I look at myself and other women as we in turn look upon a scene of our racialised others, attempting to make ourselves white feminine subjects in our acts of looking and reading. But that phrase 'looking *upon* a scene' misleads, for viewers are always *in* the scene they regard, even as they imagine themselves outside it, as the eye, the point of view. The reader-viewer always constitutes the visual field; what is visible is subjective. An image never appears 'before' us, temporally or spatially; there is no 'us' prior to, or in front of, an image. We are always implicated in it, described in the relation between the parts.[3] A viewer organises the scene, and so the scene describes her. We can know her by her lines of sight, the coordinates of her viewing position can be deduced by what she can and cannot see. In what follows, the 'subject-who-desires-to-be-white' might show herself most clearly in the moment when she fantasises herself to be outside the scene of race, looking on.

* * *

To begin with the scene from Rita and Jack's early days together, at the Boathouse on the banks of the Brisbane River, in 1950. What could I see of the scene of the Boathouse, this old building I imagine with its timber frame giving a little under the weight of men and women in motion – dancing, swinging each other around in a room made hot with bodies and breath? Can my imagined reader see this scene, of hundreds of Aboriginal men and women dressed up and doing the old waltzes? Did it take work for you to see it, as it did for me, or is it a scene you know? Could you step out onto the dance floor?

Would you have imagined, for instance, any 'Captains' in this scene? For Rita Huggins recalls her encounters in the 1950s and 1960s with the white men who sought the sexual attention of Aboriginal women, and who were manipulated in

---

[3] See for example, Judith Butler's essay 'Nella Larsen's psychoanalytic challenge' in *Bodies*, and 'Endangered/endangering: schematic racism and white paranoia', in Gooding-Williams. Seminal in the field of whiteness and the look were Gaines, and Dyer.

turn by the women who worked at extracting a material benefit from the situation: 'In those days there were plenty of "captains" who were willing to share drinks, smokes and their company with us.' But, she points out, 'they didn't get it all their way because sometimes we'd beat them at their own game. The power for once was in our court until we tired of it all, then we'd leave. They'd get gooly up, but who cared?' (66). Were these men present in the scene you imagined? Where might they have stood in this press of people? Did they touch the skins of young women, were their longing eyes staring or were they drunken and downcast? Do the young women avoid their hands but take their money? Do the women mock them?

An important contribution to understanding the sexual economies to which Rita Huggins points is made by the Indigenous visual artist Tracey Moffatt in her short film *Nice Coloured Girls*. Drawing on historical records and documents of memory, Moffatt shows that the Captains' encounters with Aboriginal women date to the earliest days of colonisation and continue into the present. The modern-day Captains are like the men who arrived on the first boats, they merely make different offerings: a drink and a cigarette, or a riff of marijuana, a meal, instead of bread or a string of beads. In *Nice Coloured Girls* contemporary young women comment that: 'We call them Captains because that's what our Mothers and Grandmothers have always called them. Our relatives don't like us to follow in their footsteps this way but what can we do when we don't have any money.' Moffatt herself will be familiar with these kinds of stories from her own family history. Her family is also from Cherbourg; Tracey Moffatt knew Rita Huggins and other women of that older generation and heard their stories. The position Moffatt describes these women as taking up might be that of her own mother or her grandmother, aunties and sisters. As in Rita Huggins's story, the women in Moffatt's film are not passive but extract what material benefit they can from the men: relieving a man's wallet of cash while he's too drunk to notice or care, bringing their own friends into the man's circle around a meal at a restaurant, spreading around his largesse so all can eat.

The figuring of the sexual economies of colonialism occurs in the course of this film's explicit critique of the limits of white settler ways of seeing. I take the film's subject to be perspective itself, which it racialises. It points to the viewing position a white subject takes up and shows its blind spots. It does this by installing elements that usually fall from the scene that is seen by a white viewing subject. To give an example: we are shown a gilt-edged drawing of ships at bay, a typical eighteenth-century scene of ships in benign languor. In front of this drawing the filmmaker installs other scenes: of the first Captains who brought Aboriginal women onto the ships; the men's hopeful offerings of money, bread and beads to the women in exchange for sex. What is outside the scene as imagined by the white colonial seer is put in the frame by the filmmaker, overlaying the white visual field with other meanings until it literally shatters under the pressure and falls from view. Those of us who desire to take up a position of a seeing subject before this scene of race are reminded of the partiality of our vision, and it is nowhere more partial than before this film itself. What can viewers see in the scene of sexual economies that

Nice Coloured Girls describes and where are we blind? How is our own subject position, with all its attendant desires, described by what we can see?

In an influential essay on *Nice Coloured Girls* the American feminist critic E. Ann Kaplan makes two moves that disavow any such blindspot in her own vision: one is to assert her capacity to see through an Aboriginal woman's eyes, an extraordinary claim that amounts to trespass of the most intimate, bodily kind; and the other is to see the white imperialist gaze as masculine, a move through which she aims to exclude herself from Australian imperialism not because she is an American but because she is a woman.

In her first move, she argues that the 'camera forces us' to look through Aboriginal women's eyes: 'we must' she says, 'adopt the Aboriginal women's perspective' (321). Kaplan's own viewing position as a white subject is taken away from her by the Aboriginal filmmaker, she claims; she has been obliged to vacate the position of white imperial subject, at least for the duration of the film. But no camera has such power. The camera cannot produce a scene through 'the black women's eyes'. Kaplan's argument assumes that what an Aboriginal filmmaker has seen with her eye at the camera is what all viewers can see, refusing the inextricable relation between the subject and the scene, between the 'I' and the 'eye'.[4] That Kaplan still sees through her own eyes is clear, for instance, when she calls the women in the film 'black prostitutes' (321) – by extension, Rita Huggins and her friends, who included Tracey Moffatt's mother, would be so named, too. But this is a naming that does not make sense in the context of the discourse on colonial sexual relations that Moffatt and Huggins have given us. This is not the name these Aboriginal women are giving themselves or each other. This is a name that suggests itself to Kaplan because of her way of seeing the scene the film describes and the place of Aboriginal women in it: it is her way of looking.

So, Kaplan believes she can occupy another's viewing position. More than that, she maintains that she is morally obliged to do so, installed into this position by an Indigenous filmmaker whose work effects 'a reversal of the imperialist gaze' (320). Still, if the white imperialist gaze is reversed, it remains the imperialist gaze; it is not made into the other's gaze. The reversal effects a change in the *object* of the gaze: now it is the white subject who is submitted to the gaze, it is whiteness itself rather than its objects that is available for scrutiny. But submitting to any gaze – either to an Aboriginal woman's gaze or the imperialist gaze – is precisely what Kaplan refuses to do. She does not allow the film to be showing an Aboriginal gaze looking at her, the white female spectator (in this she recalls Roediger's reader). She removes herself, firstly by claiming that she now stands in the position of the Aboriginal women – she is, conveniently, no longer a white woman – and

---

[4]   Judith Butler poses a challenge to the idea that the visual can be taken as simply *there*, evidential, in her essay on the notorious Rodney King case. In this essay, though, Butler continues to locate white sexual desire in men, this time in the policemen who brutalised King. She does not refer to white women's desire as spectators of the scene. What position might white women take up when viewing the footage of this crime?

secondly by gendering whiteness as masculine, making the 'Captains' stand in for whiteness, ugly and derelict. It is this white imperialist subject whom Kaplan feels the film gazes upon; Kaplan herself can enjoy a sense of her own invisibility, made possible by her feminine powers to make 'alternative identifications'.

When the imperialist gaze is reversed, what is the trajectory of looks? We might imagine this as a white subject standing before a mirror held up to her by her critics, and before this mirror she may be aided to see herself differently. But, at most, she will be able only to imagine herself as if looked at by another. This is an imagining made within the limits of her own sight: her vision always remains hers. And, if we follow our earlier arguments here concerning the gaze of whiteness, what this white subject submits to before the 'mirror' is not some*one*'s gaze at all but the gaze of the Other. Over her shoulder, somewhere behind her, out of view, is the truly imperious gaze of the Other, who of course is not there at all. This is the gaze of whiteness that is not exterior to the subject but constitutive of her.

Following the arguments I made in the previous chapter concerning the men who compiled Rita Huggins's personal files, we might say that in Australia men have made themselves white through their relations with Aboriginal women, probably since the first boats. In their sexual relationships with Aboriginal women these Captains endeavour to make themselves white. A Captain's sexual practices are always racialised ones, and we might say that his desire is not so much for the Aboriginal woman as it is for himself: an idea of what he might become, what this country might make him. In this sense, his encounter with Aboriginal women is not an expression of a self as much as its making, a moment in his being made white: that is, of becoming intelligible, visible, as white – a moment in his own appearance.

While Kaplan excises the white woman from the scene of lascivious desire by attributing to her a special kind of innocence, Aboriginal women have told us what they see: white women desiring Aboriginal men. This kind of desire is not part of the prevailing white discourse on race relations, however, and feminist interventions do not usually depart from this. In feminist discourses on sexuality in the scene of race, such as Kaplan's, desire is found on the side of men and white women's desire is not recorded. In reading the scene of sexual desire in Moffatt's film, Kaplan is writing herself into a position of whiteness again, even as she claims to have evacuated from it. Her white woman is once again a seeing subject, certain of her powers of vision, who cannot be seen desiring her others.

So, the Captain, this particular white subject, is one way of imagining desire in a postcolonial scene of race, but what about his female counterpart? For instance, do women like myself reading Rita Huggins's story see ourselves in the scene at the Boathouse? Are white women in the scene of such encounters, or do we tend to remain always spectators, standing in the observers' gallery? Are we apart, looking but not being seen? Are we imagining ourselves as never moved by the dance, not caught in a stranger's arms? In fact, as Jackie Huggins has recently told me, the Boathouse was exclusively for Indigenous patrons. Unlike Brisbane hotels, for instance, where Aboriginal and whites mixed, however desultorily, however antagonistically, the Boathouse was a more private affair, for once outside a white spectator's gaze – making its scene perhaps even more unimaginable to myself as a white seeing subject. And, perhaps the reason I cannot imagine myself on the dance floor is because there are no subjects here to whom I can attribute whiteness's gaze, and so enable my own appearance.

A White Woman's Loving Look?

I make myself white in those practices through which I install myself in a scene I have arranged into white and its others, a scene into which I inscribe myself as white through the fantasy that I am the one who looks rather than is looked at. I am never made only white, however; I am a woman, too. What part does feminine desire have in this making-white?

A white Australian woman's desire for her Indigenous others generally falls from view in prevailing discourses of race relations. As the Australian literary critic and historian Gillian Whitlock has argued, 'neither historians nor literary critics have paid much attention to the desire of women, proper or improper, in the empire' (88). Definitions of white femininity have, at least historically, been figured as the absence of desire for our others: the white woman does not look at or long for her Indigenous other. Yet, feminist discourses insist that the feminine subject does look rather than being only looked at; that she is a desiring subject and not only the object of an other's desiring. What do white-signed feminist discourses do with this desiring subject when she appears in the so-called postcolonial scene? What forms does her desire take in their accounts, and can she be permitted to maintain desire if its object is Indigenous?

Looking and longing are not always pretty, and there is no particular innocence that can be claimed for their feminine manifestations. As Vicki Kirby has argued, there can be no appeal to a feminine otherness as the grounds of a feminine goodness (Kirby 'Capitalising'). If a white woman who looks at her other is moved by desire, it is surely a desire that takes its shape within the wider contours of 'race': desire must be formed, in some manner, by the racialised discourses in which the subject comes to feel. This is to say something a little different than what Ronald Hyam, for instance, has argued for the erotics of empire, that is, that the racialised conditions of empire provided an erotic field for the *expression* of a libertarian sexuality. Sex, he says, 'is relevant not so much to the question why empires were set up as to how they were run. Empire provided ample opportunity for sexual indulgence' (Hyam 2, quoted in Whitlock). We can go further than this, and insist that empire not only provided the conditions of possibility for the expression of sexuality but also provided the conditions of its formation, too. Moreover, the erotic fields of empire are not limited to its colonised territories but are also more proximate than this; they are in the home of empire. That is, empire – in its colonial or postcolonial aspects – must be formative of the sexual desires of imperial subjects before these subjects venture into colonised spaces. The desires of a colonial or postcolonial subject are desires made in racialised discourses lived and felt in the intimacy of home and hearth. Imperialism's reach is, after all, into the most intimate places: it makes bodies who feel, who are moved by others. Both in its historical and present forms, imperialism eroticises all its subjects, and not only those who travel into colonised territories. So, can we say that in colonial and postcolonial contexts, a woman's sexuality is made in relation to her whiteness and, in turn, that her whiteness is made in relation to her sexual desire?

Feminist historians have well-documented the place of sexual constraint on white women during the Australian colony's moves towards nationhood, but the eruption of white feminine sexual desire is less familiar, less well observed. Discourses of race purity and health have been cited by feminist historians as formative of the sexual scene in the context of anxieties over the formation of a white nation and the subsequent repression of white men's but especially white women's sexuality across 'racial' divides, but what of the desire that remains nonetheless? Can we allow for the existence of a feminine desire to see and touch the body of an other? Does not something of this desire at times escape sexual repression, does it never linger, or erupt?

If we were to rely on white-signed histories of Australia, including feminist ones, we might believe that white women had never known a desire for Aboriginal men. Even when Aboriginal women have told us of this desire, it almost always fails to appear in settler accounts. On this point, we will not be corrected, it seems. As Victoria Haskins and John Maynard point out, 'Nearly every recent history of Aboriginal peoples in Australia makes some references to relationships between Aboriginal women and white men, but virtually none mentions the inverse relationships between Aboriginal men and white women' (191). Haskins and Maynard's work uncovers and celebrates these relationships: 'In the face of extreme hatred, racism and prejudice, such couples were prepared to make great sacrifice at whatever the price for their love, and their courage in the face of such opposition was truly remarkable' (216). This claim might speak of Haskins and Maynard's own love. They are themselves a couple of the kind they study: a white woman married to an Aboriginal man.

As we recognise that the history of sexual relations between Aboriginal women and white men is marked by the colonial and postcolonial relations in which they take place, so too must we complicate some white women's desire for Aboriginal men, as Haskins and Maynard go on to point out. A white woman can be moved by desires other than loving ones. This is raised by Haskins and Maynard in a question concerning power. Taking up Anne McClintock's point that 'the rationed privileges of race all too often put white women in positions of decided – if borrowed – power, not only over colonised women but over colonised men'[5], they ask: '[W]hat becomes, then, of white women's "borrowed power", when they marry a non-white

---

[5]   McClintock 6, quoted in Haskins and Maynard, 216. The notion of white women's powers being 'borrowed' from men elides the power that comes to her by dint of being white.

108   *The Postcolonial Eye*

or colonised man? Do they simply surrender this privilege and protection ... or, conversely, as some of the official records suggest, do they continue to carry some of that racial power in relation to their husbands?' (216).

To emphasise, as feminist historians have tended to do, the constraint, control and repression of white women's sexual desire, or to refuse to see this sexual desire at all, is to foreclose consideration of that which might be most troubling in some of these women's relations with their others. It is to foreclose consideration of the range of white women's desires – the provenances of these desires and in some cases their perversions. It is critical that the despotism and dereliction of some white men's desires for Aboriginal women not be captured for a feminist project that makes white women innocent of perverse desires towards others. Can we go further and ask whether some white women's sexual desires for racialised others in a settler context carry the marks of a particular perversion, that of the master-slave relation? And, if so, how have we – other white women – failed to see this?

There is one particular white Australian female figure who, in the early decades of the twentieth century, wrote about the desires a white woman might feel for a 'black' man. In this case, the 'black' men were Africans or Jamaicans but the affective possibilities for this white woman were surely formed in relation to the anxiety and desire aroused by Indigenous men at home. This woman is the novelist and travel writer Mary Gaunt, who between 1912 and 1932 published a popular series of books on Jamaica, Africa and China that are saturated with desire for a racialised and subjugated masculine other. This desire is there on the page, it is expressed quite explicitly. No 'overreading', no sophisticated interpretative practice is needed to see it. Yet, although Gaunt's writings have attracted considerable attention from Australian feminist historians and literary scholars over the last two decades, Gaunt's narratorial position has been able to remain safely immured from any suggestion of sexual desire for 'black' men. If feminism emphasises looking and desiring as integral to feminine subjectivity, some looks, some desires, remain outside our purview. Gaunt does desire; she does indeed look. On these counts she might be expected to satisfy a feminism that organises its ideal of the feminine subject around desire and the look.[6] However, contemporary feminists will not see *this* desire, *this* look. Might Gaunt's longing look at a racialised other disquiet her compatriots still?

Rehearsing the imperialist discourses of her time, Gaunt in her travel writings argues that sexual commingling between the 'races' is 'unthinkable', but she nevertheless proves herself capable of thinking about it a great deal (*Alone* 16). She notes the impossibility of sexual relations between 'black' and 'white' in the course of detailed observations of the desirability of the other:

---

[6]   Pamela Murray reads Gaunt's novel *Kirkham's Find* as offering 'an articulate and able personification of Gaunt's new woman ... a definition of Woman based on a female gaze and female desire'. Quoted in Whitlock 93.

Tall, stalwart, handsome as is many a negro, no white woman may take a black man for her husband and be respected by her own people; no white man may take a black girl, though her dark eyes be soft and tender, though her skin be as satin and her figure like that of the Venus of Milo, and hope to introduce her among his friends as his wife. Even the missionaries who preach that the black man is a brother decline emphatically to receive him as a brother-in-law. (Gaunt *Alone* 15–16)

Gaunt has an eye not only to the attractions of the men but of the women, suggesting too that her desire was rather more wide-ranging than the heterosexual desire she refers to here (Whitlock).

Gaunt admits to a pleasure in seeing the African man, the 'negro' as she insisted on calling him even while acknowledging that African was the preferred term. Her naming the African 'negro' tied her fantasises of her other back to a slave past. Her pleasure lay in the fantasy of observing the 'negro' while he was made to suffer at the hands of a white 'master' – again, Gaunt's preferred term. She fantasised about his debasement and, tellingly, also about the debasement she fancied that he desired to produce in his 'master'. There is a mobility around the master-slave relation in Gaunt's fantasies, where the 'slave' might desire and effect power over the 'master'.

Reflections – In Jamaica (1932) begins with Gaunt's imaginings of Jamaica in bygone days. In her mind's eye, she sees newly arrived slaves moving between the rows of sugar canes:

I saw them trembling and frightened; inducted into their new quarters; appraised by the planter as good or bad beasts; settling into their new place, and – though they knew it not themselves – biding their time. I saw them attracting the white man by the youthful charms of their women, bearing his children, stalwart sons and beautiful daughters; holding him; serving him; debasing him; themselves suffering cruelly; *yet after all attaining to a power and place they never could have known if they had not been sold into exile.*

I thought of slave shops, the long Middle Passage, the degrading sale; the tramp to the new home, and the cruel 'seasoning'; which to many meant death. (3, quoted Whitlock 91–2, emphasis added)

Gaunt always wrote of slavery as she has done here: in terms of the slave's suffering and debasement, on one hand, and his own cruelty and powers to debase the master, on the other. It is the 'negro', after all, who is in Gaunt's eyes 'diabolically cruel' (*Alone* 93). The cruelty and power of the master-slave relation, as Gaunt tells it, are always close to eroticism: here, the beautiful girl who holds and serves her master. In this brief passage, slaves are trembling and frightened; masters are debasing and debased; cruel suffering, degradation, and death are everywhere; and, at the heart of the story, the seductive slave and the master who has succumbed.

Earlier, in 1912, Gaunt published *Alone in West Africa*, which she wrote in order 'to tell the prowess of the men who had gone before and left their traces in great stone forts all along three hundred miles of coast' (11). These stone forts are slave castles, the men on whom she bestows 'all honour' are the slave runners who 'upheld the might of Britain, and her rights in the trade in palm oil and slaves and ivory' (28). The slave days, though, are scarcely passed for Gaunt; for her, Africa vibrates with the slave days and at every opportunity she reinstates the master-slave relation. When she cannot, when this fantasy fails, she suffers nostalgia for the days that have passed, and worries for the white man's future.

At the outset of her journey, on a crowded river boat, she feels sympathy for the slave driver of old. It is 'impossible to feel humane in the midst of such a shrieking, howling mob', she says. 'It seemed likely we should sweep away a few dozen who were hanging on in the most dangerous places to the frailest supports. Possibly they wouldn't have been missed. I began to understand why the old slaver was callous' (26). As she proceeds into West Africa, 'the continent of [her] dreams' (11), she becomes yet bolder: the 'negro', she contends, must be ruled – more than that, physically beaten where necessary. The 'negro' asks for this treatment – indeed in Gaunt's eyes is perfectly suited to it. 'The firm hand is what he requires and appreciates' (272):

> A good sound beating is of course the correct thing, and though a good sound beating is not legal in English territory, luckily, say I very luckily – for the negro does not understand leniency, he regards it as a sign of weakness – it is many a time administered *sub rosa*, and the inferior respects the kindly man who is his master, who if he do wrong will have no hesitation in having him laid out and a round dozen administered ... Because much as I admire the Germans and the wonderful fixed plan on which they have built up their colony, I have known Englishmen who would get just as good results if their hands had not been tied. And occasionally one meets or hears of a man who will not allow his hands to be tied. (273)

Running next to descriptions of howling, shrieking African men who must be ruled are descriptions of these men's nakedness, their bared buttocks and chests. Gaunt is 'wild with delight and excitement', finding herself called by Africa's 'savagery' (7), and its 'demurring men' (127). These are men reduced to boys in Gaunt's eyes by the white woman who can dominate them. Gaunt herself is one such 'uplifted' white woman; she 'purred with pride' (127). 'The first thing to be done was to look out for a boy', she says, and by this she means an African man who will take charge of her private rooms, prepare her bath, bring her an early morning cup of tea. She in turn will take pleasure dressing him in 'white shirt, khaki knicker-bockers, and a red cummerbund, and bare feet' (19). Of other men, her pleasure is in their undress: 'I shall always regret', she writes, 'that I did not take [the Captain's] photograph as he leaned over the railing ... He wore a khaki coat and very elderly tweed trousers, split behind; his feet were bare; he did not pander to that vitiated taste which demands underlinen' (25).

Gaunt desires, she looks. More than this, she desires the other's complicit gaze in return. She desires the debasement of the other and of herself in turn, in a sadistic play of looks. A stranger to her, an African man in Liberia, bare-chested, from the upper balcony of his house looks down upon her passing along in the street and 'gave her thoughts she ... deeply resented':

> Often passing along the street and looking up I saw men and women in the scantiest attire lounging on their balconies doing nothing, unless they were thinking, which is doubtful.
>
> I believed all the horrible stories of Vaudooism [sic] of America and the West Indies when I saw the naked chest and shoulders of a black man leaning over a balcony in Monrovia ... *Was it because the half-civilised man was sinking back into barbarism and looking at the white woman gave her thoughts she would deeply have resented?* Was it just an example of the thought-reading we are subconsciously doing every day and all day long without exactly realising it ourselves? (69–70, my emphasis)

In the formation of whiteness in the colonial scene white men and women fantasise themselves as the unseen observers of others. This cannot always hold, though; there will always be moments when one sees oneself being looked upon by others. When this happens in Mary Gaunt's narrative, it produces in her a mix of pleasure and terror as she suddenly discovers in herself 'thoughts she would deeply have resented'. These thoughts, however, are not of her own making, or so she wishes to believe. They have been given to her, installed in her by the 'half-civilised man sinking back into barbarism and looking at the white woman'. Even now, she cannot admit them as her own.

* * *

Mary Gaunt's writings have been read by a contemporary generation of Australian feminists in two main ways. Some have been enthusiastic in their discovery of Gaunt as exemplary of the New Woman, celebrating her independence and adventurousness against the constraints of the nineteenth- and early twentieth-century social and moral codes. In these accounts, Gaunt 'bridged the gulf between wanting and being and became all the strong, adventurous women she had written about. There is never a time when we do not delight in such a triumph of the human spirit' (Hickman 58–9). She is admired for 'her personal determination to throw herself fully into anything undertaken, and her belief that women had equal abilities and rights in any society' (Martin 192). (Also, see Bradstock 144, who notes that all of Gaunt's books 'concern the controversial question of the rights of individual women to independence and equality'. Similarly, see Robinson.) Among this generation of feminist critics, Gaunt is often taken seriously as being 'alone' in Africa, even while surrounded and assisted by so many Africans: 'She travelled alone where few Western women had ever been', claims Hickman (58). Her racism is noted but rather than being made the subject of analysis it is passed over as being no more than typical of her day, the sadism of her sexualised regard

112   *The Postcolonial Eye*

for African men entirely dropping from view.[7] It is just not seen, apparently. These accounts, too, sympathise with Gaunt's lamentations on the restrictions on a married woman's life, and the difficulties of a single woman who must choose between marriage and work (Afterword, Spender, Gaunt *Kirkham* 338–9). That these feminine dilemmas are highly particular – they are the dilemmas of the white middle classes – is not raised. Many of Gaunt's contemporaries did not have the privilege of the dilemmas about which Gaunt complains – still, Gaunt is made to stand in for the New Woman, whose race or class privileges remain generally unmarked.

It has been pointed out in some of these feminist readings that Gaunt's writing coincided with Australian federation and the formation of Australia as a white nation. *Kirkham's Find*, for instance, was published three years before Australian federation, *Alone in West Africa* a little over a decade afterwards. But there is another historical coincidence, too: this feminist rediscovery and celebration of Gaunt took place around 1988, the year of Australia's bicentenary, a time of intense antagonisms over the history of white-black relations. At the very moment of this renewed national anxiety, white feminists celebrated Mary Gaunt, this woman with a fantastic sense of her own racial entitlement, an apologist for White Australia, nostalgic for the slave trade.

If reading is a performative act, making what it says it finds, then these readers (under the sign of second wave feminism) have not so much rediscovered Gaunt as given her a life, drawn from their own idealisations. As this feminism valorised economic and sexual independence and freedom of movement, so its proponents idealise these in Gaunt; and as this feminism failed to theorise the mutuality of gender, race and sexuality, so do these readings, turning a blind eye to Gaunt's eroticisation of her racialised others. Her white supremacist views and her sadistic sexuality are put aside as if these could be separated from her pursuit of her rights as a white woman.

More recently, another kind of feminist reading, a more critical one, has insisted on the ways that such an ideal of independent Australian womanhood is formed under colonialism. Gillian Whitlock and Angela Woollacott offer the most powerful readings of this kind, each emphasising the imbrication of race, gender and sexuality in their readings of Gaunt's texts. Both of these writers look at the association between Australian race relations and Gaunt's investments in other places, and the fact that Australian race relations are themselves formed in association with the Black Atlantic and the slave trade.

---

[7]   Bradstock observes that Gaunt's novels were 'all fairly racist … Gaunt's interest in Africa was mainly in British colonization and differed little from prevailing attitudes of the time' (147). For Hickman, 'Mary was a woman of her times. But while she had narrow views and prejudices typical of her time, she could sometimes see very clearly beyond these' (60). For Martin, 'Her attitude to the black population is often without insight or understanding. Perhaps the best (or worst) that can be said is that it differed little from the prevailing attitudes of the time' (192).

For Woollacott, Gaunt 'extrapolates Australian cultural politics to other imperial sites', and her writings 'allow us to see at work assumptions of the early twentieth century about the interconnectedness of empire, the interconstitution of race and gender, and the central place of sexuality therein' (Woollacott 190). Woollacott reads Gaunt's writings for their emphasis on the 'proper racial and gender arrangements' for empire (Woollacott 190), part of a national project towards a White Australian ideal that attempted 'to fix the inherently unstable categories of race, gender and sexuality' (190). But while a consideration of imperialist discourses of 'proper' sexual arrangements is important, to continue to emphasise constraint, control and repression of white women's sexual desire is to foreclose consideration of that which might be most troubling in some white women's relations with their 'others'. It is to foreclose consideration of the range of white women's desires, the provenances of these desires and, in some cases, their perversions.

Gillian Whitlock is in no doubt that the 'empire is an erotic field, a site where fantasies could be indulged' (89). Taking up and critiquing ideas about sexual desire and empire put forward by Ronald Hyam in *Sexuality and Empire*, Whitlock genders the analysis, suggesting that Hyam's libertarianism is a perverse masculine desire. The feminine subject of empire might pursue something rather different, even if still perverse, even if still a 'most improper desire', as Gaunt professed hers to be. For Whitlock, Gaunt's 'most improper desire' is 'for liberty but not ... libertarianism'. This is still a perverse desire in the sense that it is the 'abandonment of the aim of reproduction and the pursuit of pleasure as an aim independent of it ... Gaunt found in the empire the opportunity to escape femininity and compulsory heterosexuality' (89).

This is an account of feminine perversion, though, that might very well involve no sex at all, or at least not with men. What makes Gaunt's desire 'most improper', according to this reading, might be its absence of a sexualised object: the desire for liberty from gendered constraints rather than for sexual libertarianism. I have argued that this was not the case for Gaunt, and that her sexual objects included 'black' men, captured, tied, debased, and the pleasure she reports lies in looking upon these others. Gaunt saw African men as objects through which to write herself into a position of a supreme white woman. So, what does it mean not to have seen this? Why have white Australian women repetitively not read the sexual sadism in Gaunt's writing? To not see Gaunt's narratives of sadism is after all an act in itself; it takes work not to see Gaunt's representations of her sexual desire that are written, explicitly, there on the page. This not-seeing is a moment in the formation of ourselves as white women, a moment structured by our own desires.

Chapter 8
'Matron always carried a small whip'

When we do evil,
we and our victims
are equally bewildered.
—W.H. Auden *Marginalia* (788)

We began with a photograph of two Aboriginal girls, Edna Walker and Doreen Barber, taken during the Board for Anthropological Research's Harvard and Adelaide Universities' expedition in 1938 into Aboriginal settlements in Queensland. This particular portrait is part of a series of images of children interred at Cherbourg Aboriginal Settlement. In these photographs, the children hold their arms to their sides as they have been instructed to do. They do not embrace, there is no arm resting easily along another child's shoulder, no hands linked affectionately around another's waist. In this photograph, both girls look earnestly towards the camera but Doreen Barber's mouth is the sadder one, and she frowns at the photographer's demand that she meets his eye. Her head is shaved, *shamejob*.

In addition to the white anthropologist with his eye at the camera there is someone else, too, who might have been looking at the girls: it's not hard to imagine Agnes Semple standing close by. Perhaps it is her hand that holds up the small enigmatic white card with its number – N1474. Wherever she stood that day as the girls were made to face the camera, the Superintendent's wife was deeply implicated in the production of images of race at Cherbourg, and she often held her own eye to a camera's viewfinder. She was a keen photographer and produced a series of photographs of Cherbourg in the 1920s and 1930s. Her photographs, though, are more wildly imaginative than anything Norman Tindale or Joseph Birdsell arranged during the expeditions. The photographs she took are tableaux of absurd design, scenes through which her fantasies of race are brought into view. As her husband's perspective is caught in the archive he produced (see Chapter 6), so is Agnes Semple's documented in the images she made, and in others she brought together in a family photograph collection.

Although Agnes Semple rarely appears before the camera, we can say that she makes an appearance nevertheless. She appears in these fantasies, in her dreams of others: 'the subject of the dream is the dreamer.' The photographs are composed according to the lines of her sight and desire, and from them we might be able to trace the coordinates of her viewing position, looking at her looking at her others.

(And, can you see *my* desiring, seeing 'I'?)

Fig. 8.1   'Six girls in costume', late 1920s.

Agnes Semple choreographed various compositions in black and white. 'Six girls in costume' anticipates one of the regular fancy dress concerts she held at Cherbourg in the 1920s. (The question insists itself: for whose enjoyment?) She arranges Aboriginal girls in postures of arrested flight, reflected in the shallow waters of the creek. Their bodies are draped in long delicate strands of dried grasses. But, these are not all Aboriginal girls after all. There, in the foreground, on a rock at the water's edge is a white girl with blond plaits. Her smile is more certain than the others. This is Elizabeth, Agnes Semple's daughter. (The words accompanying the images reproduced here are Elizabeth's, recorded as she looked again at these images sixty years later, in 1987, when she donated her family's photograph collection to the Queensland Museum.)

In another deliberate staging for the camera, Agnes Semple arranged other Cherbourg inmates, adults now, into a scene of the nations of the world. Here, the participants in her costume drama look unsmilingly at the camera – the arc of enjoyment does not extend to them. Among them is a 'squaw' with long black plaits and headband, and a 'Red Indian Chief' in feathered headdress and fringed tunic; a Japanese woman is signified by a paper and bamboo parasol. What figure is it, dressed like the night sky in a costume of stars and moon? I can't tell. Australia's representative does not appear in national dress as the others do. Australia is signified by the new national flag, draped over an Aboriginal woman in whose hands has been placed a little stick flag she holds joylessly.

Fig. 8.2   'Women posing in the costumes they wore to a fancy dress on the settlement, mid 1920s. The snapshot was taken in the Superintendent's garden. In the background is the sawmill.'

Fig. 8.3   'A ceremonial arch erected to welcome official visitors', 1920s.

118   *The Postcolonial Eye*

Among the photographs in the Semple family collection is Figure 8.3, of three white men in suits walking through an elaborate arboreal arch. The men pause for the benefit of the camera, one of them holding up the boomerangs that have just been given to him. The men will proceed through a guard of honour that is comprised of Aboriginal men in ceremonial paint, headdress and spears. Positioned at the top of this over-sized garden folly, this bizarre bit of topiary, are four more men, also painted up and holding raised spears. Consider the height of the arch and the resources that would have been devoted to its construction – the time, labour and timber. My fingers tend towards the keyboard's exclamation marks. What fantasies of the 'natives'! What contortion, what twist, to make Aboriginal men perform in a scene like this, men who are entirely captive, and will probably remain so for the rest of their days?

So, for whose enjoyment were such scenes staged? There exists a very important eyewitness account of William Porteous Semple's and Agnes Semple's enjoyment. This is Ruth Hegarty's memoir of her days as a dormitory girl at Cherbourg in the 1930s. In *Is that you, Ruthie?* Ruth Hegarty looks at the Semples looking at her and others, and she sees their enjoyment. In particular she sees their enjoyment in making Aboriginal men, women and children into spectacles. She offers a critique of the reserve system and its associated practices as evidenced at Cherbourg during these years: the forced removal of Aboriginal peoples from their traditional lands, the mandatory internment of men, women and children on the reserves, and the separation of children from their families, practices that were legislated under the 'Dog Act' as the *Aboriginals Protection and Restriction of the Sale of Opium Act 1897* is still referred to by Aboriginal people and which produced among other things the Stolen Generations.[1] These practices emerge in her account as sadistic, and systematically so. Against the well-rehearsed arguments that these practices were well-intentioned mistakes, Ruth Hegarty points to white men and women's enjoyment at other's subjugation and captivity and she emphasises the pleasure taken by particular white subjects in looking.

Ruth Hegarty was brought as a baby to the dormitory after the forced removal of her family from Mitchell, in southwest Queensland to Cherbourg (or Barambah as it was then called) in 1930. She was interred there for the next 22 years, under the authority of William Semple, who was Superintendent there between 1924 and 1949. Among the first memories she tells is the story of Dulcie Munro, who suffered a kind of paralysis and was unable to walk, but no wheelchair or other aid were provided for her. She developed a way of moving nevertheless: belly

---

[1]   The Stolen Generations have been documented in Australian Human Rights and Equal Opportunity Commission. The Stolen Generations have been the subject of controversy among white Australian scholars (see Chapter 1). For an Indigenous scholarly perspective, see Birch's important contribution: 'The first white man born'. An extensive body of Indigenous-signed visual and literary arts engages with the trauma of the Stolen Generations and this includes the novels of Alexis Wright (discussed in Chapter 3) and Kim Scott (discussed in Chapters 9 and 10).

up, her bent legs in front of her, her arms straight down to the floor, bearing her weight. She went everywhere like this. 'Each night she crawled up and down long flights of stairs to bed, a long and difficult climb on all-fours' (3). So begins Ruth Hegarty's account of the profound deprivations of Cherbourg under the Semples.

Semple was in charge of the reserve overall, but the administration of the dormitories fell to the Matron. During Ruth Hegarty's time in the dormitory, there were several women in this position, including Agnes Semple between 1924 and 1932. Ruth Hegarty remembers that the Matron and other white women officials carried small whips (36, 60). The Matron, with whip in hand, watched young dormitory girls every morning scramble among the piles of communal clothes, searching out a garment that might fit, a dress not too long, a pair of bloomers not too big. There were no shoes for the girls to squabble over. Then, when the girls – all in a rush – arranged themselves in military rows, she carried out her inspections of hands, ears and heads and, requiring the girls to lift their dresses, she inspected their bloomers (36).

At night, the communal ritual was repeated in reverse. Dresses were discarded and the pile of night clothes searched through, a long night dress covetted on winter nights. Bloomers were to be discarded too; the girls must wear no underclothes to bed. An inspection was held each night before the girls went upstairs to bed, requiring them to lift their night dresses to ensure they were naked underneath (39). The Matron, Ruth Hegarty recalls, was feared by everyone:

> She was caretaker and distributor of the store supplied for cooking, cleaning and washing for all of the three dormitories. She supervised the distribution of clothing to the children living in the dormitories. These were called 'free issue', we got them about three times a year. This scant issue consisted of a school uniform and blouse at the beginning of the year, and a pair of homemade bloomers and at the other times a dress and bloomers. The boys got khaki trousers and shirt, no underclothes. There were never ever any belts or braces to hold their trousers up. Most of the boys used rope or bits of rag. (18)

There was no bed linen at Cherbourg during these years, only half a dozen towels and a tub of bath water between 60 girls. Menstruating girls were provided with one sanitary belt that would not be replaced if it were lost or damaged or stolen, and since the girls had nowhere secure and private for any belongings, they wore their sanitary belts every day and every night of their lives. They were bound to it. They took especial care of the old jam tin, too, that they'd been given for boiling the little triangles of rags for their menstruation blood.

The children's heads were shaved, ostensibly in the name of hygiene but de facto for punitive purposes. Heads were shaved when there was an outbreak of lice, certainly, but also when the children did not obey the Matron's law. After a beating, the children's heads 'were shaved, and then depending on the severity of the crime (stealing food, going somewhere without permission, even making a noise) it would be the lock-up'.

120   *The Postcolonial Eye*

> Even if we were locked up for only half the night to teach us a lesson, the
> very thought of being put away on your own in a locked cell, with high barred
> windows, no lights and very little ventilation, no bed and a drum in the corner –
> this was enough to terrorise any child. Just the isolation was enough without the
> fear and trepidation that followed the scratching on the walls. Those experiences
> had the capacity to disempower any child. (43)

Children who wet their beds were forced to sleep on the verandah away from
the other children: 'the mattresses were often completely saturated as the
children slept huddled together', trying to warm themselves. 'Those poor kids
were not allowed to use sheets. Every morning after a night of bed-wetting
the children would be seen struggling down a long flight of steps dragging
heavy mattresses dripping wet' (45). Ruth Hegarty bears witness to many other
obscenities, as do other Aboriginal men and women in their memoirs of the
reserve system.[2]

Let's return, then, to Agnes Semple's photographs. Despite the desperately
impoverished conditions under which Aboriginal people were living at
Cherbourg, the materials for the relatively elaborate fancy dress concerts could
still be garnered; an arch could be built to welcome official visitors; regular
dances could be staged. There was a tight control over the issue of clothes at
Cherbourg – there were not enough clothes and these were depersonalised, a
communal collection of shabby uniforms and sack dresses – yet there were
enough resources to support the dramatisation of Agnes Semple's vision. The
point I am making here is that the deprived conditions under which men, women
and children were forced to live were not simply the outcome of economic
retreat, or 'mere' neglect. They were not the result of an absence of care. Quite
the opposite: someone cared too much. The Semples' project (exemplary of a
much wider regime) was a passionate and motivated one; it was a project that
offered the perverse enjoyment of the spectacle of men, women and children
being entirely subject to the Semples' law (or so the hope might have run). Their
fantasy was that Aboriginal men, women and children at Cherbourg were theirs
to play with. I am arguing that, if we look at Aboriginal documents of memory,
such as Ruth Hegarty's memoir, and bring these into proximity with white
officials' own documents of memory – in this case, these photographs – together
we have evidence of this logic, the logic of a perverse enjoyment in an other's
deprivation.

---

   [2]   Notable examples include Huggins and Huggins (discussed in Chapter 6); Garimara;
also see the sequel to Ruth Hegarty's *Is that you, Ruthie? – Bittersweet Journey*, St Lucia,
Qld: University of Queensland Press, 2003. See also Kinnane's story of his grandmother's
experiences in *ShadowLines*.

Fig. 8.4　　The camp at Cherbourg comprising shacks, or 'yumbas', made from discarded corrugated iron and other debris, c.1930.

Fig. 8.5　　'Both Mr Semple and his wife were keen gardeners – and the Settlement had a good water supply from the creek. Mr Semple raised all his own seeds and did most of the planting out. All white officials had a dark boy to work in their gardens three days a week. Flowers in the picture are mostly roses, English daisies and larkspurs.' 1930s.

The Intimacies of Empire

It is often said that in the colonial context, Aboriginal men and women have been infantilised. On the evidence of these photographs, I think we can go further and say that they were sometimes treated like playthings: as figures to dress and undress, to move from place to place, available to having their bodies and limbs pressed into this pose or another according to the little scenes in which they were made to appear. They were treated as a child might treat a doll that can be pulled out of a cupboard or a toy box and pushed back and forgotten when the urge to play passes. What puzzlement might this have evoked in the grown men and women who were forced to submit to this? Did they wonder what propelled their white counterparts to take pleasure in childish games? By saying childish, I don't mean to suggest innocence. I am reminded again of Toni Morrison's *Beloved*, when Stamp Paid asks in bewilderment at the white masters' capacity to do damage: 'Who *are* these people?' And were there moments when this bewilderment was echoed in the white men and women; when they too wondered about the kind of world they had made for themselves and what it had made of them?

Fig. 8.6   'Jim Fisher was one of the main performers in the concert party organised by Mrs Semple, Matron at the Settlement and wife of the Superintendent. He had a rich baritone voice, and sang Harry Lauder songs learned from the gramaphone. He also played gum leaf to perfection.'

Jim Fisher appears in a kilt, sporran and tartan hose, c.1925, dressed for one of Agnes Semple's concert parties where he will perhaps sing the Harry Lauder songs to which Elizabeth Semple refers above. William Porteous Semple was Scottish, although nowhere in this photographic collection is there an image of him in his national dress. The directness of Jim Fisher's gaze holds my attention as he looks down at his photographer who, this time, is not Agnes Semple but her young son, Jack. Many of the adult Aboriginal and Islander men at Cherbourg were made to submit to the child's eye at the camera. (Does it go without saying that this collection includes no images taken by an Aboriginal photographer?) Jack took the following photograph, too, of Jimmy Edwards in the ceremonial paint and headdress of the Torres Strait.

Fig. 8.7 'Jimmy Edwards in "war paint", and carrying spear and nulla nulla, photographed at the Superintendent's house, early 1930s.'

For the camera, the Semple children mime Aboriginality; they take up another's posture or dress. In the following photograph Jack plays at being an Aboriginal hunter, miming the adult men whom he has photographed; his sister Elizabeth plays at being an Aboriginal girl in her mother's various tableaux. These children hold their bodies in the postures of their others and bring signs of otherness into proximity with their own bodies: grass dress and headband, woomera and spear. The pleasures available to whites in acts of crossdressing – this form of blackface – is developed in the following chapter. For now, I want to point to Elizabeth Semple's interest in a more literal or explicit blackface. She took a series of photographs of the production of *The Romance of Runnimede*, a silent film made at Cherbourg in the 1920s, based on Steele Rudd's novel of the same name.

Fig. 8.8   'Jack Semple with shield, spears and woomera he made. On Saturday mornings he often went "hunting" (for goannas, bearded dragons, "white tree grubs", honey) with dark children, who were his constant playmates until he went to boarding school in Warwick.'

Fig. 8.9   'Tommy Stuckey holds aloft a four-pronged fishing spear and woomera at Cherbourg Sports Ground. In daily life, Tommy was a stockman. He came from North Queensland. He was a keen "corroboree man."'

The American actress Eva Novak appears in jodhpurs and knee-high leather boots and surrounded by adoring 'black' men on their knees before the white woman. Cherbourg men were made available to the American production company as (probably unpaid) extras, but the Aboriginal protagonist Goondi was not played by an Aboriginal man at all; the man in the centre of the photograph is a white man in blackface.

Fig. 8.10   'Eva Novak, an American actress, is in the centre, surrounded by aboriginals, with the "oracle of the race", Goondi (a white actor) at left. The scene was filmed at Red Ridge on the old Barambah-Wondai road.'

The pleasures that blackface offers to whites in the Australian scene of race is taken up in the following chapter, but I want to anticipate its argument a little here to say that in blackface is revealed the disavowed pleasures that proximity with blackness holds for white Australians. This is a pleasure that is revealed for instance in the following photograph, where the intimate pleasures of Empire are at once acted out and disavowed. Here a white man, a Mr Stopford (after whom the girls' dormitory was named) asks for a light for his cigarette from another man, Cobbo Williams, who, considering the dress codes of the day, is almost naked, an Aboriginal man with bare legs and torso among the suited and uniformed men that surround him. 'Doing a bit of play-acting for the camera', Stopford brings his body into proximity with this other man's; the men's hands are raised to their mouths. Is there not something of the intimacy of a kiss? On Stopford's left, the local Murgon policeman, Sergeant McMahon, looks on, with what kind of smile?

Fig. 8.11   'Mr Stopford, on an official visit, is doing a bit of play-acting for the camera, lighting his cigarette from one being smoked by Cobbo Williams, who dressed for a corroboree put on to entertain the visitors, 1920s.'

A White Christmas

There is one photograph which has troubled me in a peculiarly personal way for 20 years, ever since it was first put in my hands by Auntie Rita Huggins. It troubled me when I first saw it, and so I have tended to turn away from it, I have preferred not to look. But, it keeps returning to me for one reason and another. The image itself is quite benign: Christmas Day at Cherbourg, 1937. There is a little party out on the grass, there are paper hats and small baskets, filled with sweets perhaps. Wrapping paper is strewn about. The heat of the Queensland summer might not yet be fully felt – it appears to be morning still. W.P. Semple and Agnes Semple are in their night clothes. Santa Claus is with them. W.P. Semple sits in a straight-backed dining chair, hands clasped in his pyjama-clad lap. Next to him in the small circle of chairs is Agnes Semple smiling at the camera.

In the foreground, two Aboriginal men – Jack Demelin and Willie McKenzie – kneel in front of the white men and women, looking directly towards the camera. They are dignified, serious. Then there is a young woman sitting on the grass at Boss Semple's feet. She is beautiful and unsmiling. This is Rita Huggins at 17. Some light is cast on this image by Ruth Hegarty, who tells of Christmases at Cherbourg at this time. I reproduce her account in full. It is far better told in her own words than paraphrased in my own.

Fig. 8.12   Christmas Day, Cherbourg 1937. Left to right Rita Holt, Superintendent Semple, Wallace McKenzie, Mrs Semple, Miss George, Jack Demelin, Willie McKenzie.

No stockings were put out on Christmas Eve in the dorm – Santa Claus would definitely have been a figment of our imagination. We knew there'd be nothing ...

On Christmas morning we were awakened early, not to look under the tree as there was none in the dorm, but to go carolling around the white officials' houses. We'd start off from Boss Semple's with 'Hark the Herald Angels Sing'. I often wondered if he listened. He would emerge from his back door towards the end of the singing and throw (yes, throw!) a handful of nuts and lollies. As we scrambled for these we knew we were not to eat them. No one ate so much as one nut or lolly, there were kept for the Christmas table. For the next hour we went from house to house and the same thing happened. The lollies were thrown on the lawn and they, the white officials, would stand and watch as we scrambled to pick them up – as if they got some sort of amusement out of it.

With empty tummies we'd arrive back at the Home, the lollies were put away to be used for the Christmas table ... [After church we'd] run home as fast as we could just to get a first glance at the decorations and to watch the tables being set up.

With our faces pressed against the glass window we'd watch the older girls setting the tables with lollies and small cakes, all nicely iced, being put in everyone's place. After many years of watching this same scene you'd think it would lose its appeal ...

As we filed through, our eyes lit up like torch bulbs. We would sing grace. Some of the little ones didn't know it yet but the cakes and lollies were not to be eaten. The Superintendent and the Matron walked through the dining room to

128   *The Postcolonial Eye*

inspect us before we sat down to eat. After they went, the lollies and cakes were taken off the tables to be brought back for New Year's Day. Six days later we'd eat stale cake and lollies. (80–82)

Her story throws the innocence of the Semples' image of Christmas Day, reminding us again of the cost of their enjoyment.

There is, though, something else about this image that troubles me. How to say it? I disappear before this image, I feel as if I risk a kind of annihilation and I turn away. It is not only that the scene is unfamiliar to me, preventing me from locating myself in it, although it is true that I've never been able to place myself there. I can neither join that little circle of other whites nor sit with the young Rita and the Aboriginal men. (Can I catch a glimpse of my own shadow? There, falling on the grass, as if I am standing next to the photographer, looking on?) But there's something more: there's the question of the gaze, for who could see *me* in a scene such as this? The whites are blind: they avert their eyes, or are blinded by their own narcissism. They enjoy too much the staging of their own whiteness, a whiteness which, across this historical distance, pulls too far away from my own. I cannot make *these* whites invoke the knowing, seeing Other of my fantasies and without whom I cannot appear – *as a white woman*.[3]

But surely the seeing subjects in this photograph are Rita and the two men beside her on the grass; it is their serious and steady gaze that looks towards the viewer. Has that been too hard for me to see? Is it from their look that I have turned away? What is more unbearable, the blind 'white' or the seeing 'black'? So, it is not only the Semple eye/I that might be betrayed in photographs such as these, but my own.

---

[3]   See Chapter 6 for my argument concerning whiteness in the 'eyes' of a blind Other.

PART IV
Whiteness and its Veils

PART IV

Whiteness and its Verbs

Chapter 9
Darkness Casts its Light:
Australian Blackface

> As the first-born-successfully-white-man-in-the-family-line I awoke to a terrible pressure, particularly upon my nose and forehead, and thought I was blind. In fact, the truth was there was nothing to see, except – right in front of my eyes – a whiteness which was surface only, with no depth and very little variation.
>
> —Kim Scott *Benang* (11)

Australian white subjectivity is formed in proximity to blackness which it desires *and* refuses, irreducibly. This is a constitutive ambivalence: it is how a white subject can appear as white at all, it is how the whiteness to which she clings is made. The 'black' whom the 'white' Australian subject so equivocally desires and denies is the Indigenous subject made black by colonialism's imperatives. It is this black in relation to whom a white can take shape, as white tulle shows itself against a black background. But for a white subject there is a crucial distance to be observed, however, for if she becomes too close to her black other, she is not made white at all but tainted. 'I am *not* my other', she insists. 'We are opposites, black and white. I am everything that my other is not.' Out of this othering the white subject will fashion an image of herself. But this image does not hold. It flips into its negative – the white 'I' collapses into her image of her other. Her emphatic 'I am *not* that' reveals something more: the white subject does indeed believe she is her other, or might be.

No other Australian text shows this better than Kim Scott's astounding *Benang: From the Heart*, which figures white desiring subjects in irreducibly ambiguous relationship with their Indigenous others to whom they are drawn and from whom they recoil. This ambivalent white desire is shown to be at the very heart not only of white Australian subjectivities but also of Australian race policies: assimilationism on one hand and segregation on the other. *Benang* shows that in assimilationism is a desire for proximity, always disavowed, and that segregation is propelled by the anxiety that such proximity arouses. Segregation in turn brings about a renewed anxiety: what is it that we have excluded? What is 'out there'? What can we not see? There is then a retreat once more into assimilationism in the hope that it can bring inside that which is outside, cojoin the two, and so on. This is Australia's colonial and postcolonial history and it continues right into the present.[1]

---

[1] The Australian Federal Government's policies under its Northern Territory Intervention program are an example of contemporary enforced assimilationism, bringing traditional Aboriginal men and women 'in' from the so-called remote communities.

132 *The Postcolonial Eye*

Benang makes a simultaneous point: this scene of race is not wholly homegrown. For all its specificities, Australian race discourses show the hallmarks of American slavocracy and the meanings given to white-black and master-slave relations formed under those conditions. *Benang* works more effectively than any other Australian novel to show how Indigeneity in its radical difference from whiteness is felled and made into black instead. More than that, it is 'niggered'.

This Indigenous-signed novel retells the story of Australian colonialism since first contact. From this enormous novel, I begin with three associated fragments. This is not an economic move; it is suggested by the text itself which composes itself in fragments – necessarily so, ethically so, as I will argue in the following chapter. The first fragment I work with here is a blackface minstrel show, performed before a camera, where the desired proximity between whiteness and blackness is specularised (221–4). The show recalls the nineteenth-century theatrical practices of the American urban North, with its naturalisations of slavery, although some of its sartorial references are to more recent reinvigorations.[2] This first fragment is set in rural Western Australia in an indeterminate year c.1900, and it is an Aboriginal boy, a Nyoongar, rather than an African American slave, who is made to carry the blacknesss against which whiteness can be cast. The second fragment depicts scenes a day or so later when paradigmatic stories of Australian colonialism are enacted, again before a camera, and which continue to speak of the passage of race discourses across the Atlantic and Indian oceans in an arc that stretches between the Americas, Britain, Africa, India and Australia (224–5). The third fragment slips just underneath the surface of these two scenes' play with black and white (passim). It is the scene of a massacre of Indigenous men, women and children in Western Australia one Christmas in the 1880s. The American South might be heard in these descriptions, now in references to lynchings – to hanging trees and their 'strange fruit'. This time, no photographs have been taken, at least none that appear in the archive that the text's Nyoongar narrator consults, and so he relies on another kind of documentation, the documents of memory, including the memory of smell and of the sound of buzzing flies. Images of these massacres shadow the images forming on the photographic plates of white men at play.

---

[2]   According to Eric Lott:

While [blackface] was organized around the quite explicit 'borrowing' of black cultural materials for white dissemination, a borrowing that ultimately depended on the material relations of slavery, the minstrel show obscured these relations by pretending that slavery was amusing, right, and natural. Although it arose from a white obsession with black (male) bodies which underlies white racial dread to our own day, it ruthlessly disavowed its fleshly investments through ridicule and racist lampoon. Lott 3.

Darkness Casts its Light 133

* * *

White men in dinner suits with charcoaled faces draw their chairs in a semi-circle, and at their feet they place a sign – *Black and White Minstrels*.[3] Among them is Sandy Mason, dressed in women's clothes with pumpkins for breasts, sitting on another man's knee, coquettishly swinging a leg and giggling. What does he find in this scene to make him laugh so? The text doesn't say. The men sit still for the camera until the photographer's gunpowder flashes and then, breaking their pose, they grab the boy in their midst, the boy who is the son of Sandy and a Nyoongar woman known among whites as Fanny. The men grab this boy whom they call 'black' and 'half-caste' saying, 'C'mon, let's whiten him up' (223). Another flash of the camera's blinding light, and the men are in motion once more, Sandy Mason dancing to the fiddlers' music, lifting his skirts, while the young boy, known as Sandy Two, mimics the men, perfectly repeating their postures and gestures.

In the choreography of this minstrel scene, white men bring themselves into proximity with what they imagine blackness to be. They put it on, covering their skin with charcoal; one plays at holding a black woman in his lap. What speculation about such a scene does *Benang* invite? Desire is surely there, a white desire for proximity to its others, a desire so strong that at times it becomes a desire for merging, for oneness. As Eric Lott has argued of nineteenth-century American blackface minstrelsy, such acts were not based unambiguously in racial aversion, as some have argued, but founded also in cross-racial desire, a desire, Lott suggests, 'that coupled a nearly insupportable fascination and a self-protective derision with respect to black people and their cultural practices, and that made blackface minstrelsy less a sign of absolute white power and control than of panic, anxiety, terror and pleasure' (6).

This idea resonates with my opening claim, borrowed from the important work done by American critical race theorists, that whiteness is made in proximity with blackness, a proximity which the white subject desires and must deny. According to this view, it is only through blackness that whiteness can appear.

---

[3]   *Benang*'s figuring of the minstrelsy scenes recalls the traditional British and American minstrel shows of the nineteenth century with their semicircle of white male performers blacked up with greasepaint, charcoal or burnt cork, an array of instruments, fiddle, banjo and tambourine, the cross-dressed wench and the farce component, with its dancing, music and burlesque. See Lott 5–6. For other approaches to American blackface, see Ellison's notable intervention. Tuhkanen provides a useful contextualisation of the different approaches to blackface, 9–34. The equation between black and slave is brought into minstrelsy's themes, often explicitly. *Benang*'s minstrels adopt a different sartorial style, however, than the British and American nineteenth-century shows' outsized 'Negro' costumes: *Benang*'s minstrel men in their dinner suits suggests minstrelsy from the 1920s and even later, for instance, in the reinvigoration of blackface in British television's *The Black and White Minstrels* (late 1950s–1970s), which was popular viewing in Australia. This seeming historical conflation, this slippage in time, is an important move in *Benang*, as I go on to argue below.

134   *The Postcolonial Eye*

As Judith Butler powerfully argues for instance in her reading of Nella Larsen's novella *Passing*, set in Harlem in the 1920s, Larsen's white American protagonist *requires* the association with blacks that he claims repulses him; 'he cannot be white without blacks and without the constant disavowal of his relation to them. It is only through that disavowal that his whiteness is constituted, and through the institutionalization of that disavowal that his whiteness is perpetually – but anxiously – reconstituted' (Butler *Bodies* 171).

This is a blackness, however, that whiteness makes. We must insist that blackness is not already there, an object waiting to be discovered, but is a product of racial discourses. This black is made in historically specific discourses, including those that arise in the context of European expansionism and colonialism. This is to argue, then, against the tendency in some discourses on race to speak, for instance, of 'black Africans' as if they existed as black (or as African) prior to the colonial discourses of their formation. Instead, it is to insist that whiteness makes/ names the blackness that it needs for its own appearance. This is a blackness that is made and known in whiteness's terms; it is its reverse, its negative image, and as such is calculable, it can be known in advance. If whiteness is civilised, blackness *is not*; if whiteness is clean, blackness *is not*. Through such oppositional pairings, whiteness's boundaries are constituted. Blackness, then, is seen in this kind of approach as being produced not only for whites' satisfaction but for their very formation.

In the American scene of race to which Butler refers, blackness has been made through processes of blackening or 'niggering' whiteness's others – notably those subjects brought in chains from the land mass we now call Africa, but others have been blackened, too, at different times: Jews, Italians, the Irish.[4] Blackness also has been made, however, through another process and that is through the elision of Indigeneity. If American whiteness is formed in relation to blackness – blackness as it is imagined, made and named within regimes of whiteness – this is a blackness from which Indigeneity tends to be excluded. It is a black-white relation that disavows the presence of Indigeneity in relation to which both white and black are constituted.

Historically, the American scene of black and white excluded Native Americans by installing them outside the social realm, in 'nature'. They were positioned not so much as a different race as a different species. Idealised within the terms of James Fenimore Cooper's Red Nobleman of Nature, they were discursively positioned outside the cultural order. 'There was', Robert C. Toll has argued, 'literally no "place" for them within white American society' (Toll 168). American blackface minstrelsy's conventions of figuring the field of race in terms of black and white, and exclusively installing the figure of the African American slave in the position of the black, dropped the Indigenous figure from the scene.

---

    [4]   See Walter Benn Michaels on Jews and Italians as black in American discourses of race in the 1920s in *Our America*; and on arguments concerning the blackness of the Irish in America, see Ignatiev.

In the Australian case, the Indigenous subject, now and historically, also falls from the scene of black and white but for different reasons. This might seem a surprising claim to make because in Australia there has always been a tendency to bracket Indigeneity with nature; this has been a discursive possibility in Australia as it has been elsewhere. However, more forceful still has been the push in Australian discourses on race to install the Indigenous subject in the position of black. Indigeneity as such is dropped and made into blackness – where black is 'nigger' and 'coon'. Accordingly, *Benang*'s blackface minstrelsy can observe the form's conventions of black and white by dropping Indigeneity from its performance; it does this by remaking the Indigenous subject as black. There is no place for Nyoongar in this. The young boy in the minstrel show is not Nyoongar but black in the eyes of these men.

In the place of the enigmatic Nyoongar is installed the known and calculable black. This erasure of Nyoongar is important; it erases the spectre of untranslatable difference against which the colonial subject cannot appear as white. That is, by erasing Nyoongar and installing black in its place, the colonial subject has made a blackness that will enable his or her own formation as white. Nyoongar is collapsed into black because otherwise it would raise the Indigenous subject as a sovereign subject, outside the black-white binary that makes whiteness's others known within its own terms. It would make the Nyoongar incalculable, sovereign – a possibility that the coloniser/white/master must and does refuse.[5] In *Benang*, the substitution of 'black' for Nyoongar is the only way the men can see of fulfilling their desires to be white subjects.

The minstrel scene is part of the repetition of racialised discourses through which white subjects are made: it is performative. It is not merely a representation of the white men's imaginings of themselves and others, acted for their pleasure, it is a moment in their very formation as whites. Whereas Eric Lott, speaking of American blackface, resists the idea of blackface as a repetition of power relations of race, instead insisting that blackface is a signifier of race with all the distortions, displacements, condensations and discontinuities of any act of signification (Lott 8), we might make another move again and suggest that blackface *is* a

---

[5] We can go further and say that terms such as 'Native American' or 'Aboriginal' can also work as the black term in a white-black binary. These, too, are among the terms produced and deployed by coloniser subjects in order to form images of themselves as white. There were no Aboriginals before colonisation but Nyoongar, Yorta Yorta, Walpiri and so on, as there were no Native Americans but Hopi, Iroquois, Kuiu and so on before they were dispossessed of the land the colonisers called America.

In a seemingly unwitting paradox, the noted Australian historian Inga Clendinnen introduces the same logic when using the word Australians to refer to the peoples whom the British found occupying the land mass that would come to be called Australia. She goes further, calling them 'Australia's first immigrants'. In this move, she remakes the country's original subjects in the image of the colonising subjects who came after, which is to say, remakes them in her own image. Clendinnen *Dancing* 4–5. Kenny uses the term Australians to refer to Indigenous peoples throughout his *The Lamb Enters the Dreaming*.

repetition of a kind: it repeats, however approximately, the white subject's ideals of white and black and in such repetition the white subject is made. When a white subject mimics a 'black', it is still whiteness that is being spoken and gestured to. Minstrelsy's conventions that figure race in black and white specularise the wider discourses, but they are also performative. In the conventions of blackface, race as the exclusive pairing of black and white is specularised in a performative act that *makes* what it says is there to be found, with white men donning the gesture, voice and vestments of the blackness that they make in this very act.

We can go further and say that if white subjects are approximations of racialised ideals of whiteness, then whiteness is itself whiteface. A subject who desires to be white adopts the vestments, gestures and voice of an ideal whiteness. In this regime of race, subjects who desire to be white act out their ideals of whiteness and blackness – in many ways unconsciously and unknowingly. As Butler has said of the regime of gender (and she is often misquoted): drag's reversals are not peculiar performances of gender; rather, gender is already drag.[6] Gender is only and always a repetition, a mimicry of ideals, and so it is with race.

* * *

So, who is this cross-dressing Sandy One Mason sitting on another's knee? Is he white, as we might assume him to be from the minstrel scene? Sandy One Mason's placement in the binary of black and white seems to be clear for most of the text: he is a white man, isn't he? For most readers surely know of the prohibitions at this time against Indigenes and whites mixing.[7] We know, too, that traditionally blackface is a white man's act. Blackface performers have always been careful to distinguish between themselves and the black figures they play. Robert C. Toll recounts the nineteenth-century American minstrel joke: 'Why am I like a young widow? Because I do not stay long in black' (Toll 40).

Sandy One Mason enjoys privileges that mark him as white: he is literate for instance, he is a citizen (304), he is free of the various and far-reaching restrictions imposed on Nyoongars. But upon his death, his wife, Benang (referred to as Fanny for most of the book), removes Sandy One's old sea clothes from his body and replaces them with hairbelt and kangaroo-skin cloak (352). In the final pages of the novel, Sandy One's great-grandson Harley claims that Sandy One 'was no white man. Just as I am no white man' (492), and he is referred to as a *nigger* by an old man who had probably participated in the minstrel scene decades earlier (483).

According to a dualistic logic of race, one cannot be white *and* black (however much the same logic might inspire this very desire in its subjects). If, as I have

---

[6]   Judith Butler, *Gender Trouble*.

[7]   *The Aborigines Protection Act 1909* explicitly outlawed whites and Aboriginals mixing and cohabiting. For a consideration of the everyday effects of such legislated apartheid, see, for instance, *The Coolbaroo Club*, a film set in Western Australia, written by Kinnane, Marsh and Scholes.

suggested, race discourses fail to make Nyoongar a category of race because they make Nyoongar fall from their discourses and in its place install a black, then Nyoongar floats somewhat from the bindings of racialised pairs. Nyoongar and 'white' are not clearly opposites, they are not an exclusive binary pair. Some subjects, then, could be Nyoongar *and* white. And indeed while *Benang*'s Indigenous figures find themselves always represented in white discourses according to the violence of calculability – they are either 'full blood' or fractions of this: half-caste, quadroon, octoroon – we might ask whether *Benang* gives some of its Indigenous protagonists a doubled subjectivity: white and Nyoongar.

In Kim Scott and Hazel Brown's *Kayang and Me*, the term wadjela Nyoongar is translated to mean whiteman Nyoongar: 'It's a phrase with subtle increments of meaning which range, depending on tone and context, all the way from "one of us" to "one of them"' (Scott and Brown 18). Whiteman and Nyoongar are therefore not figured here as exclusive terms. To be white there must be a black but Nyoongar is independent of and prior to both these positions.

For most of *Benang*, Harley, Sandy One's great-grandson, read the evidence as I had done, believing that Sandy One was a white man *only*. As he discovers: 'Sandy One was no white man. Just as I am no white man.'[8] Certainly neither Sandy One nor Harley are white men if by white we mean an exclusive category, as prevailing discourses of whiteness would have it as being. The conjuncture 'whiteman Nyoongar', though, as Scott speaks of it above, does different work, writing against the notion of white and Nyoongar as exclusive.

In the colonial context, to be white is to be on the side of the coloniser.[9] There are times when Sandy One Mason is indeed white in this sense, forced to be so. If white is the settlers' position, if it is associated with trespass and dispossessing others of their land, Sandy One Mason is in the double position of having been dispossessed and dispossessing. He participates in a massacre, or 'spree', in which his wife's sister is killed. Sandy and the narrator refuse to clarify his involvement except to say that 'Sandy One came back drunk and stupid and snarling at [Benang], through a fog of vomit and alcohol. "It was three bullets, they put three in her" ... He spat, was sobbing, lay down snoring' (221). This is a sign of Sandy One's doubleness – and the agony of this. To suggest that Sandy One is white at these moments is not to say that he is not also and always Nyoongar. Nyoongar is another set of meanings altogether than those signifiable by the black-white binaries of race. Nyoongar is not assimilable to black. It carries meanings I do not assume to know. To say that Sandy One can only be one or the other is to make Nyoongar black to the colonisers' white, and then to insist on the binarism that

---

8   Lisa Slater reads *Benang* as a novel about miscegenation, a term that assumes and reinvigorates the discourses of race. For Slater, Harley is 'hybrid, miscegenated and polymorphous'. See Slater 'Kim Scott's *Benang*' 64.

9   See Moreton-Robinson '"I still call Australia home"'.

138   *The Postcolonial Eye*

has black and white as an exclusive pair. Sandy One Mason does not necessarily repudiate his Indigeneity when he appears as a white man.[10]

There is no pre-discursive object that we can call race, no white or black outside history; white and black are imaginary in the sense that they are images of the idealised subject and object. They are, nevertheless, materialised. In the colonising setting one of the signifiers of race is colonisation itself: to be white, a subject must be able to take up a position on the side of the colonisers. A white subject who does not always do so compromises his or her whiteness. There is no white subject already and always there to be found. A white subject is made, and remade, and sometimes 'imperfectly' so, however partial, temporary, infinitesimal are these imperfect reiterations of a white ideal. We can no longer say, therefore, that Sandy One is merely passing as a white man when he gains for himself and his family some of the privileges of whiteness.[11] He *is* a white man if he can 'pass', but this is not all he is. To 'be' white is 'merely' to pass the killing ideals of race.

Sandy One Mason, giggling in blackface and women's clothes, is crossing raced and gendered lines. Sandy's idea of the joke, however, might be different to his fellow players. Whereas their pleasure might lie in bringing themselves into (erotic) proximity with the black other of their own imagining, for Sandy might it lie in the idea of a Nyoongar wearing blackface to mimic white men mimicking black men? A cross-dressing Nyoongar in blackface mimicking white Australian men mimicking white American men mimicking black women. This scene shows Australians performing a scene of race avowedly from 'over there' but which all the same registers the structure of desire 'here', a desire that is disavowed.

The men's pleasure in Sandy One's travesty of gender raises a question mark over the relation between gender and race. Is Sandy One's cross-dressing about gender, or about whiteness? Sandy One's gesture not only mimics women but white men's pleasure at mimicking women. It is then about whiteness as well as gender: it is about white masculine pleasure, and about a racialised femininity in their eyes. Another story is told in *Benang* of white men cross-dressing:

> [There were] hundreds of white men running along a beach after one of their own, who was dressed like a woman and howling like a mad thing. His tongue was lolled from his mouth and trailed in his slipstream. The police stood

---

[10]   Lisa Slater reads Sandy One Mason differently. He is, she says, a Nyoongar who has denied his Aboriginality and whose 'anti-ethics' causes him to suffer from a cancerous tongue. See her essay 'Kim Scott's *Benang*: an ethics of uncertainty'. But to whom does he deny his Aboriginality? Presumably not to his wife or children, or other Nyoongars. After all, upon his death, Benang dresses his body in hairbelt and kangaroo-skin. When Benang first meets Sandy One she is trapped on a beach, and avoids rape by the white men who are coming towards the beach on boats by approaching one man among them, Sandy One. What did she recognise in him? See also Gauch.

[11]   For important arguments concerning whiteness as privilege and possession, see Aileen Moreton-Robinson's extensive body of scholarship, for instance her *Talkin' up to the White Woman*; and 'The possessive logic of patriarchal white sovereignty'.

Darkness Casts its Light

befuddled, and then – working like sheepdogs – they caught the madman. He protested, laughed that he was just pretending, was just bored with drinking and waiting for his miner's license ... (262)

In the white men's eyes, is Sandy One singled out for the role of a woman in their skit because as a 'black' he is already positioned as feminine? Consider again the writings of the Australian historian Inga Clendinnen and her apparent pleasure in repeating without gloss Charles Darwin's amused description of a scene in 1832 on a beach in Tierra del Fuego (as the continent was then called) when men from the *Beagle* met and danced and sang with Indigenous men who'd come down to the shore: 'one of the young men, when asked, had no objections to a little waltzing', Darwin reports.[12] The young Indigenous man was given the feminine position, then, was he, and invited to follow the white man's lead?

* * *

Blackface is a powerful specularisation of race discourses. To blacken one's face by charcoal or burnt cork – such a literal representation of 'black'! In producing this scene for its readers, however, *Benang* does more than provide an imaginative figuring of race, a spectacle intended to startle a reader into seeing the similarities between American slavery and Australian colonial relations. Certainly, it might defamiliarise the Australian scene of race, the 'already-known', setting it down among social relations of slavery and its legacies which prevailing Australian discourses always prefer to place outside Australia. 'Slavery is not part of our history', or so we prefer to believe. 'We are innocent of *that*.' This disavowal is maintained despite the nomenclature 'nigger' and 'coon' being used for Indigenous men and women, historically and into the present; despite the prevalence of colonial images of Aboriginal men in shackles and iron collars; despite the familiar fact of Indigenous men and women forcibly pressed into unpaid and indentured labour, and so on.[13]

But when *Benang* works with blackface it is not merely an imaginative strategy that invites a reader to make associations between Australian and American conditions of colonialism and slavery. Scott has not invented an Australian blackface in order to show something of the logic of race; there has been a long tradition of blackface in Australia and it has played its part in the 'blackening'

---

[12]   Charles Darwin's *A Naturalist's Voyage around the World (The Voyage of HMS 'Beagle', 1839)*. Oxford: Oxford World Classics, Oxford University Press, 1930, quoted by Inga Clendinnen, *Dancing* 7.

[13]   For instance, see Deborah Bird Rose on the use of the nomenclature 'nigger' in the Victoria River Downs area in *Dingo* 10. The word 'master' is used in Indigenous narratives to describe the missionaries and superintendents; in *Benang* Kim Scott uses the word 'slave' without gloss (491). Bruce Pascoe asks who forged the chains and necklaces, in *Convincing Ground*.

140   *The Postcolonial Eye*

and the 'niggering' of Australian Indigeneity. Blackface in Australia may never have achieved the same status as a national art that Lott suggests was the case in America in the late 1840s, but still it has had quite a life and one that continues into the present (Lott 8). *Benang* points to the fact that many nineteenth-century practices and discourses of slavery in Britain and America formed a grounding for Australian race practices: blackface is one example.[14]

Blackface minstrelsy was performed in Australian music halls and in vaudeville as well as on street corners by bands of buskers in the nineteenth century; 'nigger melodists' and other 'negroistic foolishments' were common to cheap theatres and at the horse races in Sydney and Melbourne.[15] The topography of empire and the passage of slave boats are marked in its skits and stylisations: one popular skit was called 'Plantation Frolics' and there were 'jubilee' songs, or 'Negro spirituals'.[16] There were ready sales of black varnish and white paper cuffs: for instance, in Woolloomooloo, Sydney, after the Mohawk Minstrels' opening night in 1882. The Mohawk Minstrels were English brothers who had performed shows such as 'The Cuff and Collar Coons' in London for many years in the late nineteenth-century. Their coupling of Mohawk with 'coon' shows the transnationalism of 'niggering' Indigeneity.

This mapping of empire and the passage of its ships is not only the case for the nineteenth-century varieties; it is spectacularly evident for instance in Charles Chauvel's now-iconic Australian film *Jedda* (1955) which was dubbed using the voices of English, South African and Caribbean actors over the Australian Aboriginal actors' own voices.[17] It is also clear in later restagings of blackface minstrelsy, for instance in the BBC's *The Black and White Minstrel Show* (1957–1973) that made such popular viewing in Australia (Pickering 161); and in very recent stagings of blackface minstrelsy on Australian television the old forms have been controversially reinvigorated.[18] The work these various examples of blackface does towards the 'niggering' of Australian Indigenous

---

[14]   Gilbert argues that minstrelsy was popular in Australia, Canada and New Zealand, India, Jamaica, Nigeria and South Africa.

[15]   Even Ned Kelly's gang has been loosely associated with black minstrelsy in some commentary. See Bellanta.

[16]   See Bellanta; Richard Waterhouse; Miller 146. Pickering (below) speaks of the 'niggering' of African and black people; Fotheringham.

[17]   Benjamin Miller 149–50. *Jedda*, made by Charles and Else Chauvel in 1955, was Australia's first full-length, full-colour film.

[18]   In October 2009, an Australian talent show *Hey, Hey It's Saturday* included a skit called 'Jackson Jive', billed as a Michael Jackson tribute and figuring men in blackface as the Jackson Five; the Jackson figure was played by a man in whiteface. The skit received international coverage, and more controversy outside Australia than in. In July 2010, a Western Australian court acquitted a white Australian, Simon Barker, of racial vilification after he placed on the internet a video he had made called *Noongah–Out Da Front*. The video figures white men in blackface performing as Aboriginal male rappers, where that word is brought into association with 'rapers'. While many Aboriginal men and women

men and women is not popularly acknowledged, however, and some historians, too, have been reluctant to 'over-read' Australian blackface in race's terms.[19]

Benang brings a reader's attention to other ways that the American discourses of race circulate in Australia. There are Aboriginal men who read American novels – westerns, 'cowboy-and-indian' stories, *Hiawatha* – looking for images of themselves in texts where the 'indian' will be annihilated; there are Aboriginal women who are given the names of American house slaves, Topsy, no less, the name of the young girl raised to be a house slave in Harriet Beecher Stowe's *Uncle Tom's Cabin*. In *Benang*, Topsy will hold in her hands a tin of food with a 'black mammy' on its lid, and a tin of shoe polish that bears the name and image of a 'black sambo', perhaps the very kind of shoe polish that the white men will use to 'blacken' themselves. Again, these are not inventions on Scott's part so much as imaginative uses of history. So, for instance, Topsy was a name commonly given Aboriginal women of an older generation who worked on cattle and sheep stations as domestic servants, nannies and as musterers. The link between American slavery and Australian colonial relations is there in the historical record but generally refused in prevailing Australian notions of our history. One of Scott's accomplishments in *Benang* is to bring this link to the surface, to usher it into the scene of race, to make it appear.

Benang's vocabulary works again to associate Australian and American scenes of race. For instance the word 'wagon' is used, and raises images of American western expansion, with 'indians' attacking besieged pioneers. 'Woodheap' is another word that is introduced in the text, and which raises the American antebellum South with its 'niggers in the woodheap', a phrase I have heard used in Australia. Then there are Aboriginal men with chains looped around their throats. I reproduce quite a lengthy passage here not only to offer evidence of Scott's choice of language, but also to offer a fragment of his text that, for readers as yet unfamiliar with *Benang*, will show something of the images with which it works more generally:

---

attested to the obscenity of the video and its lyrics, in the magistrate's view it was 'art'. Costs were awarded against the plaintiffs.

[19] Melissa Bellanta, in arguing against seeing blackface in terms that preclude considerations of masculinity and class, does not theorise the interrelation between gender, class and race. In trying to avoid an either/or argument that pits race against masculinity in considerations of the meanings available to blackface, Bellanta instead suggests that blackface can be read either in terms of gender or race. This misses the opportunity to comment on the ways that the production of gender (in this case masculinity) in the colonial context is always racialised. There is no masculinity possible in that setting that is not always and also racialised. For a succinct argument on the gender and race as mutually constitutive, see Judith Butler's 'Passing, queering: Nella Larsen's psychoanalytic challenge' in *Bodies that Matter* 167–8.

142 *The Postcolonial Eye*

In the darkness, among the stuff thrown from the wagon, something struggled and made noises. It was the boy she'd seen trying to escape. His eyes rolled above the gag at his mouth as he was pushed into a large hessian bag. He continued to struggle; Kathleen saw the bag swinging on the rope which suspended it from a tree.

Outside, someone chopped wood ... The axe rose and fell, rose and fell, and only its rhythm held her day together.

Shaven haired women, dressed in hessian and flour bags, stepped from the kitchen with food slops.

An old man felt his way along the wall toward her. Kathleen did not move, she held her breath, and the old man's hands found the doorframe ... The old man's eyes were sealed, and he moved slowly ...

Once he was past her, the blind one resumed feeling his way along the wall. He coughed, and seemed to tremble with each axe stroke ...

A small boy sat on the steps one afternoon. He was thin, his bones but a frame for the rags he wore, and his head seemed too heavy for his neck. He rested his chin on his knees, and turned his head to Kathleen when she sat beside him, then turned away again. His eyes were open, soft and unseeing ...

Shivering in the pale morning, Kathleen stood at the woodheap. There was yesterday's symmetrical stack of wood and two cylindrical bundles of canvas, one larger than the other. One held the body of the old blind man; and from the smaller bundle a small hand protruded, as if frozen in a secret wave of departure. (*Benang* 330–33)

But it is in *Benang*'s trope of racial uplift, metaphorised in the figure of its narrator who levitates, where the passage of racial discourses between America and Australia is most clearly and insistently enunciated. I turn to this a little further on.

The Blacks are Attacking

I have been approaching blackface as propelled by a disavowed desire for blackness. The desire for such proximity has its attendant anxieties, however, when closeness comes to be experienced as an over-proximity, when the gap between white and black collapses, and there appears what Joan Copjec after Lacan calls 'the lack of a lack'.[20] The symbolic practices that produce postcolonialism's objects are not sufficiently sustained and the objects totter and threaten to fall. Then, such proximity of black and white proves unbearable; the men's enjoyment cannot be sustained. In the days that follow the Christmas party and its minstrel show, racial lines are redrawn and a separation of black and white is enacted. The separation of white and black is performed in new skits that refer to the black object of colonial discourses from India and Africa as well as to the Australian frontier and

---

[20] 'Rather than an object or its lack, anxiety signals a lack of a lack, a failure of the symbolic reality wherein all alienable objects, objects that can be given or taken away, lost and refound, are constituted and circulate.' Copjec *Read my Desire* 119.

Darkness Casts its Light   143

its violences that often led to death. On the frontier, one's position along the line that divides white and black was fatally significant.

> Over the next few days they did scenes for the camera again and again.
> The boss, with a holstered revolver at his hip, leans on a reclining camel and looks into the distance. He wears jodhpurs, and a pith helmet. Sandy Two, in loincloth, stands at the camel's head, holding its reins.
> The men wanted photographs of themselves being attacked by the *blacks*, but the only possible male attackers on the station were very old and it was difficult to get them to participate, let alone look ferocious enough.
> A boss bathing in one of the granite pools. On the rock towering above him stands Sandy Two, and, at the very top, out of focus, his naked and charcoaled father, holding a spear, and with one foot reluctantly resting on the arch of the other. (224, original emphasis)

Blackface continues in these skits with Sandy One blacked up again, but reluctantly now. For an Aboriginal man 'passing' as white, it is one thing to black up as a 'negro' and another as a murderous 'native'. This is no longer minstrelsy's happy black fool or dandy and it recalls the farce component of American minstrelsy in the 1870s where in the context of new expansion into the West, the figure of the Native American began to make an appearance, now as vicious scalper (Toll 164–6). In *Benang*'s tableau, Sandy One blackens his skin with charcoal to represent an Aboriginal man who, with spear readied, stands above his supposedly innocent and vulnerable victim enjoying the everyday pastime of bathing. In this scene, American ideas of 'black' overlay 'native': the 'native' figure is rendered 'black' by the application of charcoal, or to put this another way, Indigeneity is 'niggered', and at the same time, 'native' aggression is incorporated into the image. The Aboriginal is the black slave, the white man's object, made and possessed by him, *and* the untrustworthy 'native', the original aggressor.

An aside: in 1921 the Australian filmmaker Charles Chauvel travelled to the United States and took acting parts in Hollywood films in blackface. Chauvel was 'in one shot galloping right-to-left as a Red Indian, the next hurtling by in the same direction, even on the same horse, as a cowboy chasing the same Red Indian (himself)'.[21] Benjamin Miller comments: 'This image of Chauvel ... chasing his own racial creations across the screen can be read as a potent comment on the Australian social imaginary's construction of race. Reading Chauvel in blackface reflects his fictions of race back onto himself – he is 'cowboy' and 'Indian.''' Although Miller's idea has the two parts, 'cowboy' and 'Indian', temporally and spatially separated, he is making a very important point about Chauvel's interest in pursuing both parts. In 1923, when Chauvel returned from Hollywood, he directed his first silent film, *The Moth of Moonbi*, in which he appears in blackface as an

---

[21]   Michael Pate 'Introduction' to Susanne Chauvel Carlsson *Charles and Elsa Chauvel: Movie Pioneers*. St Lucia, Qld: University of Queensland Press, 1989, p. x (ix–xi) quoted in Miller 140.

144 *The Postcolonial Eye*

Aboriginal stockman. All that he needed, it seems, in order to make an appearance as an Aboriginal man was to colour his skin. When he made *Jedda*, he cast the white actor Paul Clarke as the Aboriginal head stockman, blackening his skin, too: that is all that is needed to make the man's difference appear in his eyes.

Returning to *Benang*'s scene of 'native' aggression: the text locates the original violence differently than do the white men's plays with history. Underlying the men's games of black and white over this Christmas c.1900 is a massacre, one that seems to be located in the mid-1880s, although I can hardly be sure. The text's form guarantees that. Some fragments of the story of an earlier massacre appear on the same page as these days of play, and Sandy's wife, Fanny, listening to the men partying that Christmas at the turn of the century is 'reminded of the hanging tree, and occasionally she heard shots from the direction of the homestead. The buzzing of flies replayed in her head. That buzzing. She had found a sister, uncovered and dead on the ground. The stench, the buzzing flies had led her there' (*Benang* 221).

> There was just that one tree, tall above the tufted scrub which stretched away in all directions. Hanging from it, what seemed assorted shadows. But these were too solid for shadows, and although too heavy for the desert breeze they nonetheless swayed, and shifted, and probably spun on their axis if ever you got close enough to look.
>
> After each new movement, the sound of a rifle shot. There were only a few shooters. (*Benang* 184–5)

A massacre, perhaps in the mid-1880s, is given as one of the antecedents to the Christmas party with its minstrelsy show and the subsequent performances of black aggression. If readers can find their way back through this labyrinthine text, they will find another fragment of the story of the massacre, a story that takes the cause of violence back in time once more, to the treatment of women tied by ropes to a stable wall and an old man in a woodheap, tied up in the sun among the timber as if he were something 'less than a dog', with no bowl of water and a chain looped around his throat (173). When Fanny finds the key to the chain and releases him, the man moves towards the stables where a white man is working at a grindstone, his back to the door. The Aboriginal man picks up an axe and the white man's scream freezes time. His death is avenged by a massacre in which station men on horseback run down a small group of men and women and children (*Benang* 174).

Rape is a crucial element of the massacres' compositions. In one massacre, white men rape their daughters conceived in previous ones, or offer them up to other men. Sandy One recalls: 'The women, many of them the men's own daughters, were in great demand' (342). For these men, though, this seems not to be incestuous because they do not claim the girls as their own. How could they? These girls are blacks, aren't they? The men refuse to see any trace of themselves in the girls, each man resolving the girl whom he rapes into a singularity – she is a black. His relationship to the girl, and his earlier presence in her mother's body, is – for this moment – refused. His past proximity to Aboriginal women is denied

Darkness Casts its Light

in his pursuit of a new round of enjoyment of his other – an enjoyment that might very well end in the girl's death. This is one of the costs to Indigenous men and women of white desire and its disavowal.

The Perverse Assimilationist

Benang, then, points not only to a white masculine desire to put on blackness but to enter it. Its main white figure, Ern Solomon Scat, penetrates 'black' bodies – young women, young girls, his own grandson. He is fascinated by the sexual coupling of black and white. In such union, Ern Scat hopes he will find himself in possession of blackness, a blackness he can hold, press himself against, enter. Never permanently, of course. There is always the moment of parting when Ern must take his body back, retract his withered member, however reluctantly.

Yet, he claims, he does not desire blackness at all; his only wish is for its annihilation through assimilation with whiteness. For Scat is an assimilationist, aiming at the 'uplift of a despised race' (27). He is a version of A.O. Neville, the Chief Protector of Aborigines in Western Australia, who through legislated practices in the 1930s attempted the 'biological absorption' of Aboriginal peoples by whites through a program of 'breeding out' Aboriginal people.[22] Indeed, Neville makes an appearance in *Benang* as Scat's cousin and employer. In the example of Scat, we are shown assimilationism to be structured by a disavowed enjoyment of the blackness that it ostensibly aims to annihilate. After all, a program of breeding *out* requires a breeding *with*.

The allure that Indigenous women hold for Ern Scat emerges as soon as he steps off the boat onto Australian shores, when he discovers what sex with Indigenous women might make of him: 'How he spurted his ecstasy that night. And he had felt so powerful, even as he turned his back and returned to the light' (79). His passage to Australia from Britain has been via South Africa: 'He left his home town and the scrawny women of its streets and brothels and, stopping off in South Africa, discovered young and *coloured* women. The differing hues of flesh. Various entrances' (44, original emphasis). South Africa offers an opportunity for Scat to position himself as white coloniser *cum* master, a position that is inexorably associated with sex. Australia offers another such opportunity.

In Australia he seeks out Indigenous women for more domesticated sexual relations and he attempts to whiten these women, but his is a literal reading of whiteness: he wishes to whiten their skin with face powder and bleach and to hide their skin from the sun under hats and gloves. There is a series of such women. He first marries Kathleen, but sends her away when his hopes for her are not fulfilled, and he replaces her with the child Topsy with whom he has a son, Tommy. Of Topsy he demands that she cover her face when she leaves the house (154); and he submerges her in a bath of bleach: he 'poured bleach into the hot water, placed

---

[22] Auber Octavius Neville, Chief Protector of Aborigines Western Australia 1915–1936; and Commissioner of Native Affairs 1936–1940.

146   *The Postcolonial Eye*

his hand on the top of Topsy's head and pushed her under' (158). He kills his own daughter, Ellen, because she is not white enough but installs in her place one 'black' girl after another, all of whom he calls Ellen and with whom he has sexual relations. He finds a series of 'black' girls each of whom he seeks to whiten, before discarding and moving on to the next 'black' girl.

We might say that Scat *veils* these women's bodies in whiteness. Like any veil, however, it is a lure. Traces of what lies underneath can be peeped at through the veil, luring him to look, holding his gaze with the promise of an unveiling. And, indeed, in obscene rituals of looking, Scat repeatedly lifts the veils of whiteness he has put in place.[23]

Perhaps the most obscene example of his perverse practices, though, is the way in which he subjects his own grandson, Harley, to this searching gaze. Scat thinks of Harley as the 'first-born white', the result of his private experiments in assimilationism. Scat has sought to 'breed out' blackness by 'breeding with' Indigenous women. Unlike the men in the 'sprees', he claims the children born of these alliances as his own; he wants to find his whiteness marked on their bodies. At the same time, though, he examines the secret recesses of his grandson's body for traces of 'blackness' – not with distaste but with desire. He ferrets out the blackness. He wants to *see* it. This is how he will maintain his interest; blackness is alluring to him.

As the superintendents and matrons did to children on the reserves, Ern investigates the colour of his grandson's skin where the sun had not reached, including as Harley says, 'my black hole, that last aureole of my colour, my black insides. To think this lured grandfather!' (159).

> He used to part my hair and see the scalp beneath and – when I was older, and recovering under his care – run his fingers through my curls, and all over me. 'Looking for traces of colour', he'd mutter, stretching my cheeks apart. 'There (mumble, mumble), a purple tint where we are pink, and that bluish tint to the whites of your eyes.'
>
> He would begin this way, clinical, but – soon enough – was shouting, urgent with power.
>
> 'Keep your eyes open. Eyes open,' he would say, one hand clamping the back of my neck, the other my shoulder. 'Keep them open.' At least he accepted that I could not look directly at him on such an occasion, and so I stared at the wall as he thrust, in his stilted way, trying to get deeper within me, and if that was not violation enough, wanting to remain there even as he shrivelled. (77–8)

The text alerts us to the perversion that propels Scat's acts by the demand he makes of his grandson – 'Keep your eyes open. Eyes open.' This recalls Parveen Adams when she points out that a Lacanian approach to perversion figures the

---

[23]   I am not arguing that this disavowed enjoyment in blackness is men's only. Recall Ruth Hegarty's memory of the Matron at Cherbourg requiring girls to lift their dresses for her (see Chapter 8).

other's acquiescing gaze. 'It is', she writes, 'in general a supplementary feature of any perversion to incite a spectator, as if the aura of the perversion is made up of a consumption of vision that demands that a spectator restore the visual energy which is exhausted in the scene' (Adams *Emptiness* 92). There is another important way, though, in which Scat's assimilationism is figured as perverse in the Lacanian sense and that is that he 'breeds with' Indigenous women in the name of duty; his enjoyment has become a law that he has a duty to obey. The question of assimilation and the 'racial uplift' at which it ostensibly aims is for Scat an 'onerous, but strangely engaging issue' (*Benang* 72). He disavows his pleasure and recasts it as a duty he performs, a duty inscribed in Law. On the matter of perversion and duty, Joan Copjec is very helpful. She refers us to Deleuze on the pervert's relation to pleasure where he argues that: 'Pleasure ceases to motivate the will and is abjured, disavowed, "renounced", the better to be recovered as ... a law.' Copjec continues:

> As [the pervert's] relation to the Other assumes the form of a contract and the Other takes the form of an actual person, only crueller, 'ferocious in his demands and invulnerable', the pervert (according to Lacan's characterization, which is surprisingly close to Deleuze's) surrenders his *right* to jouissance in order to assume it as a *duty* that he has contracted to carry out. Enjoyment becomes a service he performs for the Other. (Copjec *Imagine* 224–5)

For a Freudian and Lacanian ethics, the proper place for a subject is above *and* below the law at once: or, another way of putting this, always on that line where above and below meet. This is the place of an impossible or irresolvable dialectic. This approach suggests that a perverse subject does not maintain the dialectic but flouts the Law by always putting the Law elsewhere: 'I was only following orders.' This position, this seeming acquiescence to the Law, makes the Law elsewhere. The perverse subject is only subjected to the Law, embodied in the figure of the Dictator, for instance, who becomes/embodies/is the Law for his perverse subjects.

* * *

One of the fantasies played out in blackface minstrelsy in Australia as elsewhere is that blackness is essential and unambiguous, and always knowable – it is marked on the skin, it can be read from the body. This fantasy can never be satisfactorily shored up, of course, because biological essentialism has blackness as comported 'in the blood', in sly droplets that might not show themselves, or that show themselves unexpectedly, say in the unwelcome colour of a newborn's skin and hair. Traces of blackness, according to these discourses, remain in the body, however hidden. No 'breeding out' is without its remainder.

While the American 'one-drop rule' is well-known for its institutionalisation of these ideas, it has its counterpart in Australian segregation policies that criminalised marriage and cohabitation between whites and Indigenous men and

148 *The Postcolonial Eye*

women, with a view to avoiding the contamination of the white race. As Robert Manne reports: 'In several Australian states sexual relations between European males and Aboriginal females were banned. Several states gave "the chief protector" of Aborigines the power to approve or disapprove of all Aboriginal marriages. In Queensland racial intermarriage was discouraged.' A.O. Neville-styled assimilationism in the Northern Territory and Western Australia made an exception in the case of marriages between 'half-caste' women and white men. As Manne points out, these were 'regarded with special favour by the state in the interest of "breeding out the colour"' (Manne Foreword xiii–xiv). The form of assimilation pursued so enthusiastically by Neville in the 1930s was indebted to other American race practices, such as those proposed by Frank H. Haskins in *The Racial Basis of Civilization* where he argued for 'racial mixture, including intermarriage between blacks and whites. Mulattoes … had a good chance to adapt to "advanced culture", and if they were light enough to pass for white, so much the better' (Fredrickson 161).

All notions of race work with ideas of the pure and the impure, and enunciate themselves through a lexicon of wholeness and division, fractions and traces. In America, for instance, there is the 'half-breed', in Australia its counterpart in the 'full-blood' and 'half-caste' and more – 'quadroon' and 'octoroon'. In *Benang* Scat obsessively tracks his children and grandchildren's passage from black, to partially black, and through to white in the eyes of the Law which he obeys. In 'clear diagrams and slippery fractions' (37), on cards and files and photographs, he records the success of his project of racial uplift, numbering, reckoning, calculating, producing an archive of assimilation. His grandson, Harley, the first white-born, the 'uplifted' issue of Scat's eugenicism.[24]

The language of racial 'uplift' from the American lexicon of race runs through the entire book; it is its trope, imaginatively refigured as a literal lifting up, an elevation of Harley's body as it floats. Harley levitates, without any wish to do so. He literally rises off the ground, and floats. He doesn't fly or sail, his levitation has not this kind of wilfulness to it. He is being forced upwards, as if in a topsy-turvy world where gravity pushed up rather than pulling down. In this he is an embodiment of his grandfather's project to 'uplift the Aboriginal race'. Harley has been so uplifted that he is now 'white', or so Ern would have it. From the 1930s Scat has been assiduously following his duty to obey the law of assimilation and here is his successful issue, the 'first white man born'. (His 'white' is always a legal category, he wishes to satisfy the law. As the law changes its definitions of 'white' or a 'native', so do Scat's perceptions and ambitions. Any child will need to be white according to the legal statutes.)[25]

---

[24] On eugenicism, see Copjec *Imagine* 152.

[25] Morrissey refers to Scott's characters suffering from a 'fallen corporality', in his untitled review of *Benang*.

As a young man, Harley accidentally discovers Scat's archive and the power of his grandfather's words to carve him, shaping him into his ideal, 'uplifting' him. He discovers that he is merely a 'fraction':

> I found myself hovering over sets of documents, things filed in plastic envelopes in rumbling drawers and snapping files. Certificates of birth, death, marriage; newspaper clippings, police reports; letters (personal; from this or that historical society); parish records; cemetery listings; books, photographs ...
>
> Photographs. As before, I shuffled idly through them. I was careless, letting them fall to the floor. Various people, all classified as *Aboriginal*. There were portraits arranged in pairs; one a snapshot labelled *As I found them*, the other a studio photograph captioned *Identical with above child*. There were families grouped according to skin colour. And, sudden enough to startle me, my own image.
>
> Captions to the photographs; *full-blood, half-caste (first cross), quadroon, octoroon*. There was a page of various fractions, possible permutations growing more and more convoluted. Of course, in the language of such mathematics it is simple; from the whole to the partial and back again. This much was clear; I was a fraction of what I might have been.
>
> A caption beneath my father's photograph:
> *Octoroon grandson (mother quarter caste [No.2], father Scottish). Freckles on the face are the only trace of colour apparent.*
>
> I saw my image inserted into sequences of three or four in which I was always at the end of the line (even now, I wince at such a phrase). Each sequence was entitled, *Three Generations (Reading from Right to Left)*, and each individual was designated by a fraction. (25–6, original emphasis)

'I understood', Harley goes on to say, 'that much effort had gone into arriving at me ... I was intended as the product of a long and considered process which my grandfather had brought to a conclusion' (28). This process starts with Scat having a son with Topsy, the Indigenous woman whom Scat reckons to be a 'quadroon' (1/4 'black') based on the assumption that her grandfather was a white man. On Scat's reckonings, that makes her son Tommy an 'octoroon' (1/8 'black') and Tommy's son Harley (at 1/16 'black') 'the first white man born': legally 'white'. But here's the catch: Harley's great-great-grandfather is not the white man Scat always took him to be and on whose whiteness his calculations depend. Harley's great-great-grandfather is Sandy One Mason, whose father was a shepherd, presumed to be 'white', and whose mother was an Indigenous woman (*Benang* 483). The paradox to which *Benang* points is that Scat cannot read his own system of signs. To his horror, he discovers too late that he made a mistake in his reckonings, and that he cannot, after all, read blackness and whiteness as if they were written on the skin.

Chapter 10
Resisting a White Spectator's Enjoyment:
Benang's Aesthetics

> You dreamt that you were punished, like the boy you'd seen put in a bag and suspended from a rope high in a tree. Swinging. Trying to keep your head above your feet. Feeling that you were not quite drifting, but released; set free, thrown out and abandoned. It was dark, the weave of the Hessian making rectangles of light ... Cut down, crawling out of the bag. You could not walk, and fell, kept falling; the earth had moved away, rolled away ...
>
> —Kim Scott *Benang* (91–3)

What positions are open to a reader of *Benang*, preoccupied as this text is with acts of sadism against Indigenous men, women and children? How to persevere with reading? If, as some psychoanalytic approaches suggest, perversion demands a fascinated spectator, is a reader placed in just this position and thereby implicated in the acts of perverse enjoyment upon which she gazes?[1] In other words, if to read is always to look, how does one read of obscene acts without committing another act of perversion? And how does one write of sadism without either exciting a reader's sadistic traits, or torturing her in turn?

Practices of writing and reading are themselves among the perverse acts to which *Benang* requires its readers attend. *Benang* draws intimate associations between sadism and writing and reading, raising Kafka-like scenes in which technologies of writing figure as means of punishment and education: the prisoner will learn from writing carved into his skin (Kafka *The Penal Colony*). The writing of history and the production of the historical record are particularly implicated.

But writing and reading about perversion are not always perverse, of course, as *Benang* also shows. There are other possibilities and these lie not only in the stories that are told but the way of their telling, that is, in a text's formal qualities. *Benang*'s own form is fragmentary and in some senses excessive. It offers a repetitive and incoherent telling of the stories of colonisation. Fragments recur many times over, imperfectly repeated. The variation between tellings, the places where fragments fall, the disordering of historical time, the figuring of psychic time as troubled and fractured make the scene of reading full of uncertainty and doubt. Far from being an empty aesthetics, it is through its formal qualities that *Benang* effects an ethics whereby the reader herself is repositioned before the events which the narrative describes. It is through its form that *Benang* resists a reader who might maintain

---

[1]   'It is a general supplement of any perversion to incite a spectator, as if the aura of the perversion is made of a consumption of vision that demands that a spectator restore the visual energy which is exhausted in the scene.' Adams *Emptiness* 91.

152   *The Postcolonial Eye*

a hope that different histories can be cohered into one, or that the unspeakable in the past can be spoken after all, or that what is unknowable and ungraspable across differences can at last be held in the mind.[2] It is also through this aesthetic form that *Benang* effects an ethical practice through which a reader's pleasure before the spectacle of another – a reader's scopophilia – is stalled.

In what follows, I consider some of the reading positions that *Benang* offers and forecloses. By returning to a consideration of the crimes and misadventures of Ern Scat – this historian, archivist and sadist – I look again at questions of historical practice and the colonial archive, arguing that *Benang* shows the limits of these by deploying aesthetic forms that fill the scene of reading with profound doubt. Readers cannot maintain a masterful position of knowledge and certainty before this text, however carefully they might trace a course through the facts. And then I turn explicitly to the text's treatment of sadism and argue that, again, it is through *Benang*'s aesthetic form that a separation is enacted between a reader's look and the scenes of perversion that it describes.

The Reader and the Historical Record

Given how mostly obscene are the causes of Ern's enjoyment, it is not hard to imagine readers distancing themselves from these, wishing to remain unpleasured and unmoved, but this is not the only possible reading effect. We might also say that in some crucial ways *Benang* very pointedly invites a reader into a position much like Ern's, albeit to frustrate and disappoint. So for instance there is Ern's looking for the trace of blackness that he so much enjoys finding. As a reader, I might avert my eyes when Ern penetrates Harley's body, but all the same didn't I attempt to trace Harley's blackness by other means, finding its tracks throughout the text, in the family trees that Ern's record implies? Didn't I wish to pursue the hidden figure of the 'Aboriginal' in the text, uncovering him from his hiding place? The task of searching out white and black in this way proves to be impossible, of course, and not only for Ern, whose project unravels so dramatically. It is impossible for us, too, as readers. If we desire to pursue black and white through the generations, it will only end in dead ends. A reader's efforts at calculation, her tracing with pen and paper the complex family relations – such reckonings are derailed.

The text, though, points to something other than the fact that Ern, and perhaps a reader, has made a mistake in thinking that Sandy One was a white man, a mistake that might be corrected before continuing to make more calculations. It shows that the calculations themselves are impossible because the figures (in both senses of the word) are always uncertain. There is no sure ground here, no origin where the meanings of 'white' and 'black' can finally come to rest. We can say, as I did at the end of the last chapter, that Sandy One Mason's father was a shepherd and his

---

[2]   *Benang*'s aesthetic refuses the reader who desires to capture an other. Slater puts this so well when she says that Scott 'resists entrapping Indigenous people in his textual empire' (Slater 'Kim Scott's *Benang*: monstrous (textual) bodies' 69).

Resisting a White Spectator's Enjoyment 153

mother a Nyoongar, but what does this tell us, except that the quest for a racially pure origin is fantasmatic? After all, a quest for race origins can hardly be arrested there. It only leads further back, to more questions: who were this shepherd's father and mother? Who was this Nyoongar woman's parents? And so on.

The ambitions of Ern the archivist do not add up to much in the end, for all 'his notes and rough drafts, his clear diagrams and slippery fractions' (37). Yet some of Kim Scott's readers still argue for the promise that the archive holds for an Indigenous subject who desires to recover his history and identity. Inga Clendinnen, for instance, reads Scott's writing as showing the generative possibilities the archive holds. While she suggests that Indigenous men and women's memory and the colonial record are both best understood as myth – 'selected experiences recast into memory-stories which, through devoted repetition, takes on lustrous authority' (Clendinnen 'Brown skin' 55) – she nevertheless hopes that such mythic accounts might be 'exceeded' by a proper kind of cultural history that can glean the truth by putting the two together, one supplementing the other (Clendinnen *History Question*). The tension between Indigenous memory and the colonial written record is not, in this approach, taken as an opportunity to deconstruct the *logic* of the colonial archive: instead the archive offers Scott 'hefty findings'.[3] For Lisa Slater, too, while agreeing with arguments that the colonial archive can only be used to deconstruct colonial historiography, still invests it with reconstructive possibilities. So, in *Benang*, the archive will enable Harley to 'go on to recover and "flesh out" … the limited identity that his grandfather bequeathed him' (Slater 'Making strange' 358).

In this regard, Slater says, she takes her lead from Harley himself, who, near the close of the novel, ponders: 'Few thought [Ern] a worthy man in his own time. But, he helped us read and write. He chose to put us on paper. A strange gift' (457). But I read those words 'strange gift' as being far too ambiguous to offer anything like a lead and against these kinds of arguments suggest that *Benang* figures the archive as a technology of colonialism, productive of the very colonising relations that it ostensibly merely records. Harley as the-first-white-man-born, Harley as Ern Scat fantasises him to be, was *made* in the archive; this image of Harley, this white man's fantasy, is a Frankenstein monster, he is the archivist's own creation. The paradigm of the archive – its surveillance of the other, its making the other an object of scrutiny, its records and reckonings – this paradigm is productive of the very problem that Clendennin and Slater wish it could solve. The archive is no mere re-presentation of colonialism and its subjects; it is one of the moments of their formation.[4]

---

[3]   Clendinnen 'Brown skin' 55. See Philip Morrissey's important response to Clendinnen's methods in 'Dancing with shadows' 65–74.

[4]   So whereas Madeleine Byrne suggests that the documents from the archive *interrupt* the narrative, I see them as at the heart of the narrative. Then there is the other story, the one that is not in the archive, the story 'behind and between'. See Byrne 110–15.

154 *The Postcolonial Eye*

It is not, then, in this laboratory that Harley will be able to pinch his own flesh or return to earth, be once more subject to gravity's force, once more a human subject rather than a number or a fraction. It is in the places where Ern's logic fails to take hold that lie the possibilities of Harley's substantiation. Harley must 'grow ... from that fraction of life which fell' (28). He will not find himself in the archive; he will find a space that the archive cannot fill. It is in this gap that hope lies; it is the space which opens onto other worlds of meaning, worlds in which he might come to appear. That is to say, Harley's hopes and possibilities lie in what fails to be rendered, in what is *not* written in the archive; they lie among all the men and women who fall from view in the violent processes through which the 'first white man' was born. As Scott writes elsewhere: 'Sometimes, in writing and rewriting the language of the archives it seems possible ... to hint at what language can't say; as if something existed behind and between the lines' (Scott 'Disputed Territory' 12). *Benang* at the height of its considerable powers achieves this – a hint that something exists behind and between what language can say. This is its great accomplishment. As Harley says: 'I thought of all those the papers named, and of how little the ink could tell' (347).

Benang does not only tell us, through Harley, that ink has its limits. It is not only Harley who discovers this. A reader who aspires to make sense of all this paper and ink is defeated, too. A reader's attempt to track the details is to enter a mire of 'facts' that might not add up to very much. One discovery is undone by the next, dates slide around, more gaps open up, men and women disappear with no account given. It is hard to imagine what reading practice it is that could fix meanings out of all of this.

If *Benang* writes against relying on the archive, and if it writes against hopes for complete and full knowledge of the past, it also writes against taking recourse in the imagination – which, anyway, can only repeat what is already known. The historian faced with the archival record who tries to fill in its gaps, imaginatively if necessary, forecloses the historical truth that *Benang* points to: the fact of irrecoverable loss. *Benang*, then, can be read not only against certain historical practices but against the historical novelist, too: it is an *anti*-historical novel. It is structured according to a subjective rather than historical time, refusing the historical novel's distinctions and discretions between past, present and future. As Harley says: 'And I further acknowledge, and nod to, the demands of Historical Fiction. And I nod with the resentment which those I will call my people felt, still feel. Nod nod nod' (323).

In this, *Benang* recalls another great late twentieth-century novel, Morrison's *Beloved*, surely one of *Benang*'s intertexts. *Beloved*, too, is a meditation on the past, on loss and on memory – or 'rememory' as *Beloved* has it, the neologism emphasising the ways that history and memory are always active processes, reassemblages of fragments, re-membering. Morrison's writing practice in *Beloved* is an unsettling of conventional ways of coming to knowledge, including those of a positivist historical practice which aims to recover the past in the archive. Morrison refused the archive and its written record for her 'rememory' of slavery, and racialised the archives' claims to knowledge. The historical record through which a view on slavery might be reconstructed is itself produced within the same racial discourses about which Morrison writes, but by which she refuses to be captured. For her, the past cannot be found carried into the present in documents, in the written historical record – in transcripts of trials, in newspaper reportings, in the registers of births, deaths and marriages, or even in the documents that describe the trade in African slaves. Traces of the past can be found elsewhere, carried in song and story for instance; carried by the body – in touch, voice, gesture; and in the beloved one who has 'passed on' but cohabits with the living nevertheless, carrying the past into the present, but in a form which renders the past as another world, mysterious and unfathomable. This is the nature of the past according to *Beloved*. The hold *Beloved*'s protagonists have on the past is only and necessarily partial and incomplete: neither memory nor the historical record can fill in this gap for some of its meanings remain irrecoverable. For Morrison, there is always a gap in the record and it should not be stopped up. She refuses to satisfy such a desire in her readers.

In the white Australian literary scene, a willingness to work with ideas of radical and irrecoverable loss, and to do this work at the level of form, is exceedingly rare: it is more often found, however, in Indigenous literary practices. It seems that many Indigenous writers are able to bear the unknown and unknowable, and not as temporary states that can be reversed if only one were careful and persistent enough in searching out the historical facts. The political significance of an aesthetics that inscribes silence, invisibility and irrecoverable loss is nowhere clearer than in the division between those who practice it and those who does not.

Writing Towards Whiteness; or, Just Who Tortures Whom?

Writing and reading are crucial to Ern's project of racial uplift – Harley must be literate if he is to be made white. These practices, however, also become the conditions of Ern's failure and the instruments of his own torture.

Benang makes a clear connection between whiteness and the written word. The written word and its associated practices are the property of and passage to whiteness.[5] In *Benang* whites assume that any Aboriginal is illiterate, and should remain so. To be without writing is a just and proper deprivation: 'So, the boy can read? Where'd he learn that? ... that upstart little *darky*' (208). 'Jack read old newspapers he had collected, and – in the very act of doing so – dispelled and

---

[5]   By this I do not mean that *Benang* argues that writing is an exclusively white, or European, practice. Indigenous cultures were never exclusively oral: marks on earth and rock, on body and now canvas are forms of writing. I am referring here to the ways that *Benang* figures European notions of literacy and the ways these have been used into relations of racialised power (see Chapter 2).

156   *The Postcolonial Eye*

disproved what those very same papers said about him and his people' (137).[6]
This recalls once more that other scene that is so proximately drawn throughout
Benang, the scene of American slavocracy where literacy is associated with being
human, and therefore with whiteness and its rights to liberty. Henry Louis Gates
Jr describes the case of the enslaved and literate Phillis Wheatley, who in 1772
faced a jury in a Boston courthouse that would determine whether she had written
a collection of poems, and the case of George Moses Horton of Chapel Hill whose
book of poems was published in the mid-1820s. For men and women such as these,
writing was 'a commodity which they were forced to trade for their humanity'
(Gates 9). '[M]ost Europeans privileged *writing* ... as the principal measure of the
Africans' humanity, their capacity for progress, their very place in the great chain
of being ... Learning to read and to write, then, was not only difficult, it was a
violation of a law' (9).

When Phillis Wheatley and George Moses Horton proved themselves to be not
only literate but authors, they were (reluctantly) manumitted. Their belonging to
an irrational inhumanity was challenged by their writing. Here was a visible sign of
reason, the most privileged, valorised, human characteristic in post-Enlightenment
discourse (Gates 2). They became subjects in the eyes of whites, although only
barely so, perhaps: the continuing recognition of their subjectivity was always at
risk. And they proved themselves not only able to write, but capable of writing
within the literary genres of those European men and women who claimed to have
rightful mastery over them.[7]

Ern recognises the place of education in his project of making Harley the first
white man born, but it is through this that Ern inadvertently produces the instrument
of his own torture. Harley discovers for himself his grandfather's assimilationist
project. He can now read Ern's archive, and he can also write, and he writes on
Ern's skin, carving words with a knife into Ern's flesh, recalling the work that the
sentence must do in *The Penal Colony* where the Officer becomes the prisoner
of his own machine. (Kafka) Ern, by this time physically disabled by age, is
Harley's prisoner. Like Kafka's prisoner he might understand the words inscribed
on his skin just before death. Harley tells his reader that: 'It may have been my
desire to transform myself, or even self-hatred, which suggested I slash and cut

---

[6]   Ruth Hegarty reports that Cherbourg residents 'were considered "primitives"
and not fit subjects to be properly educated or civilised' (74). Ruth Hegarty also reports
Queensland Governor Leslie Wilson's views on visiting Cherbourg in 1934: 'It seems far
more important to me, that they (Aboriginal children) should be instructed in this practical
work (that is, labourers and servants) than in history or geography. Once they learn to read
and write and do simple arithmetic that would seem all that is required' (96). See Blake's
research into Cherbourg Aboriginal Settlement.

[7]   These genres reinscribe the very constraints from which the individual subject has
sought freedom. So, in *Benang*, Harley's Uncle Will gives shape to his own image through
reading American westerns, cowboy novels, *Hiawatha*. What contortionism did he practise to
make himself appear in these texts' scenes, with their 'indians' who disappear from the text,
who disappear into death. Was he instead lured by the position of a white figure, the cowboy?

words into my own skin.' 'But', he continues, 'I soon turned to my grandfather's flesh. I wanted to mark him, to show my resentment at how his words had shaped me' (37). Harley's acts of sadism are referred to many times more: 'My blade drew letters with a fine white line, but in an instant all precision would be lost in gushing blood', he says. 'I bandaged his wounds to conceal what I wrote and, bathing them, considered how they grew, how they altered and elaborated on what I had intended' (287). 'I bathed him in salty water, was slow and gentle with my touch. The wounds I had given him grew, and in unforeseen ways.'[8] The script he had taken so much trouble over 'changed shape, and the words became hard to decipher' (78).

> At one stage, full of frustration and anger at my place in Grandad's story, I wrote END, CRASH, FINISH into his skin. I poured black ink and ash into the wounds, and tended them carefully so that the skin would heal and seal the letters stark and proud.
>
> I read through his notes, and all I could do was ... tend him, treat him, tie him down and occasionally write a word or two in the way I have indicated above. 'Here', I would poke and prod him, 'quite white where the skin does not touch. This soft skin.' And I sliced my words, not so deep, but just enough, as it were, to scar and tattoo him.
>
> Thinking again of his plans, his words, I added the lines of ink. How the dirty tributary joins the great river. (445)

But Harley cannot maintain his interest in torturing his grandfather. He has exhausted the energy that the scene once held for him, and he no longer has the desire to restore it. He is spent, and he turns instead to another kind of writing. He glimpses another story, another scene, one in which he can appear as Nyoongar, and he writes towards this. This is writing that will bind him quite differently, knotting together a new arrangement of signifiers, grounding him, and he will be able to turn finally towards love.

A Reader's Look

The question of the look is central to *Benang*. So, for instance, while Ern Scat desires to enter Aboriginal men's and women's bodies, while he desires to occupy them, he also desires to occupy their field of vision, to be looked at in his illicit pursuits, to capture the other's look. When he sexually penetrates his grandson, his enjoyment depends on his grandson's look. To recall what Parveen Adams says about perversion and the look: 'It is in general a supplementary feature of

---

[8]   Kim Scott is quoted by Madeleine Byrne as saying in interview that writing is like 'trying to whisper in someone's ear ... In some ways it hurts more, if you let it seep in' (Byrne 114). This idea of writing as propelled by a sadistic impulse is very close to Harley's own writing practices for much of the book. But this aim is transformed in *Benang*, as I go on to argue.

any perversion to incite a spectator, as if the aura of the perversion is made up of a consumption of vision that demands a spectator restore the visual energy which is exhausted in the scene' (Adams *Emptiness* 91). Adams goes further, though. She says that not only do acts of perversion demand this fascinated viewer but so do representations of perversion or, to put this another way, representations of perversion enact what they represent: "'Look at me", says any representation of perversion in a structure of fascination. One's eye does not fall on such a representation; it is seized by the representation. It is clear how our horror and enjoyment go together' (Adams *Emptiness* 91).

This returns us to the question with which we began: is a reader's eye seized by *Benang*'s representations of perversions? Does *Benang* demand that we keep our eyes open, that we are fascinated witnesses of the perversions it describes?

Harley as the text's narrator points to his imagined readers whom he addresses directly and for the most part with the same mix of intimacy and hatred that can be heard in his address to Ern. When Harley recalls the perverse acts that his grandfather committed on the younger man's body, and when in turn he reports his own cruelties towards Ern, is he figured as taking a perverse enjoyment in his imagined reader's attention? Does he seek his readers' fascination? 'I hope you are not falling asleep' (323), Harley says, as if he would like to prod his readers into a state of wakefulness, needling them into optimal arousal so as to torment them again, just as he does to his grandfather when he slumps exhausted from Harley's words.

Harley, however, cannot maintain his own interest. As he averted his eyes from Ern's obscenities, Harley in the end turns away from the torture scene he has invented. He can't go on with it. He looks back at Ern, not with fascination or hatred but with disinterest. In this way, *Benang* shows us the structure of the perverse look, and Harley's final refusal of it. Harley enters into a scene of perversion, but he can't keep his enjoyment alive, and he lets it fall.

Benang does something more, though, than *narrativise* the structure of perversion. It obviously does that: through the writing that it attributes to Harley, *Benang* describes very effectively the exchange of looks between Harley and Ern, showing when perversion is aroused and when it falls. But *Benang* does something more, too. It represents perversion and the look not only at the level of the narrative, but at the level of form. *Benang* has its own structure of the look, which cuts a reader's scopophilia, so that even as it persists in pointing to obscene acts it does so without seizing the gaze of a fascinated spectator. In particular it does this by the oblique way it figures the spectacle of another's suffering. That is to say, there are acts of perverse cruelty represented in *Benang* as anamorphotic forms, that morph into their devastating shapes only at some distance from the scene of reading.

This occurs through a combination of *Benang*'s formal qualities. Firstly, there is the effect of its size. It is a gigantic text that does not submit to the familiar supporting structures of other large texts – it is not an epic, for instance[9] it is made up of fragments without clear chronological arrangement; it is anarchic, following Harley's discoveries and his free associations of ideas. The relations between people across the generations is often impossible to follow: 'But again, I digress and confuse all of us, one with the other' (367). There is rupture in the grammar, too, that often mitigates ordinary reading. The pronouns are not always clear, the subjects of sentences slide around. There is a repetition of sentences and a stumbling, a stuttering. Sentences begin and begin again, unfinished, foreshortened, and in that abridgement their grammatical subject is sometimes missing. There is not only repetition but backtracking, too, and stories jumble together, so that historically discrete events come up against each other on the same brief passage.

One important effect is that the text is often illegible. Its objects are indiscernible, one's eye passes over them in the attempt to bring some other part of the scene into focus. Arranging the text into object and ground is hard work. There is always something obscuring one's vision. What is it that I am peering at? Is what I am looking at now part of the story or is it superfluous detail that I should look past?

In writing about *Benang* and some of the obscene acts that it describes, I've had to bring these acts into view. They are not always as apparent as my writing so far might suggest. So, one stumbles upon a fragment that refers to the rape of children in an orphanage, or to a young woman tied to a bed, or to massacres. There are many references to these crimes but they are in fragments that are jumbled with other fragments and scattered across hundreds of pages. In places it is very unclear what it is that is being shown to a reader. In other places, something comes more clearly into view so that a reader might be able to immediately discern the outlines of the object being described, or the crime being committed, but then be unable to decide who is doing this, or how, or when, or to whom. A reader might not be able to make easy sense, say, of why white women tar and feather a boy (99–100), or what it is that swings from a tree. Is it a dead man or a woman, or is it some other 'strange fruit'? What *is* it that I am looking at now?

To work with the example with which this chapter begins: of a boy swinging up high, tied up in a hessian bag. This brief passage has been extracted from the vast text in which it is embedded, we might even say hidden. *Benang* allows a reader to pass over it. In some sense we could say that no great significance rests on it; the story will go on much the same whether one has seen it or not, or at least a reader will be no more or less confused if it falls into the background or is not seen at all. This event is returned to much later on in the text, but again it almost slips from view, appearing in a passage that describes a scene of great confusion as people from town are forcibly removed to a reserve.

---

[9]   See Carlos Fuentes on the epic and anti-epic.

160 *The Postcolonial Eye*

> In the darkness, among the stuff thrown from the wagon, something struggled and made noises. It was the boy she'd seen trying to escape. His eyes rolled above the gag at his mouth as he was pushed into a hessian bag. He continued to struggle; Kathleen saw the bag swinging on the rope which suspended it from a tree. (330)

Why is it so difficult to see, read, remember this suspended boy? For I know no reviewer who has referred to it, and, anecdotally, I know of no reader who can recall reading it. What position does *Benang* offer us before this scene, such that the boy in the hessian sack can scarcely be seen? Or, to put this another way, in what position would we have to stand for him to come into view, to enter the story that we *can* read? (There will be readers who remember it well, of course, and there will be scenes in *Benang* that I cannot see or remember that have great clarity for other readers. I am speaking here of a general phenomenon before a text such as *Benang* in which things fall from view, and there will be differences between readers' vision.)

The figure of the boy in the hessian sack might be read as an anamorphotic form in the sense that it is largely indiscernible; the boy is a figure through which one can peer, a 'stain', an obstacle through or around which one looks, dropping him out of the scene, out of *Benang*. I said earlier that there is no major narrative significance resting on this figure: one can read *Benang* without him. But there is another way of looking at this: we could say that *Benang* is in fact organised around that boy, and the Australian history that still cannot produce a story in which that boy has a place. That boy still belongs to another story. *Benang* organises itself around such obscure or hidden figures, the figures who cannot be seen, and whose lives have not been recorded in the archive. The obscene story of that boy in a hessian sack has still to be written. What archive holds *that* story? What missionary, archivist or Superintendent's wife recorded a scene like that in their collections?

Bibliography

All references are to print, unless otherwise stated.

Adams, Parveen. *The Emptiness of the Image: Psychoanalysis and Sexual Differences*. London and New York: Routledge, 1996.

Adams, Parveen (ed.). *Art: Sublimation or Symptom*. New York: Other Press, 2003.

Adelaide, Deborah (ed.). *A Bright and Fiery Troop: Australian Women Writers of the Nineteenth Century*. Ringwood: Penguin, 1988.

Adorno, Theodore. *Negative Dialectics*. Trans. E. Ashton. New York: Seabury, 1996.

Agamben, Giorgio. *Remnants of Auschwitz: The Witness and the Archive*. Trans. Daniel Heller-Roazen. New York: Zone Books, 1999.

Ahmed, Sara (ed.). *Uprootings/Regroundings*: *Questions of Home and Migration*. Oxford: Berg Publishing, 2003.

Améry, Jean. *At the Mind's Limits: Contemplation by a Survivor on Auschwitz and its Realities*. Trans. by Sidney Rosenfeld and Stella P. Rosenfeld. New York: Schocken Books, 1986.

Anderson, Don. 'Bound for glory'. *The Bulletin*, 12 June 2007, vol. 125 no. 6573: 58–9.

Auden, W.H. *Collected Poems*. Edited by Edward Mendelson. New York: The Modern Library, 2007.

Australian Human Rights and Equal Opportunity Commission. *Bringing them Home: Report of the National Inquiry into the Separation of Aboriginal and Torres Strait Islander Children from their Families*. Sydney: HREOC, 1997.

Baldwin, James. 'On being "white" ... and other lies'. In David Roediger (edited and introduced), *Black on White: Black Writers on What it Means to be White*. New York: Schocken Books, 1998: 177–80.

Banks, Marcus and Howard Morphy (eds). *Rethinking Visual Anthropology*. New Haven: Yale University Press, 1997.

Barta, Tony. 'After the Holocaust: consciousness of genocide in Australia'. *Australian Journal of Politics and History*, vol. 31, no. 1, 1985: 154–61.

———. 'Discourses of genocide in Germany and Australia: a linked history', *Aboriginal History*, vol. 25, 2001: 37–56.

———. 'Sorry, and not sorry, in Australia: How the apology to the stolen generations buried a history of genocide'. *Journal of Genocide Research*, vol. 10, no. 2, 2008: 201–14.

———. 'With intent to deny: on colonial intentions and genocide denial'. *Journal of Genocide Research*, vol. 10, issue 1, March 2008: 111–19.

Bartlett, Francesca. 'Clean, white girls: assimilation and women's work'. *Hecate* vol. 25 no. 1, May 1999: 10–38.

Bellanta, Melissa. 'Leary kin: Australian larrikins and the blackface minstrel dandy'. *Journal of Social History*, vol. 42, no. 3, Spring 2009: 677–95.

Bennett, Tegan. 'Abused and beaten'. *The Australian*, 10 May 1997: 9.

Bhabha, Homi K. *Nation and Narration*. Boston: Routledge, 1990.

———. 'The Third Space. Interview with Homi Bhabha'. In Jonathan Rutherford (ed.), *Identity: Community, Culture, Difference*. London: Lawrence & Wishart, 1990: 207–21.

———. *The Location of Culture*. London and New York: Routledge, 1994.

———. 'Cultures in-between'. In Stuart Hall and Paul du Gay (eds), *Questions of Cultural Identity*. London: Sage, 1996: 53–60.

Biddle, Jennifer. 'Breasts, bodies, art: Central Desert women's paintings and the politics of aesthetic encounter'. *Cultural Studies Review*, vol. 12, no. 1, March 2006: 16–31.

Birch, Tony. '"The first white man born": contesting the "Stolen Generations" narrative in Australia'. In Judith Ryan and Chris Wallace-Crabbe (eds), *Imagining Australia: Literature and Culture in the New World*. Cambridge, MA: Harvard University Committee on Australian Studies, 2004: 137–57.

———. *Shadowboxing*. Melbourne: Scribe, 2006.

Blake, Thom. *A Dumping Ground: A History of the Cherbourg Settlement*. St Lucia, Qld: University of Queensland Press, 2001.

Bliss, Carolyn. Review of *Plains of Promise*. In *World Literature Today*, vol. 72, no. 3, July 1998: 681–2.

Bowers, Maggie. *Magic(al) Realism: The New Critical Idiom*. London and New York: Routledge, 2004.

Bradstock, Margaret. 'Mary Gaunt' entry in Australian Literature, 1788–1914, *Dictionary of Literary Biography*, vol. 230. Edited by Selina Samuels. Detroit: Bruccoli Clark Layman Book, the Gale Group, 2001: 143–51.

Brennan, Teresa. *Exhausting Modernity: Grounds for a New Economy*. London and New York: Routledge, 2000.

Butler, Judith. *Gender Trouble: Feminism and the Subversion of Identity*. London and New York: Routledge, 1990.

———. *Bodies that Matter: On the Discursive Limits of 'Sex'*. New York and London: Routledge, 1993.

———. 'Endangered/endangering: schematic racism and white paranoia'. In Robert Gooding-Williams (ed. and trans.), *Reading Rodney King: Reading Urban Uprising*. New York and London: Routledge, 1993: 15–22.

Byrne, Madeleine. 'How Australian is it? Reading *Benang*'. *Antipodes*, vol. 15, no. 2, December 2001: 110–15.

Carlsson, Susanne Chauvel. *Charles and Elsa Chauvel: Movie Pioneers*. St Lucia, Qld: University of Queensland Press, 1989.

Carter, Denise. 'Novel idea pays off'. *The Cairns Post*, 18 August 2007: 35.

Chanady, Amaryll Beatrice. *Magical Realism and the Fantastic: Resolved versus Unresolved Antinomy*. New York: Garland, 1985.

Clendinnen, Inga. *Reading the Holocaust*. Melbourne: Text, 1998.

—. *Dancing with Strangers*. Melbourne: Text, 2003.

—. 'Brown skins, black hearts'. In *The Monthly*, June 2005: 54–6.

—. *The History Question: Who Owns the Past?* Quarterly Essay issue 23, Melbourne: Black Inc., 2006.

Copjec, Joan. *Read My Desire: Lacan Against the Historicists*. An October Book, Cambridge, MA; London, England: MIT Press, 1994.

—. *Supposing the Subject* (ed.). London and New York: Verso, 1994.

—. *Imagine There's No Woman: Ethics and Sublimation*. Cambridge, Massachusetts; London, England: MIT Press, 2004.

Dart, Jonathan. 'Alexis's book helps break the mould'. *Central Advocate*, 25 May 2007: 1.

Davison, Liam. 'Phantasmagorical tale fills a legendary landscape'. *Sydney Morning Herald*, 16 September 2006: 32.

Devlin-Glass, Frances. 'Broken songs and ecology: writing on the Gulf of Carpentaria'. *Táin*, no. 44, December 2006–February 2007: 28–9.

—. 'Alexis Wright's *Carpentaria*'. *Antipodes*, vol. 21, no. 1, June 2007: 82–4.

—. 'A politics of the Dreamtime: destructive and regenerative rainbows in Alexis Wright's *Carpentaria*'. *Australian Literary Studies*, vol. 23, no. 4, 2008: 392–407.

Diprose, Rosalyn. *Bodies of Women: Ethics, Embodiment and Sexual Difference*. New York: Routledge, 1994.

DuBois, W.E.B. *The Souls of Black Folk*. Edited and introduction and notes by Brent Hayes Edwards, New York: Oxford University Press, 2007.

Dussart, Françoise. 'A body painting in translation'. In Marcus Banks and Howard Morphy (eds). *Rethinking Visual Anthropology*. New Haven: Yale University Press, 1997: 186–202.

—. 'Shown but not shared, presented but not proffered: redefining ritual identity among Walpiri ritual performers 1990–2000'. In *Australian Journal of Anthropology*, 15(3) 2004: 253–66.

Dyer, Richard. 'White'. *Screen*, vol. 29, no. 4, Autumn 1988: 44–65.

Edwards, Coral and Peter Read (eds). *The Lost Children: Thirteen Australians taken from their Aboriginal families tell of the Struggle to find their Natural Parents*. Sydney: Doubleday, 1989.

Elder, Catriona. 'Staging "white" Australia: representations of race and sexuality in the north'. In Jane Long, Jan Gothard and Helen Brash (eds). *Forging Identities: Bodies, Gender and Feminist History*. Nedlands, WA: University of WA Press, 1997: 29–46.

Ellinghaus, Katherine. 'Margins of acceptability: class, education, and interracial marriage in Australia and North America'. *Frontiers*, 23, no. 3 (Dec 2002): 55–75.

Ellison, Ralph. 'Change the joke, slip the yoke'. In *Shadow and Act*. London: Secker and Warburg, 1967: 45–59.

England, Katharine. 'Small-town dreaming'. *The Advertiser*, 30 September 2006: W10.

England, Katharine and Deborah Bogle. 'Place of hope and desperation'. *The Advertiser*, 30 June 2007: W8.

Evans, Mari (ed.). *Black Women Writers*. New York: Anchor Books, 1984.

Fanon, Frantz. *Toward the African Revolution*. Harmondsworth: Pelican, 1970.

———. *Black Skins, White Masks*. London: Pluto Press, 1991.

Ferrier, Carole. 'The best Australian novel for years'. *Australian Women's Book Review*, 18(2) 2006: 20–21.

———. 'Disappearing memory'. *JASAL*, special issue 2008: 37–55.

Fichte, Hubert. *Detlev's Imitations*. London and New York: Serpent's Tail, 1991.

Fitzgerald, Michael. 'Crossing the Gulf'. *Time* International South Pacific edition, 2 October 2006, issue 39: 62.

Foord, Kate. 'The fantasy of the modern Australian nation: travelling to the "empty centre"'. *Australian Feminist Studies*, vol. 18, no. 42, 2003: 273–83.

Foreman, P. Gabrielle. 'Past-on stories: history and the magically real, Morrison and Allende on call'. In Lois Parkinson Zamora and Wendy B. Faris (ed. and introd.), *Magic Realism: Theory, History, Community*. Durham and London: Duke University Press, 1995.

Fotheringham, Richard. *Australian Plays for the Colonial Stage 1834–1848*. St Lucia, Qld: University of Queensland Press, 2006.

Frankenberg, Ruth. 'Mirage of an unmarked whiteness'. In Birgit Brander Rasmussen, Eric Klinenberg, Irene J. Nexica and Matt Wray (eds), *The Making and Unmaking of Whiteness*. Durham and London: Duke University Press, 2001.

Fredrickson, George M. *Racism: A Short History*. Foreword by Robert Manne, Melbourne: Scribe, 2002.

Freud, Sigmund. *The Standard Edition of the Complete Psychological Works of Sigmund Freud*, volume XVII (1917–1919): An Infantile Neurosis and Other Works. Trans under the general editorship of James Strachey, in collaboration with Anna Freud. London: Vintage/The Hogarth Press, 2001.

Frow, John. 'In the penal colony'. *Australian Humanities Review* issue no. 13 April 1999, http://www.australianhumanitiesreview.org/archive/Issue-April-1999/frow3.html. Online.

Fuentes, Carlos. *Don Quixote: Or, The Critique of Reading*. Austin: Institute of Latin American Studies, University of Texas at Austin, 1976.

Gaines, Jane. 'White privilege and the right to look'. *Screen*, vol. 29, no. 4, 1988: 13–27.

Garimara, Doris Pilkington. *Follow the Rabbit-Proof Fence*. St Lucia, Qld: University of Queensland Press, 2001.

Gates, Henry Louis Jr (ed.). *'Race', Writing and Difference*. Chicago: Chicago University Press, 1986.

Gauch, Suzanne. 'Telling the tale of a body devoured by narrative'. *Differences*, vol. 11, no. 1, 1999: 179–202.

Gaunt, Mary. *Alone in West Africa*. London: T. Werner Laurie, 1912.

———. *Reflection – in Jamaica*. London: Benn, 1932.

—. *Kirkham's Find.* Introduction by Kylie Tennant, afterword by Dale Spender. Ringwood: Penguin, 1988: 338–9.

Gelder, Ken (ed.). *Oxford Book of Australian Ghost Stories.* Melbourne: Oxford University Press, 1994.

Gelder, Ken and Jane M. Jacobs. *Uncanny Australia: Sacredness and Identity in a Postcolonial Nation.* Carlton: Melbourne University Press, 1998.

Gibson, Ross. *South of the West: Postcolonialism and the Narrative Construction of Australia.* Bloomington and Indianapolis: Indiana University Press, 1992.

Gilbert, Helen. 'Black and white and re(a)d all over again: indigenous minstrelsy in contemporary Canadian and Australian theatre'. *Theatre Journal,* 55(4) 2003: 679–98.

Ginibi, Ruby Langford. *My Bundjalung People.* St Lucia, Qld: University of Queensland Press, 1994.

—. *Don't Take Your Love to Town.* Ringwood: Penguin, 1998.

Griffiths, Tom. *Hunters and Collectors: The Antiquarian Imagination in Australia.* Cambridge and Melbourne: Cambridge University Press, 1996.

Grossman, Michele. 'Reading Aboriginal writing: editing, Aboriginality, textuality'. *Meanjin* 60(3) 2001: 146–60.

—. 'Xen(ography) and the art of representing otherwise: Australian Indigenous life-writing and the vernacular text'. *Postcolonial Studies,* 8(3) 2005: 277–301.

—. 'Risk, roguery and revelation'. *The Australian,* 4 October 2006: 10.

Hage, Ghassan. *White Nation: Fantasies of White Supremacy in a Multicultural Society.* Sydney and Kent: Pluto Press and Comerford and Millers Publishers, 1998.

Hancock, Geoff. *Magic Realism.* Toronto: Aya Press, 1980.

Haskins, Victoria and John Maynard. 'Sex, race and power: Aboriginal men and white women in Australian history'. Special issue *Histories of Sexualities,* edited by Steven Angelides and Barbara Baird, *Australian Historical Studies,* 37(126) October 2005: 191–216.

Hegarty, Ruth. *Is that you, Ruthie?* St Lucia, Qld: University of Queensland Press, 1999.

Hickman, Bronwen. 'Mary Gaunt, an Australian identity'. *Overland,* no. 158, 2000: 58–62.

hooks, bell. *Black Looks: Race and Representation.* Boston: South End Press, 1992.

Horton, David (General Ed.). *The Encyclopaedia of Aboriginal Australia: Aboriginal and Torres Strait Islander History, Society and Culture.* Canberra, ACT: Aboriginal Studies Press for the Australian Institute of Aboriginal and Torres Strait Islander Studies (AIATSIS), 1994.

Huggins, Rita and Jackie Huggins. *Auntie Rita.* Canberra, ACT: Aboriginal Studies Press, 1994.

Hyam, Ronald. *Sexuality and Empire.* Manchester: Manchester University Press, 1990.

Ignatiev, Noel. *How the Irish became White*. New York: Routledge, 1995.

Jacobs, Jane M. 'Editorial: Difference and its other'. *Transactions of the Institute of British Geographers*, New Series, vol. 25, no. 4. (2000): 403–7.

Jacobus, Mary. *Reading Woman: Essays in Feminist Criticism*. London: Methuen, 1986.

Jose, Nicholas. 'Generations suffer the agony and the exodus'. *Sydney Morning Herald*, 17 May 1997: 9.

Kafka, Franz. *The Penal Colony: Stories and Short Pieces*. Translated by Willa and Edwin Muir. New York: Schocken Books, 1964.

Kamuf, Peggy. 'Writing like a woman'. In Sally McConnell-Ginet, Sally and Ruth Borker, and Nelly Furnam (eds), *Women and Language in Literature and Society*. New York: Praeger, 1980: 284–99.

Kaplan, E. Ann. 'The "look" returned: knowledge production and constructions of "whiteness" in humanities scholarship and independent film'. In Mike Hill (ed.), *Whiteness: A Critical Reader*. New York and London: New York University Press, 1997: 316–28.

Kasack, Hermann. *Die Stadt hinter dem Strom*. Frankfurt am Main, 1978.

Kenny, Robert. *The Lamb Enters the Dreaming: Nathanael Pepper and the Ruptured World*. Melbourne: Scribe, 2007.

Kidd, Rosalind. *The Way We Civilise: Aboriginal Affairs, the Untold Story*. St Lucia, Qld: University of Queensland Press, 1997.

Kinnane, Stephen. *Shadow Lines*. Fremantle, WA: Fremantle Press, 2003.

Kinnane, Stephen, Lauren Marsh, and Roger Scholes. *The Coolbaroo Club*. Produced by Penny Robins; directed by Roger Scholes. Australia: Australian Film Finance Corporation, The Coolbaroo Club and Australian Film Commission, 1995. Film.

———. 'Capitalising difference: feminism and anthropology'. *Australian Feminist Studies*, vol. 4, no. 9, Autumn, 1989: 1–24.

Kirby, Vicki. *Telling Flesh; The Substance of the Corporeal*. New York and London: Routledge, 1997.

Kristeva, Julia. *About Chinese Women*. Trans. Anita Barrows, London: Marion Boyars, 1977.

Lacan, Jacques. *The Ethics of Psychoanalysis 1959–1960: The Seminar of Jacques Lacan*. Edited by Jacques-Alain Miller, Book VII translated with notes by Dennis Porter. London: Routledge, 1992.

———. *The Four Fundamental Concepts of Psychoanalysis, Seminar xi, 1964*. Trans. A. Sheridan. London: The Hogarth Press and the Institute of Psychoanalysis, 1998.

LeClair, Thomas. 'The language must not sweat: A conversation with Toni Morrison'. *The New Republic*, 21 March 1981: 25–9.

Lingis, Alphonso. *Translator's Preface*. Maurice Merleau-Ponty. *The Visible and the Invisible*. Edited by Claude Lefort and trans. by Alphonso Lingis. Evanston, IL: Northwestern University Press, 1968: xl–lvi.

Lott, Eric. *Love and Theft: Blackface and the American Working Class*. New York: Oxford University Press, 1993.

Macintyre, Stuart (ed.). *The Historians' Conscience: Australian Historians on the Ethics of History*. Carlton, Vic.: Melbourne University Press, 2004.

Manne, Robert. 'The Stolen Generations'. In Peter Craven (ed.), *The Best Australian Essays 1998*. Melbourne: Bookman, 1998: 23–36.

———. Foreword to George M. Fredrickson, *Racism: A Short History*. Carlton North: Scribe, 2002: ix–xvi.

———. *Whitewash: On Keith Windschuttle's Fabrication of Aboriginal History*. Melbourne: Black Inc., 2003.

———. 'Sorry business: the road to recovery'. In David Marr (ed.), *The Best Australian Essays 2008*. Melbourne: Black Inc., 2008: 101–17.

Martin, Susan. 'Sad sometimes, lonely often ... dull never'. In Debra Adelaide (ed. and introd.), *A Bright and Fiery Troop: Australian Women Writers of the Nineteenth Century*. Ringwood: Penguin, 1988: 183–97.

McClintock, Anne. *Imperial Leather: Race, Gender and Sexuality in the Colonial Contest*. New York: Routledge, 1995.

McConnell-Ginet, Sally, Ruth Borker, and Nelly Furnam (eds). *Women and Language in Literature and Society*. New York: Praeger, 1980.

McGrath, Ann. *Born in the Cattle: Aborigines in Cattle Country*. Sydney: Allen & Unwin, 1987.

Merleau-Ponty, Maurice. *The Visible and the Invisible*. Edited by Claude Lefort and trans. by Alphonso Lingis. Evanston, IL: Northwestern University Press, 1968.

Michaels, Eric. *Bad Aboriginal Art: Tradition, Media and Technological Horizons*. St Leonards: Allen & Unwin, 1994.

Michaels, Walter Benn. *Our America: Nativism, Modernism, and Pluralism*. Durham: Duke University Press, 1995.

———. 'Autobiography of an ex-white man: why race is not a social construction'. *Transition* no. 73, Spring 1997: 122–43.

Miller, Benjamin. 'The mirror of whiteness: Blackface in Charles Chauvel's *Jedda*'. In *JASAL* Special Issue 2007 *Spectres, Screens, Shadows, Mirrors*, edited by Tanya Dalziell and Paul Genoni: 104–56.

Moffatt, Tracey (producer, director, scriptwriter). *Nice Coloured Girls*. 17 mins video, colour, 1987.

Morgan, Sally. *My Place*. Fremantle, WA: Fremantle Arts Centre Press, 1987.

Moreton-Robinson, Aileen. *Talkin' up to the White Woman: Aboriginal Women and Feminism*. St Lucia, Qld: University of Queensland Press, 2000.

———. '"I still call Australia home": Indigenous belonging and place in a white colonising society'. In Sara Ahmed (ed.), *Uprootings/Regroundings: Questions of Home and Migration*. Oxford: Berg Publishing, 2003.

———. 'The possessive logic of patriarchal white sovereignty: The High Court and the Yorta Yorta decision'. *Borderlands e-journal*, vol. 3, no. 2, 2004. Online.

168   *The Postcolonial Eye*

———— (ed.). *Whitening Race: Essays in Social and Cultural Criticism.* Canberra, ACT: Aboriginal Studies Press, 2004.

———— (ed.). *Sovereign Subjects: Indigenous Sovereignty Matters.* Series editors Rachel Fensham and Jon Stratton. Crows Nest, NSW: Allen & Unwin, 2007.

Morphy, Howard. *Aboriginal Art.* London: Phaidon Press, 1998.

Morrison, Toni. 'Rootedness: the ancestor as foundation'. In Mari Evans (ed.), *Black Women Writers: Arguments and Interviews.* London: Pluto, 1985: 339–45.

————. *Beloved.* London: Picador, 1988.

————. *Playing in the Dark: Blackness and the White Literary Imagination.* Cambridge, MA: Harvard University Press, 1992.

Morrissey, Philip. Untitled review of *Benang* in *Meanjin*, 1 (2000a): 200.

————. 'Dancing with shadows: erasing Aboriginal self and sovereignty'. In Aileen Moreton-Robinson (ed.), Rachel Fensham and Jon Stratton (series eds), *Sovereign Subjects: Indigenous Sovereignty Matters.* Crows Nest, NSW: Allen & Unwin, 2007.

Morton, John. 'Tiddalik's travels: the making and remaking of an Aboriginal flood myth'. *Advances in Ecological Research*, vol. 39, 2006: 139–58.

Moses, A. Dirk (ed.). *Colonialism and Genocide.* London: Routledge, 2007.

———— (ed.). *Genocide and Settler Society: Frontier Violence and Stolen Indigenous Children in Australian History.* New York: Berghahn Books, 2004.

Muecke, Stephen. *Ancient and Modern: Time, Culture and Indigenous Philosophy.* Sydney: University of NSW Press, 2004.

Mumbulla, Percy. 'The Bunyip'. *Black-Feller, White-Feller.* Edited by Roland Robinson. Sydney: Angus & Robertson, 1958: 124–5.

Pascoe, Bruce. *Convincing Ground: Learning to Fall in Love with your Country.* Canberra, ACT: Aboriginal Studies Press, 2007.

Pickering, Michael. 'The BBC's Kentucky Minstrels 1933–1950: blackface entertainment in British radio'. *Historical Journal of Film, Radio and Television*, vol. 16, no. 2, June 1996: 161–95.

Pierce, Peter. 'Once again all credit to Giramondo'. *Canberra Times* 23 July 2006: B4.

Read, Peter. *The Stolen Generations: The Removal of Aboriginal Children in NSW 1883 to 1969.* Sydney, NSW: Ministry of Aboriginal Affairs, 1984.

Renes, Cornelis Martin. 'Discomforting readings: uncanny perceptions of self in Alexis Wright's *Plains of Promise* and David Malouf's *Remembering Babylon*'. *Eucalypt* 2, 2002. Barcelona: Australian Studies Centre: 76–102.

Reynolds, Henry. *An Indelible Stain? The Question of Genocide in Australia's History.* Ringwood, Vic: Penguin, 2001.

Robinson Jane. *Wayward Women: A Guide for Women Travellers.* New York: Oxford University Press, 1990.

Robinson, Roland (ed.). *Black-Feller, White-Feller.* Sydney: Angus & Robertson, 1958.

Roe, Paddy. *Gularabulu: Stories from the West Kimberley.* Edited by Stephen Muecke. Fremantle: Fremantle Arts Centre Press, 1983.

Roediger, David (ed. and introd.). *Black on White: Black Writers on What it Means to be White*. New York: Schocken Books, 1998.

Roh, Franz. 'Magical Realism: Post-Expressionism'. Translated from Spanish to English by Wendy B. Faris in *Magic Realism: Theory, History, Community*. Edited and with an introduction by Lois Parkinson Zamora and Wendy B. Faris, Durham and London: Duke University Press, 1995.

Rose, Deborah Bird. *Dingo Makes Us Human: Life and Land in an Australian Aboriginal Culture*. Cambridge: Cambridge University Press, 2000.

———. 'Dance of the Ephemeral: Australian Aboriginal Religion of Place'. In Mary N. Macdonald (ed.), *Experiences of Place*. Cambridge, MA: Harvard University Press, 2003: 163–86.

Russell, Lynette and Margery Fee. '"Whiteness" and "Aboriginality" in Canada and Australia'. *Feminist Theory*, vol. 8, no. 2, 2007: 187–208.

Ryan, Judith. *Colour Power: Aboriginal Art Post 1984*. Melbourne: Council of Trustees of the National Gallery of Victoria, 2004.

Sartre, Jean-Paul. *Being and Nothingness*. Translated Hazel Barnes. New York: Washington Square Press, 1992.

Scott, Kim. *Benang: From the Heart*. Fremantle, WA: Fremantle Arts Centre Press, 1999.

———. 'Disputed territory'. In Anne Brewster, Angeline O'Neill and Rosemary van den Berg (eds), *Those Who Remain Will Always Remember: An Anthology of Aboriginal Writing*. Fremantle: Fremantle Arts Centre Press, 2000: 161–71.

———. 'Capture'. *Southerly*, vol. 62, no. 2, Summer 2002: 24–33.

———. 'Covered up with sand'. *Meanjin*, vol. 66, no. 2, June 2007: 120–24.

Scott, Kim and Hazel Brown. *Kayang & Me*. Fremantle, WA: Fremantle Arts Centre Press, 2005.

Sebald, W.G. *On the Natural History of Destruction*. Translated by Anthea Bell. New York: Random House 2003.

Shoemaker, Adam. 'Hard dreams and Indigenous worlds in Australia's north'. *Hecate*, vol. 34, no. 1, 2008: 55–62.

Slater, Lisa. 'I found myself among paper' (Review of Kim Scott *Benang from the Heart*). *Southerly*, vol. 61, no. 1, Spring 2001: 220.

——— 'Making strange men: resistance and reconciliation in Kim Scott's *Benang*'. In Bruce Bennett, Susan Cowan, Jacqueline Lo, Satendra Nandan and Jennifer Webb (eds), *Resistance and Reconciliation: Writing in the Commonwealth*. Canberra: ASLALA (The Association for Commonwealth Literature and Language Studies at ADFA), 2003: 358–70.

——— 'Kim Scott's *Benang*: an ethics of uncertainty'. In *JASAL* 4, 2005: 147–58.

——— 'Kim Scott's *Benang*: monstrous (textual) bodies'. *Southerly*, vol. 65, no. 1, 2005: 63–73.

——— '*Benang*, this "most local of histories": annexing colonial records into a world without end'. *The Journal of Commonwealth Literature*, vol. 41, no. 1, Spring 2006: 51–68.

170 *The Postcolonial Eye*

Slemon, Stephen. 'Magic realism as postcolonial discourse'. In Lois Parkinson Zamora and Wendy B. Faris (ed. and introd.), *Magic Realism: Theory, History, Community*. Durham and London: Duke University Press, 1995.

Smith, Sidonie. 'Performativity, autobiographical practice, resistance'. *A/B: Auto/ Biography Studies*, vol. 10, no. 1, Spring 1995: 17–33.

Sorensen, Rosemary. 'Problems with victim support' (Review of Alexis Wright, *Plains of Promise*). *Sunday Age*, Agenda/Review: 4 May 1997: 8.

Stanner, W.E.H. 'Religion, totemism and symbolism'. In Max Charlesworth, Howard Morphy, Diane Bell and Kenneth Maddock (eds), *Religion in Aboriginal Australia: An Anthology*. St Lucia, Qld: University of Queensland Press, 1984: 137–72. Reprinted from Ronald M. and Catherine H. Berndt (eds), *Aboriginal Man in Australia*. Sydney: Angus & Robertson, 1965: 207–37.

Steger, Jason. 'Humanity's voice rises'. *The Age*, 23 June 2007: 2.

Stoler, A. *Carnal Knowledge and Imperial Power: Race and the Intimate in Colonial Rule*. Berkeley: University of California Press, 2002.

Strelau, Marilyn. 'Whose image? Whose mirror? (Aboriginal writing)'. *Antipodes*, vol. 14, no. 2, December 2000: 163–65.

Sullivan, Jane. 'From here to Carpentaria'. *The Age*, 9 September 2006: 26.

Sutton Mary-Jean. 'Re-examining total institutions: a case study from Queensland'. *Archaeology in Oceania*, no. 38, 2003: 78–89.

Sykes, Roberta. *Snake Cradle*. St Leonards, NSW: Allen & Unwin, 1997.

————. *Snake Dreaming*. St Leonards, NSW: Allen & Unwin, 1998.

————. *Snake Circle*. St Leonards, NSW: Allen & Unwin, 2000.

Sylvester, David. *The Brutality of Fact: Interviews with Francis Bacon*. New York: Thames & Hudson, 2009.

Syson, Ian. 'Uncertain magic'. *Overland*, no. 187, 2007, 85–6.

Takolander, Maria. *Catching Butterflies: Bringing Magical Realism to Ground*. Bern: Peter Lang, 2007.

Thurston, Luke. 'Meaning on trial: sublimation and *The Reader*'. In Parveen Adams (ed.), *Art; Sublimation or Symptom*. New York: Other Press, 2003: 29–48.

Toll, Robert C. *Blacking Up: The Minstrel Show in Eighteenth-century America*. New York: Oxford University Press, 1974.

Trees, Kathryn. 'Kim Scott shouting back: Kathryn Trees talks to Kim Scott about his writing'. *Fremantle Arts Review* 10(1), August/September 1995: 20–21.

Tuhkanen, Mikko. 'Of blackface and paranoid knowledge: Richard Wright, Jacques Lacan and the ambivalence of black minstrelsy'. *Diacritics* 31(2), 2001: 9–34.

Waterhouse, Richard. 'Minstrel show and vaudeville house: the Australian popular stage 1838–1914'. *Australian Historical Studies* 23 (93), October 1989: 366–85.

West-Pavlov, Russell. *Transcultural Graffiti: Diasporic Writing and the Teaching of Literary Studies*. Amsterdam and New York: Rodopi, 2005.

Whitlock, Gillian. 'A most improper desire: Mary Gaunt's journey to Jamaica'. *Kunapipi*, vol. XV, no. 3, 1993: 86–95.

Windschuttle, Keith. *The Fabrication of Aboriginal History*. Paddington, NSW: Macleay Press, 2003.

Wolfe, Patrick. 'On being woken up: the Dreamtime in anthropology and Australian settler culture'. *Comparative Studies in Society and History*, vol. 33, no. 2, April 1991: 197–224.

———. 'Robert Manne, the apology and genocide'. *Arena Magazine*, no. 94, April–May 2008: 31–3.

Woollacott, Angela. 'Creating the white colonial woman: Mary Gaunt's imperial adventuring and Australian cultural history'. In Hsu-Ming Teo and Richard White (eds), *Cultural History in Australia*. Sydney: UNSW Press, 2003: 186–200.

Wright, Alexis. *Plains of Promise*. St Lucia, Qld: University of Queensland Press, 1997.

———. 'The serpent's covenant'. In Katerina Akiewenzie-Damm and Josie Douglas (compilers), *Skins: Contemporary Indigenous Writing*. Alice Springs, NT, and Wiarton, Ont: Jukurrpa Books and Kegedonce Press, 2000: 115–22.

———. *Carpentaria*. Artarmon, NSW: Giramondo, 2006.

———. 'On writing *Carpentaria*'. *Heat*, 13 new series, 2007: 79–95.

Wyndham, Susan. 'Undercover'. *Sydney Morning Herald*, 30 June 2007: 30.

Zamora, Lois Parkinson and Wendy B. Faris (ed. and introd.). *Magic Realism: Theory, History, Community*. Durham and London: Duke University Press, 1995.

Zizek, Slavoj. *The Sublime Object of Ideology*. London, New York: Verso 1989.

Index

The Aboriginals Preservation and Protection Act 1939, 95–6
Aboriginals Protection and Restriction of the Sale of Opium Act 1897, 93–6, 93n3, 101–2, 118;
  see also sovereignty
The Aborigines Protection Act 1909, 136n7
Adams, Parveen, 19n13, 43, 45, 45n1, 49, 146–7, 157–8
  The Emptiness of the Image, 31, 34n3, 54, 57, 66n23, 151n1
Adorno, Theodor, 18, 19
aesthetics, aesthetic form, 1–2, 13, 68–70, 151–2, 155
African Americans, 65–7, 98–100, 132, 134;
  see also American, racial policies
Agamben, Georgio
  Remnants of Auschwitz, 8n3, 11
alterity, 82–3, 86
American, racial policies; *see also* colonialism; racial binarisms; slavery
  and African Americans, 65–7, 98–100, 132, 134
  assimilationism, 131–2, 148
  and *Benang: From the Heart*, 139–42
  and blackface, minstrelsy, 132–5, 132n2, 133n3, 139–43
  and literacy, 155–6
  and slavery, 66, 98–9, 132
Améry, Jean
  At the Mind's Limits, 12, 13–14
anamorphosis
  in *Benang: From the Heart*, 158–9
  and image, imaginary, 22–3, 42–3
  and Indigenous art, 44
  and Jacques Lacan, 22–3, 42–3
  and Parveen Adams, 43
  in *Plains of Promise*, 46, 54–6
Anderson, Don, 60n6
anthropology

and anthropological discourse, 47, 62, 79
Muecke, Stephen, 32, 33, 41n6, 64n18
and Stanner, W.E.H., 11, 12, 18, 22, 36–7, 76
anthropometrics, 9n4
anxiety; *see also* desire/dread
  and difference, radical difference, self-same, 20–21
  and 'the lack of a lack,' 142–3, 142n20
  and the other, 19
  settler, displacement, 85–8
  and the uncanny, 82–3
aporia, 2, 20–23, 56
archives, colonial; *see also* colonialism
  colonialism and formation of, 153–4
  and Indigenous Australians, surveillance, 92–3, 93n2, 93n3
  and the past, recovery of, 17–18, 153n4
  reserve system and white male desire, 94
art, 19, 19n13, 40, 41–4, 56n13, 61–2, 79
artefacts, Indigenous, 79–80
assimilationism
  Australian and American racial policies, 131–2, 148
  in *Benang: From the Heart*, 131–2, 145–9, 156
Auden, W.H.
  Marginalia, 115
Australian, race policies; *see also* Cherbourg Aboriginal Reserve; colonialism; reserve system; slavery, Stolen Generations
  assimilationism, 131–2, 148
  Benang: From the Heart, 131–2, 139–42
  blackface, minstrelsy, 132, 132n2, 133n3, 139–40
  and segregation, 131–2, 147–8
  and slavery, 132, 139
  white desire/dread, 131–3

174   *The Postcolonial Eye*

Australian Human Rights and Equal
    Opportunity Commission, 118n1
autobiography; *see also* Hegarty, Ruth;
    Huggins, Rita; Ginibi, Ruby
    Langford
    narratives, Indigenous, 92
    and omission, 17–18
    as performative, 27, 91–3

Bachelard, Gaston, 24
Bacon, Francis, 19, 19n13
Baldwin, James, 25
Barber, Doreen, 10, *10*, 115
Barta, Tony, 8n2
Bartlett, Francesca, 50n4
Beckett, Samuel, 18–19
Bellanta, Melissa, 140n15, 140n16, 141n19
Bennett, Tegan, 55n10, 57
Bhabha, Homi
    The Location of Culture; *Nation and*
    Narration, 81n1
Biddle, Jennifer L., 37–40, 41–2, 44, 52n7
biography, as performative, 92–3
Birch, Tony, 10n6
Birdsell, Joseph, 9n4
black and blackness, 65–70, 98–100; *see*
    also Indigeneity; racial binarisms
    black 'looking,' as controlled, 98–100
Black Atlantic, 112
blackface, minstrelsy; *see also* racial
    binarisms, scopophilia,
    spectacle, specular
    and American, racial policies, 132–5,
        132n2, 133n3, 139–43
    in Australia, 133n3, 139–40
    Benang: From the Heart, 132–3,
        133n3, 135, 139–41, 143
    and desire/dread, 132–3, 132n2
    and disavowal, 125–6, 139, 142–3
    and Elizabeth Semple, 123
    in film, 125, 140–41, 143–4
    and gender, 141n19
    and race, construction of, 134–8
Blake, Thom, 48n3, 156n6
blindness, blind spots; *see also* vision and
    the visual field
    and disavowal, 77
    and standpoint theory, 77
Bliss, Carolyn, 52n8, 55n10

the Boathouse, 101, 102, 105–6
body, embodiment, 31, 35–40, 79;
    see also Indigeneity
body, as object, 11, 12–15, 96–7
Bowers, Maggie, *Magic(al) Realism*,
    61n10, 63, 64n15, 66–7, 66n22
Bradstock, Margaret, 111, 112n7
Brennan, Teresa
    Exhausting Modernity, 45
Brown, Hazel
    Kayang and Me, 8n2, 17, 18, 137
Bunyip, The, 83–5
Butler, Judith
    Bodies that Matter, 25, 27, 46, 50n5,
        91, 94, 102n3, 134, 141n19
    Gender Trouble, 49, 136
Byrne, Madeleine, 153n4, 157n8

calculability, 12–13, 15, 135, 137, 152–3
Carpentier, Alejo, 67
Carter, Denise, 60n8
Chauvel, Charles
    Jedda, 140, 144
    The Moth of Moonbi, 143–4
Chanady, Amaryll Beatrice
    Magical Realism and the
        Fantastic, 61n10
Cherbourg Aboriginal Reserve, 9, 9n4,
    93, 95–6, 103, 156n6; *see also*
    Australian, race policies; reserve
    system; Stolen Generations
    productions of race at, 115–16,
        116, *117*, 118–20, *121*, 122–3,
        122–7, 126–8
    reserve system as sadistic, 115–16,
        118–20, 126–8
    The Romance of Runnimede (film),
        123, 125
Clarke, Paul, 144
Clendinnen, Inga, *Dancing with Strangers*
    17n11, 135n5, 139, 153, 153n3
colonialism; *see also* American, racial
    policies; archives, colonial;
    Australian, race policies;
    Indigeneity; postcolonialism;
    reserve system; slavery
    formation of and the colonial
        archives, 153–4
    as holocaust, 8, 8n2, 8n3

Index

infantilisation of Aboriginals, 122–3
massacre, in *Benang: From the Heart*,
132, 137, 144–5, 159
and perversion, 8
and racial discourse, 134–6
reading practice, as repetition of
relations of, 19–20
and sadism, 115–16, 118–20, 126–8
sexual economies of, 102–6
and state surveillance, 92–3,
93n2, 93n3, 101–2
trauma of, 15, 15n7
Cooper, James Fenimore, 134
Copjec, Joan
Imagine There's No Woman, 41, 97–8,
147, 148n24, 209
Read my Desire, 1, 24, 24n14, 25, 34,
35, 41, 46n2, 55, 55n11, 59, 142n20
Supposing the Subject, 17n11
Coronation Hill, 87
country, 38–40; *see also* Indigeneity
and embodiment
Indigeneity and, 17, 31–4, 44,
52n7, 55
reading of, and white settlers, 34–5
as text, 1–2
and the *Yawulyu* ceremony, 37–8

dance, and the *Yawulyu* ceremonies, 38
Dart, Jonathan, 60n8
Darwin, Charles, 139
Davison, Liam, 60n8
Deputy Director of Native Affairs in
Brisbane, 93–6
Derrida, Jacques, 86
desire/dread, 88, 131–3, 132n2, 138,
142–5, 146n23; *see also* anxiety;
blackface, minstrelsy; white
women's sexuality
Devlin-Glass, Frances, 59n1, 59n2, 60n7,
60n8, 75–9
difference, radical difference, self-same;
see also sovereignty; uncertainty,
radical; white and whiteness
and Aboriginal art, 44
and anxiety, 20–21
and embodiment, 39–40
and Indigenous creativity, 59–61
and language, 21–2

and magic realism, 60–68, 67n24, 67n26
white creativity, as prototype,
59–60, 65, 76–7
whites, understanding of Indigenous
world, 76–7, 79–80
differend, 86
Diprose, Rosalyn, 39
disavowal
and blackface, 125–6
of empire, violence of, 139–40
feminists, of white imperial gaze, 104–5
in *Plains of Promise*, 50–51
of radical difference, 20–22
of slavery, 139
in *Uncanny Australia*, 83
white desire/dread, 131–2, 144–5,
146n23, 151
dislocation, 13–15, 55, 81–3, 85–8, 118–20
and Stolen Generations, 55,
118–20, 118n1
the Dog Act, 93–6, 93n3, 101–2, 118;
see also sovereignty
the donkey devil, 32–5
the Dreamtime, 11, 18, 24, 36–7, 62–3, 69, 74
DuBois, W.E.B., 16
Dussart, Francoise, 41n7

Edwards, Jimmy, 123, *123*
Ellison, Ralph
Shadow and Act, 133n3
England, Katherine, 59n1, 60n8, 71n28
enjoyment, white spectator and, 96–7, 118,
120, 157–8
eye, and the I, 1, 20, 25, 42, 104–5; *see
also* the gaze

Fanon, Frantz
African Revolution; *Black Skins*, 81n1
Faris, Wendy, 61n10, 64
feminists
and Gaunt, Mary, feminist critique
on, 111–13
literary criticism, feminist, 26,
104–8, 111–13
of white imperial gaze, disavowal, 104–5
Ferrier, Carole, 55n10
Fichte, Hubert, 12–14
Detlev's Imitations, 12–14
Fisher, Jim, *122*, 123

176   *The Postcolonial Eye*

Fitzgerald, Michael, 59n2
Foord, Kate, 66n23
Foreman, P. Gabrielle, 65, 66
Fotheringham, Richard, 140n16
Frankenberg, Ruth, 99, 99n10
Freud, Sigmund, 61, 68, 81, 82–3, 83n3
Fuentes, Carlos, 159n9

García Márquez, Gabriel, 64, 64n16, 65, 67
Garimara, Doris Pilkington
    Follow the Rabbit-proof Fence, 120n2
Gates, Henry Louis, Jr, 156
Gaunt, Mary
    Alone in West Africa, 109–10, 112
    feminist critique on, 111–13
    Kirkham's Find, 108n6, 112
    and master-slave, in writings of,
        109–10, 112
    Reflections – In Jamaica, 109
    and sadism/perversion, 109–13
    white women's desire and colonial
        power relations, 108–9, 110–12,
        112n7, 113
the gaze, 17, 97–100, 104–6; *see also* eye,
    and the I; the other, otherness
Gelder, Ken
    and settler anxiety, 85–8
    on 'The Bunyip', 83–5
    Uncanny Australia, 80n35, 81–3,
        86, 88
gender, 26, 37–8, 91, 104–5, 113, 138–9,
    141n19; *see also* white
    women's sexuality
genocide, 8, 8n2; *see also* holocaust
German post-war literature, 7–11
Gibson, Ross, 82
Gilbert, Helen, 140n14
Ginibi, Ruby Langford, 9n3, 75n31
Glennie, Evelyn, 32, 35–6
Glowczeski, Barbara, 42
González Echevarría, Roberto, 63, 64n16
the Great Serpent, 24
Griffiths, Tom
    Hunters and Collectors, 79–80
Grossman, Michele, 16n9, 56n13, 59n3

Hage, Ghassan
    White Nation, 25
Hancock, Geoff, 61n10

Hardy, Frank, 59
Haskins, Frank H.
    The Racial Basis of Civilization, 148
Haskins, Victoria, 107–8
Hegarty, Ruth
    Is that you Ruthie? (memoir), 9,
        50n4, 118–20, 120n2, 126–8,
        146n23, 156n6
heimlich and *unheimlich*, 81, 82, 85; *see
    also* the uncanny
Herbert, Xavier
    Capricornia, 59, 59n1, 70n27
    Poor Fellow, My Country, 76
Hickman, Bronwen, 111, 112n7
Hindmarsh Island, 87
history, 15, 15n7, 17n11, 132–5
history wars, 15, 15n7
Hoffmann, E.T.A.
    'The Sand-Man', 82, 82n2
Holbein, Hans, *The Ambassadors*, 23, 43,
    54, 66, 66n23, 78
holocaust, 8, 8n2, 8n3, 11, 12–14
Holt, Rita *see* Huggins, Rita
Hookey, Gordon, 7, 18
hooks, bell, 98–9
Horton, George Moses, 156
Huggins, Jack, 101–3
Huggins, Jackie
    Auntie Rita, 16n9, 16n10, 50n4,
        92, 102, 105–6, 120n2
Huggins, Rita; *see also* narratives,
    Indigenous
    Auntie Rita (autobiography), 16n9,
        16n10, 50n4, 92, 102,
        105–6, 120n2
    Cherbourg Aboriginal Reserve,
        internment, 93–6, 126–8
    and the Deputy Directors of Native
        Affairs, 93–6
    and the Dog Act, 93–6, 101–2
    and Jack Huggins, 101–3
    and Semple, William Porteus, 93–6
    and the sexual economies of
        colonialism, 102–4
    and state surveillance, 92–3,
        93n2, 93n3, 101–2
    and trauma, writing, 16–17
Hyam, Ronald, 106
    Sexuality and Empire, 113

Index

Ignatiev, Noel
    How the Irish Became White, 134n3
image and imaginary
    and Aboriginal art, 41–4
    and anamorphosis, 22–3, 42–3
    construction of, 102
    imagining, Western, limits of, 77
    and self-formation, racial, 25–7,
        97–100, 134–8
    and the unimaginable, 12, 20, 34, 45,
        55–6, 70–71, 74–7
Indigeneity; *see also* black and blackness;
        colonialism; desire/dread; the
        Dreamtime; narratives, Indigenous;
        'niggering'; reserve system;
        sovereignty; white women's
        sexuality
    art, 41–4, 56n13
    artefacts, Indigenous, 80–81
    and the black/white binary, 50–51,
        134–8
    colonialism and infantilisation
        of, 122–3
    and country, 17, 31–4, 44, 52n7, 55,
        70–71, 76–8
    creativity and difference, 59–60,
        65, 76–7
    disavowal of white desire, impact
        on, 142–5
    and Dreamtime, 11, 18, 24, 36–7,
        62–3, 69, 74
    embodiment, conceptions of,
        35–40, 79
    the irrational, associated with, 59n2,
        60–62, 68, 156
    knowledge, protection of, 17
    'niggering' of, 132, 134–6, 139–41,
        139n13, 143
    radical difference and white
        understanding of, 2, 20–22, 39–40,
        60–63, 77–9, 132
    the sacred, and false equivalence,
        21–2, 75–80, 86–8
Indigenous Law, 12, 55, 62–3, 74–5,
    77–9, 78n33
interpellation, 27
interpretation, 20, 93
invisibility; *see also* blindness, blind spots;
    vision and the visual field

and reading, writing practice, 18–20,
    24–5, 34, 45–6, 46n2, 51
in visual fields, 11, 22–3, 33–5, 43–4,
    46n2, 51, 55–6, 103–4, 160

Jacobs, Jane
    on self and other, 80
    on 'The Bunyip,' 83–5
    Uncanny Australia, 80n35, 81–3, 86, 88
Jacobus, Mary, 26
Jose, Nicholas, 55n10, 57
Joyce, James, 70

Kafka, Franz
    The Penal Colony, 151, 156
Kamuf, Peggy, 26
Kaplan, E. Ann, 104–5
Kasack, Hermann
    Die Stadt hinter dem Strom, 7
Kenny, Robert
    The Lamb Enters the Dreaming,
        21–2, 135n5
Kngwarreye, Kame, Emily, 40, 41, 44
Kidd, Rosalind
    The Ways We Civilise, 48n3
Kinnane, Stephen
    Shadow Lines, 120n2
Kirby, Vicki,
    and feminine otherness, 106
    Telling Flesh, 31n2, 35–6, 39, 106
knowledge, 1, 17, 20, 33–4, 40, 61, 73–9,
        154–5; *see also* nonknowledge
    and the construction of the self, 40
    Indigenous, protection of, 17
    and language, 61
    limits to, 20, 74–9
    and unintelligibility, 1–2
    and the unknowable, 18–20, 24–5, 54,
        61, 77–9, 155
Kow Swamp, 87
Kristeva, Julia, 87–8, 63n14

Lacan, Jacques, 22, 23–4, 42–3, 46, 54, 98,
    142, 146–7
    The Ethics of Psychoanalysis, 23, 42–3
    The Four Fundamental Concepts, 54
    on perversion, 146–7
lack, 33–4, 142–3, 142n20
language, 21–2, 24, 61

178   *The Postcolonial Eye*

Larsen, Nella
   Passing, 134
Levi, Primo, 8n3
literacy, 136, 155–6, 155n5
literary criticism
   feminist, 26, 104–8, 111–13
   magic realism, 61–3
   and radical difference, 47, 62
   white critics of Indigenous signed
      texts, 56–7, 56n13, 59–63,
      59n1, 59n2, 59n3, 60n6
   Wright, Alexis, *Plains of Promise*,
      47, 56–7
literature
   lo real maravilloso, 67n26
   modernist, 19, 69–70
   post-war German, 3, 7–14, 18–19
Llosa, Vaagos
   *La Novella en America Latina,
      Dialogo*, 64n16
loss, 11, 16–18, 17n11, 154–5
Lott, Eric, 132n2, 133, 133n3, 135, 140
Lyotard, Jean-François, 86

Macintyre, Stuart
   The Historians' Conscience, 15
magic realism
   and *Carpentaria*, 52n9, 60, 62–3,
      64n16, 69–70, 73–4
   ontological, 63–4, 66–7
   in *Plains of Promise*, 56
   and postcolonial literary
      criticism, 61–3
   and radical difference, 60–68, 67n24,
      67n26, 77
   Slemon, Stephen on, 60, 61n9, 64,
      65–6, 73–4, 73n29
   word origin, definition, 61–2, 66n22
Manne, Robert, 8n2, 15n7, 148
manngyin, 79
mark, make, making, 2, 25–6, 37–40
Martin, Susan, 111, 112n7
massacre, in *Benang: From the Heart*, 132,
      137, 144–5, 159
matter, 31–2, 38–40
Maynard, John, 107–8
McClintock, Anne, 107, 107n5, 108
Merleau-Ponty, Maurice, *The Visible and
      the Invisible* 39, 44n8, 50n5, 91

Michaels, Eric, 56n13
Michaels, Walter Benn, 91, 134n4
Miller, Benjamin, 140n16, 140n17, 143
mining industry, 87
Moffatt, Tracey; *see also* narratives,
      Indigenous
   Nice Coloured Girls, 103–4
Moreton-Robinson, Aileen 137n9, 138n11
Morgan, Sally, 75n31
Morphy, Howard, 41n7
Morrison, Toni
   Beloved, 75n31, 122, 154–5
   and magic realism, reading truth as,
      65–9, 67n25
   Playing in the Dark, 101
   Songs of Solomon, 65
Morrissey, Philip, 148n25, 153n3
Morton, John, 74n30
Moses, A. Dirk
   Genocide and Settler Society, and
      Colonialism and Genocide 8n2
Muecke, Stephen, 32, 33
   Ancient and Modern, 41n6, 64n18
Mumbulla, Percy, 'The Bunyip'; *see also*
      narratives, Indigenous
   analysis of, Gelder and Jacobs, 83–5
   text, 83–4
Murray, Pam, 108n6
Murrie, 11
Murrinh-patha, 36

Napangardi, Dorothy, 40
narratives, Indigenous; *see also* Hegarty,
      Ruth; Huggins, Rita; Indigeneity;
      literature; magic realism; Moffatt,
      Tracey; Mumbulla, Percy; Roe,
      Paddy; Scott, Kim; Wright, Alexis
   aporia in, 22–3
   autobiography, 91–2
   blind spots and white readers, 22–3,
      33–5, 44, 45–6, 78–9, 128
   and Indigenous Law, 74–5, 77–9
   and Indigenous/settler hybridity, 22–3
   and trauma, 8–11, 14–18
   and the uncanny, 83–5, 87–8
   and understanding, gaps in, 8–10, 22,
      33–4, 45, 51–2, 54–6, 73–4
   and the unknowable, 18–20,
      24–5, 77–9

white reading practice and, 34, 45–7,
51–7, 63–7, 74–9
narratives, Jewish, 12–13
narratives, of
deprivation, 7–15, 154–5
loss, 11, 16–18, 17n11
trauma, 8–20, 22, 66
Native American, 134, 135n5
Neville, A.O., 148
'niggering,' 132, 134–6, 139–41, 139n13,
143; *see also* Indigeneity
nonknowledge, 15, 24–5, 46n2;
see also knowledge
Novak, Eva, 125, *125*
Nyigina, 32
Nyoongar, 17, 132, 133, 135, 136–8,
138n10, 153, 157

ontology, breasted, 37–8
the other, otherness; *see also* the gaze
and anxiety, 19
the black other as unseeing, 98–100
and the gaze, 17, 97–100, 104–6
and the Other, 97–8, 105
and radical difference, 1, 20, 50–51,
83, 88
and reading practice, 25
and uncertainty, 15

pan-Aboriginality, 47, 76–7, 135n5
Pascoe, Bruce
Convincing Ground, 140n13
passing, 138, 143
perception, 20, 22–3, 41–3;
see also anamorphosis
performativity
autobiography as, 26–7, 91–3
biography as, 92–3
construction of race, 49–50, 135–6
reading as, 2, 25–7, 47
self-formation as, 49–50, 135–6
Yawulyu ceremony as, 37–40
perspectival art, 41–2
perversion; *see also* sadism
in *Benang: From the Heart*, 145–7,
151–2, 151n1, 157–8
and colonisation, 8
deprivation, enjoyment of, 118–20
and postcolonial white masculinity, 97

sadism, and Gaunt, writings, 109–13
and white women's desires, 108, 113
Petyarre, Kathleen, 40
Pickering, Michael, 140n16
Pierce, Peter, 59n1, 59n2
poiesis, 47; *see also* reading, the reader,
reading practice
positivism, 11, 24, 47, 63, 154; *see also*
difference, radical difference,
self-same
postcolonialism; *see also* colonialism
and academic postcolonial
writing, 20–22
Australia, settlers and feelings of
home, 81–3, 85–8
literary criticism and magic
realism, 61–3

racial binarisms; *see also* American, racial
policies; black and blackness;
blackface, minstrelsy;
self-formation; slavery, white
and whiteness
Carpentaria, reversal of in, 69–70
as constructed, 46–7, 50–51, 131–6
desire/dread and production of, 131–3
doubleness, in *Benang: From the
Heart*, 137–8
Gaunt, Mary, and sex and, 108–9
and gender, 138–9
'niggering' of Indigeneity, 135,
136–7, 143
production of, at Cherbourg, 115–16,
116, *117*, 118–20, *121*, 122–3,
122–7, 125–8
racial self-formation, 25–7, 97–100,
131–2, 134–8, 143–4, 147
reserve system, 115–16
and self-formation, 25–7, 46–7, 50–51,
97–100, 131–6, 143–4, 147
Rainbow Serpent, 75–6, 77
rape, 49–51, 53, 73, 144–5, 159;
see also sadism
readers and reading practice; *see also*
writing practice
and aporia, 20–23, 56, 61
and autobiography, 26–7, 91–3
Benang: From the Heart, and
uncertainty, 151–2

180 *The Postcolonial Eye*

and blind spots, white readers, 22–3,
33–5, 44, 45–6, 77–8, 128
Carpentaria, 69–70
as colonialism, repetition of relations
of, 20
gaps in narrative, and white readers,
34, 45–7, 51–7, 63–7, 74–9
Indigenous and white readers, 22–3,
33–5, 44, 45–6, 78–9, 103–5, 128
and invisibility, 18–20, 24–5, 34, 45–6,
46n2, 51
as performative, 2, 25–7, 47
postivitism, 47, 63
radical uncertainty, 14–15, 20, 46, 63,
69–70, 73–4, 151–2
and self-formation, 25–8, 91–3
as a visual practice, 1–2, 25–7, 45
Reck, Friedrich, 12, 14
Renes, Cornelis Martin, 52n8
reserve system; *see also* Australian, race
policies; Cherbourg Aboriginal
Reserve; Indigeneity;
Stolen Generations
in *Benang: From the Heart*, 8
and colonial archives and white male
desire, 94
and inmates (term), 92n1
in *Plains of Promise*, 48–51, 50n4
racial binarisms, 115–16
and Ruth Hegarty's memoir of, 9,
115–16, 118–20, 126–8, 156n6
settlement system, 1938 expedition
into, 115
Reynolds, Henry, 8n2, 15n7
Robinson, Jane, 111
Roe, Paddy, *Gularabulu*, 32–5; *see also*
narratives, Indigenous
Roediger, David
*Black on White: Black Writers on
What it Means to be White*,
99–100, 99n10
Roh, Franz, 61–2, 78
Rose, Deborah Bird, *Dingo Makes Us
Human,* 8, 8n2, 52n8, 56n12, 75,
78n33, 78n34, 79, 139n13
Rudd, Steele
The Romance of Runnimede, 125

sadism; *see also* perversion; rape; torture
in *Benang: From the Heart*, 145–7,
151–2, 156–60
and colonisation, 116, 118
fiction, writing practice, 151,
157, 157n8
reserve systems, 115–16, 118–20, 126–8
writing practice, in *Benang: From the
Heart*, 151–2
in writings of Mary Gaunt, 109–13
Sartre, Jean-Paul, 97–8
scarification, rituals of, 39
scopophilia, 97–100, 138, 146–7, 151–2,
151n1, 157–8; *see also* blackface,
minstrelsy
productions of, Cherbourg, 115–16,
116, 117, 118–20, *121,* 122–3,
122–7, 125–8
Scott, Kim
Benang: From the Heart; *see also*
narratives, Indigenous
Aboriginality, denial of, 138n10
aesthetic form, 151–2, 152n2
anamorphosis, and, 158–9
assimilationism, 131–2, 145–9, 156
Australian, American race,
discourses, 131–5, 139–42
blackface, minstrelsy, 132–3,
133n3, 135, 139–41, 143
calculability, 137, 152–3
and the colonial archives, 153–4
cross-dressing, white men, 138–9
desire/dread, 133
doubleness in, 137–8
literacy, 155–6, 155n5
massacre, in, 132, 137, 144–5, 159
and miscegenation, 137n8
perversion in, 145–7, 151–2,
151n1, 157–8
and race, 131–8
rape, in, 144–5
reading practice, and
uncertainty, 151–2
reserves, descriptions, 8
sadism in, 145–7, 151–2, 156–60
text, formal qualities of, 158–60
Kayang and Me, 8n2, 17, 18, 137

Index 181

Sebald, W.G., *On the Natural History of Destruction*, 7–9, 11–12, 13–15
segregation, Australian race policies, 131–2, 147–8
self-formation; *see also* racial binarisms
  holocaust, as, 14
  and knowledge, 40
  performativity of, 49–50, 135–6
  racial, 25–7, 97–100, 131–2, 134–8
  and readers and reading practice, 25–8, 91–3
Semple, Agnes
  productions of race at Cherbourg, 115–16, *116, 117,* 118–20, *121,* 122–3, *122–7,* 125–8
  reserve system, sadistic, 115–16, 118–20, 126–8
Semple, Elizabeth, 116, 123
Semple, Jack, 123
Semple, William Porteus, 123
  reserve system, sadistic, example, 118–20, 123, 126–8
  and Rita Huggins, correspondence, 93–6
settle, settler, settlement
  and belonging, 81–3, 85–8
  country, reading of, 34–5
  hybridity, Indigenous/settler, 22–3
  and settler anxiety, 85–8
sexuality and empire, 106–7
  and Gaunt, Mary, writings, 108–9, 110–12, 112n7, 113
semiotics, 1, 33–4, 39
Slater, Lisa, 137n8, 138n10, 152n2, 153
slavery; *see also* American, racial policies; Australian, racial policies; colonialism; racial binarisms
  and American, racial policies, 66, 98–9, 132
  and 'black looking,' 98–100
  and Australian racial policies, 132, 139
  disavowal of, Australia, 139
  and Morrison, Toni, *Beloved,* 154–5
  and sadism, Gaunt, Mary, as example, 109–13
Slemon, Stephen, 60, 61n9, 64, 65–6, 73–4, 73n29
Sorensen, Rosemary, 55n10, 56, 57
Smith, Sidonie, 91–2

sovereignty, 2, 27, 50–51, 87–8, 101–2, 135; *see also* difference, radical difference, self-same; the Dog Act; Indigeneity
spectacle, specular, 97–100, 138–9, 146–7, 151–2, 151n1, 157–8; *see also* blackface, minstrelsy; scopophilia
  productions of race, Cherbourg, 115–16, *116, 117,* 118–20, *121,* 122–3, *122–7,* 125–8
Spender, Dale, 112
standpoint theory, 77
Stanner, W.E.H., 11, 12, 18, 22, 36–7, 76
Steger, Jason, 59n2
Stolen Generations, 8–9, 10, 48, 55, 115, 116, 118–20, 118n1; *see also* Australian, racial policies; reserve system
Stowe, Harriet Beecher
  Uncle Tom's Cabin, 141
Stuckey, Tommy, *124*
subjectivity, 23–5, 35
Sullivan, Jane, 59n1, 60n8, 71n28
Sutton, Mary-Jean, 48n3
Sykes, Roberta, 75n31
Syson, Ian, 59n1, 59n4, 60n6, 60n8

Takolander, Maria, 62n13, 64n17, 67, 67n24, 74n31, 77
Thurston, Luke, 19n12, 23, 54
Tindale, Norman 9n4
Toll, Robert C., 134, 136, 143
torture, 8, 13–14, 48–9, 73, 155–8; *see also* sadism; trauma
trauma; *see also* torture
  in *Benang: From the Heart,* massacre, in, 132, 137, 144–5, 159
  of colonialism, 15, 15n7
  narratives of, 8–20
  and Rita Huggins, 16–17
Tuhkanen, Mikko, 133n3

Uluru, 87
the uncanny; *see also heimlich* and *unheimlich*
  and alterity, 82–3, 86
  disavowal and disavowed narrative in *Uncanny Australia,* 83
  Jacobs and Gelder on, 83–5

narratives, Indigenous and the, 83–5, 87–8
and Sigmund Freud, 61, 68, 81, 82–3, 83n3
Uncanny Australia, 81, 83, 86, 88
uncertainty, radical; *see also* difference, radical difference, self-same
in *Carpentaria* by Alexis Wright, 63, 69–71, 73–4, 78–80
the reader, reading practice, 14–15, 20, 46, 63, 69–70, 73–4, 151–2
unrepresentable, unreadable, incommensurability, uncertainty, unknowability, undecidability
and absence, 33–4
in fiction, 48–9, 69–71, 73–4, 77–8, 159–60
gap, and space for the enigmatic, 18–20, 45, 54, 56–7, 77–9
and knowledge, 1–2, 17, 20, 33–4, 40, 61, 73–9, 154–5
narratives, Indigenous and the unreadable, 159–60
and silence, 17–18
and the unimaginable, 11, 12, 20, 34, 45, 55–6, 74–7

vision and the visual field; *see also* blindness, blind spots; invisibility
as constructed, 1–2, 24–5, 34, 102, 104–5, 104n1
gaps in, and invisibility, 11, 22–3, 33–5, 43–4, 46n2, 51, 55–6, 103–4, 160
reading practice as, 1–2, 25–7, 45

Waanyi/Waanji, 18, 76–8
Walalu, the Whirlwind Serpent, 76
Walker, Edna, 11, 115
Warlpiri, 37–40, 42, 52n7, 135n5
Warumungu, 36
Waterhouse, Richard, 140n16
West-Pavlov, Russell, *Transcultural Graffiti*, 33–4, 35, 39
Wheatley, Phillis, 156
White, Patrick, 60
white and whiteness; *see also* racial binarisms
Aboriginal art, white viewers of, 44

blindness, blind spots and, 22–3, 33–5, 44, 45–6, 77–8, 128
construction of, 49–51, 92–3, 97–8, 128, 133–6, 135n5
desire/dread and the production of race, 131–2, 138, 142–5, 146n23, 151
gaps in narrative, and white readers, 34, 45–7, 51–7, 63–7, 74–9
Indigenous world, understanding of, 76–80
and literacy, 136, 155–6, 155n5
magic realism, 65–70
other as spectacle, 97–8, 100, 118, 120, 157–8
and the rational, 60–62, 68, 70–71, 74
and reading practice, 34, 45–7, 51–7, 63–7, 74–9
viewing position of, 101–4
white creativity, as prototype, 59–60, 65, 76–7
white men and colonialistic sexual economy, 102–6
white women's sexuality; *see also* gender; Indigeneity
and Indigenous men, desiring, 104n4, 105–8
and Mary Gaunt, 108–9, 110–12, 112n7, 113
Whitlock, Gillian, 106, 109, 112–13
Williams, Cobbo, 125, *126*
Windschuttle, Keith
The Fabrication of Aboriginal History, 15n7
Wolfe, Patrick, 8n2, 36n4, 62, 74
Woollacott, Angela, 112–13
Wotjobaluk, 22
Wright, Alexis; *see also* narratives, Indigenous
Carpentaria
and country, 31n1
and 'Aboriginal realism', 65n20
and Indigenous knowledges, 65n20, 74–5, 78n34
and magic realism, 52n9, 60, 62–3, 64n16, 69–70, 73–4
radical uncertainty in, 63, 69–71, 71n28, 73–4, 78–80

and white critics, 59–61,
  59n1, 59n3, 60n6, 70n27
Plains of Promise, 9n5
  anamorphosis in, 46, 54–6
  disavowal in, 50–51
  reserve system in, 48–51, 50n4
  reviewers, and literary critics,
    47, 56–7
  and white readings of Indigenous
    narratives, 34, 45–7, 51–7,
    63–7, 74–9

writing practice, 9–10, 14, 18, 151–2; *see
    also* readers and reading practice
Wyndham, Susan 59n2

Yanner, Murrandoo, 75
Yanyuwa, 76–8
Yarralin, 52n8, 78n33, 79
Yawulyu ceremony, 37–40

Zamora, Lois, 61n10, 64
Zizek, Slavoj, *The Sublime Object of
    Ideology*, 50n6

CPSIA information can be obtained
at www.ICGtesting.com
Printed in the USA
BVHW042015211219
567454BV00005B/27/P